Foreign Direct Investment and Economic Growth in China

NEW HORIZONS IN INTERNATIONAL BUSINESS

General Editor: Peter J. Buckley
Centre for International Business,
University of Leeds (CIBUL), UK

This series is aimed at the frontiers of international business research. The study of international business is important not least because it gives researchers the opportunity to innovate in theory, technique, empirical investigation and interpretation. The area is fruitful for interdisciplinary and comparative research. This series is established as a central forum for the presentation of new ideas in international business.

Titles in the series include:

The Struggle for World Markets
Edited by Gavin Boyd

Japanese Multinationals in the Global Economy
Paul W. Beamish, Andrew Delios and Donald J. Lecraw

Direct Investment in Economies in Transition
Klaus Meyer

Taiwanese Firms in Southeast Asia
Networking Across Borders
Edited by Tain-Jy Chen

Global Competitive Strategies in the New World Economy
Multilateralism, Regionalization and the Transnational Firm
Edited by Hafiz Mirza

Foreign Direct Investment and Corporate Networking
A Framework for Spatial Analysis of Investment Conditions
Robert L.A. Morsink

Structural Change and Cooperation in the Global Economy
Edited by Gavin Boyd and John H. Dunning

Managing the Multinationals
An International Study of Control Mechanisms
Anne-Wil Käthe Harzing

The Origins of the International Competitiveness of Firms
The Impact of Location and Ownership in the Professional Service Industries
Lilach Nachum

Deepening Integration in the Pacific Economies
Corporate Alliances, Contestable Markets and Free Trade
Edited by Alan M. Rugman and Gavin Boyd

The Global Integration of Europe and East Asia
Studies of International Trade and Investment
Edited by Sang-Gon Lee and Pierre-Bruno Ruffini

Foreign Direct Investment and Economic Growth in China
Edited by Yanrui Wu

Foreign Direct Investment and Economic Growth in China

Edited by

Yanrui Wu

University of Western Australia

NEW HORIZONS IN INTERNATIONAL BUSINESS

Edward Elgar
Cheltenham, UK • Northampton, MA, USA

332.6730951
F714

Published by
Edward Elgar Publishing Limited
Glensanda House
Montpellier Parade
Cheltenham
Glos GL50 1UA
UK

Edward Elgar Publishing, Inc.
6 Market Street
Northampton
Massachusetts 01060
USA

A catalogue record for this book
is available from the British Library

Library of Congress Cataloguing in Publication Data

Foreign direct investment and economic growth in China / edited by
    Yanrui Wu.
    (New horizons in international business)
    Includes bibliographical references and index.
    1. Investments, Foreign—China. 2. China—Economic
conditions— 1976-   . I. Wu, Yanrui. II. Series.
    HG5782.F67   1999
    332.67'3'0951—dc21   99–17600
                                                          CIP

ISBN 1 84064 022 7

Printed and bound in Great Britain by MPG Books Ltd, Bodmin, Cornwall

Contents

Contents

Figures

Tables

Contributors

Chunlai Chen is Research Economist, the Rural Development Institute of the Chinese Academy of Social Sciences, Beijing, China.

Leonard K. Cheng is Professor and Head of Economics, Hong Kong University of Science and Technology, China.

Yum K. Kwan is Assistant Professor, Department of Economics and Finance, City University of Hong Kong, China.

Yisheng Lan is Professor, Department of Economics, Shantou University, China.

Qi Luo is Research Fellow, East Asian Institute, National University of Singapore, Singapore.

Jordan Shan is Lecturer, Department of Applied Economics, Victoria University of Technology, Australia.

Fiona Sun is Postdoctoral Research Fellow, Centre for Strategical Studies, Victoria University of Technology, Australia.

Haishun Sun is Research Fellow, Department of Economics, Deakin University, Australia.

Gary Tian is Lecturer, Department of Economics, Flinders University of South Australia, Australia.

Yanrui Wu is Lecturer, Department of Economics, University of Western Australia, Australia.

Xiaoguang Zhang is Lecturer, Department of Economics, University of Melbourne, Australia.

Preface

This edited volume contains a collection of research reports prepared by authors in Australia, Hong Kong, mainland China and Singapore. Most papers appear here for the first time. Some papers were presented at the International Conference on the Economies of Greater China held in Perth on 12–13 July 1997. The conference was organised jointly by the Department of Economics, University of Western Australia (UWA) and the Chinese Economic Studies Association of Australia (CESAA). Several contributors, – Chunlai Chen, Yisheng Lan and Haishun Sun – were awarded small grants from the above–mentioned conference so that they could present their work. The conference was generously supported by the Executive Dean's office (Faculties of Economics & Commerce, Education and Law, UWA), Department of Economics (UWA), the Vice–Chancellor's office (UWA), Asia Research Centre (Murdoch University), Ford Foundation (Beijing Office), AusAID (Canberra), Australia–China Council (Department of Foreign Affairs and Trade, Canberra), Education Section (People's Republic of China Embassy, Canberra), China Economy Program (Australian National University), Access China Centre (Macquarie University) and the Economic Society of Australia (WA Branch).

I thank all contributors for their participation in this project and for their cooperation in finalising the chapters in the past twelve months. I also thank Yew Liang Lee, Lee Kian Lim, Paula Madsen, Leanne Neo, Wana Yang and Qiang Ye for their excellent research assistance. My work on this volume was partly supported by an Australian Research Council Small Grant.

Finally, I am indebted to my colleagues at the Department of Economics for their support and encouragement, in particular to Paul Miller, Head of the Economics Department, for fighting to ensure the department's mission of fostering original and scholarly research.

Yanrui Wu
University of Western Australia
Perth

F2I
F23 047   1- 8
F23
P33 079

1. FDI and Economic Growth: An (China) Introduction

Yanrui Wu

During the past two decades, China's actually used foreign direct investment (FDI) increased from zero in 1978 to over US$45 billion in 1997, with a compound rate of growth of about 40 per cent annually (SSB 1998). This phenomenal development is indeed impressive. No doubt, the massive injection of foreign funds into China has important implications for trade, economic growth and societal development in the country. This book attempts to shed light on some of these issues. In this introductory chapter, I shall first examine the potential factors which have made China successful in attracting FDI. Then I shall present a brief survey of the debates on the role of FDI in economic growth. This is to be followed by an outline of the chapters.

WHY CHINA HAS BEEN SUCCESSFUL IN ATTRACTING FDI

China's FDI appears in two forms, for example, foreign sole ownership and joint ventures (foreign control through shareholdings). Geographically, the lion's share of China's FDI is from Hong Kong, Taiwan and other Asian economies. In recent years, however, North American and European investors have continuously increased their activities in China. By the completion of this book (in mid–1998), China's FDI from Southeast Asia had fallen. In the meantime, investment from the US and European countries has increased significantly. This trend has helped offset the negative impact of the Asian economic meltdown on China, and hence ensured a continuous flow of FDI into China.

Thus, what has made China so successful in attracting FDI? Several approaches, that is, market power, internalisation, international competitiveness, and the production–cycle model, have so far been developed to explain the determinants of FDI (Cantwell 1991, Lan 1996).[1] Dunning (1979) also proposed an approach in order to integrate various theories.

1

However, as Plummer and Montes (1995) pointed out, the theories of FDI are still incomplete in their application to China's recent experience. Empirical experience and economic theories have shown that the size and growth of the market in the host country encourage FDI (Rueber et al. 1973). This is particularly pertinent if the production is primarily for sale in the host country and if investment is made because of the size and growth potential of the domestic market. Following this line of thinking, rapid growth and the potentially large size of the domestic market in China may have played a role in attracting foreign investors at least in the 1990s.[2] The existence of abundant cheap labour has often been cited as the key factor attracting manufacturing activities to be relocated to China (Broadman and Sun 1996). However, these factors are not unique to China, for example, India is also a large country and cheap labour is available in other developing countries too.

Some authors have also emphasised the unique role of overseas Chinese firms, including firms controlled by Chinese mainland funds.[3] It is argued that the commonality of culture and language reduces the communication costs of business transactions. Most importantly, overseas Chinese have long operated their businesses in the Asian 'contractual' or 'informal' business institution that is similar to the one in post–reform China (Plummer and Montes 1995).

Challenged by China's FDI experience, economists have turned their attention to economic policy. It is pointed out that the Chinese government has made considerable efforts to improve the investment environment for foreign investment. Fan (1998) identified three types of policies, that is, preferential tax treatment, flexible contractual forms and the establishment of special economic zones (SEZs). One of the consequences of implementing the above policies is that China has had a competitive edge over its neighbouring countries in corporate tax rates. The establishment of a few special economic zones allowed the Chinese government to mobilise limited resources and to concentrate on infrastructure construction in the SEZs. Thus, according to this school of doctrine, it is management and policy that really matter to economic development as rightly pointed out in conventional economic textbooks (for example, Todaro 1997). Economists are still fine tuning their tools in explaining China's FDI growth. This book is an important addition to the literature.

ROLE OF FDI IN ECONOMIC GROWTH

As the term implies, 'foreign direct investment' distinguishes itself from other types of international capital flows, for example, portfolio diversification or debt purchases, because it involves some degree of ownership control (Plummer and Montes 1995). In the light of the new growth theory, parallel to domestic investment, FDI is an important factor which contributes to economic growth through technology transfer, efficiency improvement, its intricate link with trade flows and foreign exchange demands in a country. Specifically, FDI affects economic growth in several ways.

First, it is argued that FDI has been a major channel for the access to advanced technologies by recipient countries and hence plays a central role in the technological progress of those countries (Borensztein et al. 1998). Findlay (1978) asserts that the host countries can benefit from the 'contagion effects' associated with the advanced technology, management practices and marketing skills used by the foreign firms.

Second, outputs from FDI activities are often destined mainly to third-country markets outside the host and source countries. As inputs, FDI activities have used capital goods and other intermediate inputs supplied by host and other foreign countries. Thus, FDI is associated with both import and export trade in goods, and the hosting country can benefit from an investment–led export growth.

Third, FDI is an agent for the transformation of both the host and source economies (Lloyd 1996). Multinationals have played a central role in developing the host countries' production capacities which are often directed towards export–oriented activities. As a result, FDI contributes to the transformation of the industrial structure of the host economy and the commodity composition of its exports.

Finally, the presence of foreign firms in the economy with their superior endowments of technology and management skills will expose local firms to fierce competition. Foreign firms will progressively induce plant managers and government officials to adopt the rules of a market economy, through the diffusion of management and marketing skills and the adoption of legislation aimed at promoting greater reliance on the market (Chen et al. 1995). Local firms may also be under pressure to improve their performance and to invest in research and development (R&D). Thus, FDI enhances the marginal productivity of the capital stock in the host economies and thereby promotes growth (Wang and Blomstrom 1992). In addition, Lahiri and Ono (1998) observed that higher efficiency of foreign firms may help lower prices and hence increase consumers' surplus. Furthermore, FDI raises employment by either creating new jobs directly or using local inputs (thus creating more jobs indirectly).

However, empirical evidence has shown that the effect of FDI on economic growth is dependent upon a set of conditions in the host country's or local economy, for example, the level of human capital, location and infrastructure. Thus, it is argued that the geographical distribution of FDI in

China is mostly determined by initial income, infrastructure development, extent of general education and coastal location (Chen 1996, Broadman and Sun 1996). In the absence of these preconditions, FDI may serve to enhance the private return to investment only while exerting little positive impact in the recipient country (Balasubramanyam et al. 1996). It may even thwart rather than promote growth.

Borensztein et al. (1998) have shown empirical evidence that the contribution of FDI to economic growth is related to its interaction with the level of human capital in the recipient country. They argue that a minimum threshold stock of human capital is required to ensure that FDI is more productive than domestic investment. Balasubramanyam et al. (1997) further observe that FDI augments existing human capital, and thus effective utilisation of human capital in conjunction with FDI requires an adequate domestic market for the goods produced. It is also argued that, other things being equal, an export–promotion strategy is likely to both attract more FDI and promote more efficient utilisation thereof than an import substitution strategy. This hypothesis is supported by empirical evidence (Balasubramanyam et al. 1996).

In addition it is pointed out that foreign firms do not generate enough linkages, and are unlikely to make local purchases of inputs particularly if firms engage in labour–intensive processing of components for export (Rueber et al. 1973). Furthermore, foreign firms may suppress indigenous entrepreneurship and crowd out domestic investment due to technical superiority, superior tax and import advantages and by creating effective entry barriers through the monopolist exploitation of market power and control of patents and trademarks (Papanek 1973). Therefore, economic theory and empirical evidence postulate that FDI can contribute both positively and negatively to economic growth. On the one hand, some authors have admitted that foreign investment is more important than domestic investment in terms of its individual contribution to the growth rate. On the other hand, it is disputed that technology and skill spillovers from FDI do not materialise from the mere presence of FDI, and they have to be engineered with effective policies.

OUTLINE OF THE CHAPTERS

The main body of the book consists of three parts dealing with three core topics, namely, the general issues of FDI in the Chinese economy (Part I), the impact of FDI on economic growth (Part II) and the role of FDI in regional economic development (Part III). Part I begins with Chapter 2 by Xiaoguang Zhang. This chapter investigates the impact of the rapid ex–

pansion of FDI on the Chinese economy. It first surveys the main features of FDI, that is, its sources and destinations, sectoral and regional allocations. It then examines the importance of FDI as a source of saving and as an agent of technological transfer. This is followed by an empirical analysis of the contribution of FDI to the growth of the Chinese economy, in particular the growth of foreign trade. Finally, this chapter sheds some light on the spill-over effects of FDI on China's domestic industries.

Chapter 3 looks at foreign capital stock and its determinants. The authors, Leonard Cheng and Yum Kwan, are particularly interested in the effect of wages, education, infrastructure, income, initial foreign capital stock, and economic policy on the formation of foreign capital stock in China's 29 regions during the period 1984–94. The results show that there was a strong locational effect. The distance from Hong Kong is found to be inversely related to investment activity. It is also found that wages had a negative impact on FDI, and that infrastructure but education was important. The importance of special economic zones (SEZs) decreased over time whereas that of open coastal areas increased.

In the final chapter of Part I, Yanrui Wu investigates the performance of FDI, that is, how efficiently FDI, as one of the factor inputs, is utilised in China. Within the new growth theory framework, the author applies an input–oriented distance function approach to estimate the efficiency of FDI in China's coastal regions over the period 1983–95.

The theme of Part II is FDI, trade and economic growth. The three chapters in this part focus on the relationship between FDI and foreign trade (Chapter 5), foreign–invested enterprises and trade deficits (Chapter 6) and the causality between growth and FDI (Chapter 7), respectively. Since the early 1980s, together with the fast growth and huge amount of FDI inflows, China's international trade has grown very rapidly. What are the sources of China's rapid trade expansion since the early 1980s? Chapter 5 by Chunlai Chen attempts to investigate and answer this question by focusing on the relationship between FDI and trade. Simple regression techniques are employed to examine the relationship between FDI and trade in China. The main finding is that FDI has a positive impact on both China's provincial and bilateral trades.

While recognising that FDI, in particular foreign–invested enterprises (FIEs), has been one of the major driving forces for China's trade expansion, Haishun Sun in Chapter 6 observes that the net impact of FDI on China's trade balance is negative. In the past 18 years, with the exception of one year, the trade deficit of FIEs has increased. These deficits have significantly offset the surplus generated by Chinese domestic enterprises. Chapter 6 investigates the factors which led to the chronic trade deficits of FIEs. Those factors include (i) disproportionate imports relative to exports, (ii) importa-tion of capital goods as investment in FIEs, and (iii) transfer pricing manipulated by multinational corporations (MNCs), that is, over–invoicing imports and under–invoicing exports.

Causality between FDI and economic growth has for a long time been of interest to economists. There is an abundant literature on developed and developing economies with the exception of China. Chapter 7 by Jordan Shan, Gary Tian and Fiona Sun fills the void in the literature by applying modern econometric techniques to Chinese data. It attempts to test the causal link between the inflow of FDI and real industrial output growth. The results emerging from this research indicate a two–way causality between FDI and economic growth which is contrary to the conventional wisdom assuming a one–way causality running from FDI to GDP growth.

China has been well known for its regional disparity. The impact of FDI on the regional economies has also shown tremendous diversity. For this reason, Part III presents three case studies examining the role of FDI in regional economic development. The first chapter, Chapter 8, investigates the changing patterns of FDI in Shanghai. Since 1994 Shanghai has become China's second–largest recipient of FDI, only behind Guangdong Province. The unique feature of Shanghai's FDI is that MNCs have increasingly concentrated their investments in capital or skill–intensive manufacturing and service sectors while in other coastal provinces FDI has been involved predominantly in labour–intensive activities. In this chapter Gary Tian explains why Shanghai has become a location for FDI from MNCs. He also examines the factors which influence the inflow of FDI in Shanghai.

The focus of Chapter 9 by Qi Luo is Xiamen, one of the four special economic zones set up by the Chinese government under the leadership of Deng Xiaoping. In the 1980s, the Xiamen authority implemented a policy to use FDI to facilitate the restructuring of local, long–established enterprises. But the implementation of that policy was plagued by three main problems. First, the electronics industry has had little economic and technological linkage with other industries and hence could not function as a 'leading industry'. Second, most of the FIEs have been engaged in an enclave–type of export–processing operation and have hence never been integrated into the local economy. Finally, the generally high labour intensity of the FIEs has further restricted their role in the local industrial restructuring. These problems indicated that the strategy of using FDI to facilitate local industrial restructuring was unfeasible, highlighting the importance of having a correct understanding of the nature and characteristics of FDI projects in developing countries and hence a realistic expectation of the role of FDI.

Finally, Chapter 10 by Yisheng Lan presents a case study of foreign direct investment in Guangdong. Guangdong has been the largest recipient of China's FDI since the early 1980s. With the rising labour and land costs and the removal of some preferential policies, Guangdong is now facing more difficulties in attracting FDI. Can Guangdong maintain its growth momen–

tum and continue to be the top recipient of China's FDI? Yisheng Lan argues that, with its achieved economic progress, better infrastructure, more–educated and skilled labour force, well–developed economic integration with Hong Kong and close ties with overseas Chinese, Guangdong may be able to maintain rapid economic growth and its top position in hosting FDI for at least another decade.

NOTES

1. For more details, see Hymer (1976), Kojima (1973) and Dunning (1981).
2. For earlier studies of China's FDI, see Pomfret (1991), Kueh (1992), La Croix et al. (1995), Lardy (1995), Qu and Green (1997), Park (1997) and Sun (1998).
3. Some authors have estimated that round–tripping funds from mainland China amounted to 25 per cent of China's total FDI (Broadman and Sun 1996).

REFERENCES

Balasubramanyan, V.N., Salisu, M. and Sapsford, D., 1996. 'Foreign direct investment and growth in EP and IS countries', *Economic Journal*, **106**, 92–105.

Balasubramanyan, V.N., Salisu, M. and Sapsford, D., 1997. 'Foreign direct investment as an engine of growth', Mimeo, Department of Economics, Lancaster University.

Borensztein, E., Gregorio, J.D. and Lee, J.W., 1998. 'How does foreign direct investment affect economic growth', *Journal of International Economics*, **45**, 115–35.

Broadman, H.G. and Sun, X., 1996. 'The distribution of foreign direct investment in China', *Policy Research Working Paper*, China and Mongolia Department, World Bank.

Cantwell, J., 1991. 'A survey of the theories of international production', in C. Pitelis and R. Sugden (eds), *The nature of transnational firms*, Routledge, London.

Chen, C., 1996. 'Regional determinants of foreign direct investment in mainland China', *Journal of Economic Studies*, **23**, 18–30.

Chen, C., Chang, L. and Zhang, Y., 1995. 'The role of foreign direct investment in China's post–1978 economic development', *World Development*, **23**, 691–703.

Dunning, J.H., 1979. 'Explaining changing patterns of international production: in defence of eclectic theory', *Oxford Bulletin of Economics and Statistics*, **41**, 269–96.

Dunning, J.H., 1981. 'Explaining the international direct investment position of countries: towards a dynamic or development approach', *Weltwirtschaftliches Archiv*, **117**, 30–64.

Fan, C.S., 1998. 'Why China has been successful in attracting foreign direct investment: a transaction cost approach', *Journal of Contemporary China*, **7**, 21–32.

Findlay, R., 1978. 'Relative backwardness, direct foreign investment, and the transfer of technology: a simple dynamic model', *Quarterly Journal of Economics*, **92**, 1–16.

Hymer, S., 1976. *The international operation of national firms: a study of direct foreign investment*, MIT Press, Cambridge, Massachusetts.

Kojima, K., 1973. 'A macroeconomic approach to foreign direct investment', *Hitotsubashi Journal of Economics*, **14(1)**, 1–21.

Kueh, Y.Y., 1992. 'Foreign investment and economic change in China', *China Quarterly*, **131**, 637–89.

La Croix, S.J., Plummer, M. and Lee, K. (eds), 1995. *Emerging patterns of East Asian investment in China, from Korea, Taiwan and Hong Kong*, M.E. Sharpe, Armonk, New York.

Lahiri, S. and Ono, Y., 1998. 'Foreign direct investment, local content requirement, and profit taxation', *Economic Journal*, **108**, 444–57.

Lan, P., 1996. *Technology transfer to China through foreign direct investment*, Avebury, Aldershot.

Lardy, N.R., 1995. 'The role of foreign trade and investment in China's economic transformation', *The China Quarterly*, **144**, 1065–82.

Lloyd, P., 1996. 'The role of foreign investment in the success of Asian industrialisation', *Journal of Asian Economics*, **7(3)**, 407–33.

Papanek, G.F., 1973. 'Aid, foreign private investment, saving and growth in less developed countries', *Journal of Political Economy*, **1**, 120–30.

Park, J.D., 1997. *The special economic zones of China and their impact on its economic development*, Praeger, Westport.

Plummer, M., and Montes, M.F., 1995. 'Direct foreign investment in China: an introduction', in Sumner J. La Croix, M. Plummer and K. Lee (eds), *Emerging patterns of East Asian investment in China, from Korea, Taiwan and Hong Kong*, M.E. Sharpe, Armonk, New York.

Pomfret, R., 1991. *Investing in China: ten years of the open door policy*, Iowa State University Press, Ames, Iowa.

Qu, T. and Green, M.B., 1997. *Chinese foreign direct investment: a subnational perspective on location*, Ashgate, Aldershot.

Rueber, G.L, Crookell, H., Emerson, M. and Gallais–Hamonno, G., 1973. *Private foreign investment in development*, Clarendon Press, Oxford.

SSB (State Statistical Bureau), 1998. *Statistical survey of China 1998*, Statistical Publishing House of China, Beijing.

Sun, H., 1998. *Foreign investment and economic development in China, 1979–1996*, Ashgate, Aldershot.

Todaro, M.P., 1997. *Economic development*, 6th edition, Longman, London.

Wang, J. and Blomstrom, M. 1992. 'Foreign investment and technology transfer: a simple model', *European Economic Review*, **36**, 137–55.

PART I

Foreign Direct Investment in the Chinese
Economy

2.   Foreign Investment Policy, Contribution and Performance

Xiaoguang Zhang

INTRODUCTION

Foreign capital investment played a major symbolic role in the opening up of the Chinese economy 18 years ago when China embarked upon a journey to the market economy.[1] China immediately abandoned its doctrine of 'no internal and external debit' and began to embrace foreign capital and investment for the first time since 1949. Despite both the government and domestic enterprises having little knowledge of foreign investment and international financial markets, China had its unique advantages: a potentially huge domestic market attractive to overseas investors, an almost unlimited supply of relatively well–educated and low–cost labour, and extensive connections with overseas Chinese business communities in Asia and around the world, and, more importantly, a strong government committed to economic reform and an open–door policy.

China's utilisation of foreign capital began with official borrowing from the World Bank, the Asian Development Bank and through bilateral development assistance programmes of foreign countries and from international financial markets by issuing bonds. The legal framework for foreign direct investment (FDI), however, was absent in 1978 and had to be built from the scratch. Since 1979 when the first law on foreign joint venture was passed, China has made great efforts to establish a legal framework for foreign investment which is compatible with the international standard. The laws and regulations concerning foreign investment ventures have been constantly improved as the economy moves towards the market. By the early 1990s, China's foreign investment policy was compared favourably with other Asian countries and regarded as the most liberal in the developing world (Lardy 1994).

Since 1979, foreign capital inflows have been growing continuously. Between 1979 and 1996, China had actually received a total of more than

US$283.9 billion in foreign capital. Despite being a major borrower from the World Bank for years, FDI has always served as an important source of external capital and modern technology. As the domestic investment environment improves, the inflows of FDI have accelerated (see Table 2.1). By the end of 1996, China had actually received US$174.9 billion in foreign direct investment, which made up for more than 61.6 per cent of the total foreign capital inflow into China. Since 1992, FDI has rapidly expanded to become by far the single most important source of external capital for China, surpassing the combination of bilateral development assistance and bor-rowing commercially from international organisations.

*Table 2.1   Annual foreign capital inflows into China, 1979–95
             (US$ billion)*

Year	Foreign borrowing*		Foreign investment	
	Committed	Utilised	Contracted	Utilised
1979–82	13.55	10.69	6.01	1.17
1983	1.51	1.07	1.73	0.64
1984	1.92	1.29	2.65	1.26
1985	3.53	2.69	5.93	1.66
1986	8.41	5.01	2.83	1.87
1987	7.82	5.81	3.71	2.31
1988	9.81	6.49	5.30	3.19
1989	5.19	6.29	5.60	3.39
1990	5.10	6.53	6.60	3.49
1991	7.16	6.89	11.98	4.37
1992	10.70	7.91	58.12	11.01
1993	11.31	11.19	111.44	27.52
1994	10.67	9.27	82.68	33.77
1995	11.29	10.33	91.28	37.52
1996	7.96	12.67	73.28	41.73
Total	115.92	104.11	469.14	174.88

Note: * Includes securities sales and other types of investment, such as the equipment supplied by foreign businesses in transactions involving compensation trade, processing and assembly, and the value of equipment supplied in financial leasing transactions.

Source: SSB (1997a, p.132).

It is also worth noting that, after 18 years of economic reforms, China is no longer a closed and centrally planned economy. It is now the tenth–largest trading nation in the world. In 1996, China exported more than US$151 billion worth of goods, equivalent to 18 per cent of China's GDP, the highest among large countries. The central plans for production have been replaced by markets: 90 per cent of goods and services are now ex-changed in the marketplace.

How has China's foreign investment policy been formulated over the past 18 years? What are the current patterns of foreign investment in China? How have foreign invested enterprises (FIEs) performed? These are the main questions that will be addressed in this chapter. The focus will be on FDI because of its importance in China's long–term development.

EVOLUTION OF FOREIGN INVESTMENT POLICY

The development of foreign investment policy in China can be divided into three phases: the initial phase (1979–85), the continuous development stage (1986–91) and the high–growth period (1992 onwards).

The Initial Phase (1979–85)

The passage of the 'joint–venture law' by the National People's Congress in July 1979 marked the beginning of China's open–door policy. It set the legal framework for foreign direct investment by permitting foreign investors to form equity joint ventures with Chinese partners. In the following years, a number of related laws and regulations were soon formulated in regard to taxation and management of foreign–invested firms.

Almost from the very beginning, China's foreign investment policy had a very strong regional characteristic. The policy was deliberately biased towards the southeast coastal region. The intention was clear: to take locational advantage to attract foreign capital from Hong Kong and Macau. Between 1979 and 1980, Guangdong and Fujian provinces were granted special autonomy in dealing with foreign trade and investment. These two provinces soon established four special economic zones (SEZs) at Shenzhen, Zhuhai, Shantou and Xiamen, primarily for attracting foreign investment in export–processing production. Special policies were adopted within the zones to give foreign–invested firms most favourable treatment in terms of tax concessions, access to credit and raw materials.

Foreign investment grew modestly after the passage of the joint venture law in 1979 and the establishment of SEZs in 1980. Due to lack of a well–defined legal framework and poor infrastructure, between 1979 and 1982, only 922 foreign investment projects were approved. The contracted investment funds totalled US$6.01 billion and only US$1.17 billion was actually received. This averaged only a few hundred million dollars a year.

In May 1983, the State Council held the first working meeting on utilisation of foreign capital and decided to further liberalise foreign investment regulations. In 1984, 14 coastal cities, including Shanghai, Tianjin, Dalian, Qingdao and Guangzhou (Canton) were selected to be the first group of 'open cities', opening for foreign investment. They were allowed to adopt some special policies used only by the SEZs in relation to foreign investment. These open cities soon established their own zones, the 'economic and technological development zones'. Foreign firms investing in these zones could enjoy favourable treatment similar to that offered by the SEZs.

In 1985, the Yangtze River Delta and the Pearl River Delta and the Xia(men)–Zhang(zhou)–Quan(zhou) Triangle in South Fujian Province were declared as the coastal economic open areas.[2] The authorities of these open areas were given extended administrative power in regard to trade and investment. They were allowed to adopt certain policies and regulations similar to that of the coastal open cities.

These measures improved the investment environment within these designated cities and areas and encouraged the local authorities to compete with each other for foreign capital by offering additional incentives or better infrastructure. As a result, foreign investment expanded. Between 1983 and 1985, the total value of contracted foreign investment reached US$10.32 billion, an average of about US$3.44 billion annually. The value of realised investment was US$3.56 billion, an average of US$1.19 billion annually. Foreign investment during this period came mainly from Hong Kong and Macau. The investment projects were mostly labour–intensive manufacturing, hotels and restaurants. Guangdong and Fujian provinces and other coastal cities received most investment.

Although committed foreign investment reached the one billion US dollar mark in 1984 and continued to grow afterwards, the contracted investment funds peaked in 1985 and slipped back in 1986. This was because, despite the 1979 Law of Joint Ventures permitting foreign investment, the legal environment for foreign investors was not well defined and little attention was paid to attracting foreign investors. Thus, despite the publicity given to the opening up of China's huge potential market, the amount of foreign investment grew very slowly during the early 1980s, partly due to the long and uncertain negotiation and approval process.

Problems cited by foreign investors in the 1980s varied according to the size of the joint venture, its product and the investors' country of origin, but a few problems seemed quite common. These included the high cost of doing business in China due to an outdated communications and transport system, serious delivery problems for domestic inputs, labour practices and lack of a market for land. Some of the most serious problems were policy induced. Foreign investors complained of high valuations of land, labour and other Chinese–contributed inputs, which are in breach of the contracts, and local authorities seeking to maximise short–run returns. Perhaps most restrictive of all was the requirement to earn foreign exchange, which limited access to China's huge domestic market. The initial foreign investment law also contained many provisions that potential foreign investors regarded as being onerous: access by joint ventures to the Chinese domestic market was limited; no provision for wholly foreign–owned companies was made; the law required that the chairman of each joint venture be Chinese rather than a foreign national, and it put a finite life on all joint ventures, after which ownership had to revert to the Chinese partner.

Continuous Development Stage (1986–91)

In view of the above–mentioned problems, the Chinese government soon took action to ease these restrictions. In April 1986, the state promulgated a new law on wholly foreign–owned enterprises: the Law on Enterprises Operated Exclusively with Foreign Capital, which lifted the restriction on foreign ownership. It indicated a more relaxed attitude towards foreign control of FDI projects. The practical effect of this law was enhanced when implementation regulations were promulgated in 1988.

Meanwhile, the long–awaited Law on Cooperative Ventures was finally passed by the National People's Congress in April 1988. By then over 5,000 such ventures had already been approved in the absence of any legal framework. Similarly, in the spring of 1990, an amendment to the 1979 joint–venture law eased the initial limit on the formation of joint ventures: foreign nationals were allowed to chair the ventures and a finite life limit was not a necessary requirement for a joint venture. These laws all declared formally that the state shall not nationalise or expropriate foreign–invested ventures under normal circumstances.

In October 1986, the State Council promulgated the 'Provision on Encouraging Foreign Investment'. This important document demonstrated that serious attention had been given to providing investment incentives. It also marked a new stage in foreign investment policy development. The new measures addressed some of the problems cited by early investors, and improved the investment climate both by adding new incentives and by removing uncertainties. Joint ventures received preferential treatment for tax and imports of materials, equipment and vehicles used in production. Explicit encouragement was given to joint ventures involving advanced technology and producing exports. Export–oriented and technologically advanced joint ventures could receive additional tax benefits. In December 1987, the first state investment guideline was issued in which priority industries were highlighted and prohibited areas were also specified. It represented an attempt by the government to channel foreign capital into priority sectors.

The new measures also clarified the existing arrangements that joint ventures had autonomy in making decisions outside of plan targets in setting salaries and bonuses and in hiring senior management personnel. Equity joint ventures were granted privileged access to supply of water, electricity and transportation, paying the same price as state–owned enterprises, and to low interest loans. Probably the most important policy initiative was to give foreign ventures the right to swap foreign exchange among themselves. Balancing the foreign currency account had been the major difficulty facing many early investors. In 1985, China formally opened a swap market for foreign exchange. Initially operating only in a handful of cities, these markets quickly spread, and the transaction volume rose remarkably. By 1989, trade turnover involving foreign–invested firms exceeded US$2.3 billion. Taking advantage of the more favourable price they could receive in the market than the official exchange rate, sellers actually outnumbered buyers. Thus foreigners were net sellers of foreign exchange.

In regard to regional open policy, between 1988 and 1990, the govern–ment took three important steps to extend open economic areas. First, in 1988, it extended the coastal open areas to North China, including the Liaodong Peninsula and the Shandong Peninsula along the Bohai Sea Rim. Second, the Hainan Island was separated from Guangdong and became the thirtieth province of China and the fifth special economic zone. Third, in April 1990, the State Council approved Shanghai's plan to develop the Pudong New Area (*Pudong Xinqu*).[3] Pudong was expected to become an international economic, financial and transport centre. The development of the Pudong New Area marked an important turning point in China's foreign investment policy. The focus of foreign investment was now shifted from peripheral areas to China's industrial centres.

Foreign investors responded favourably to the new policy initiatives. Investment started to pick up again. In 1987 and 1988, China encountered serious inflation which led to the political unrest in 1989. However, foreign investment continued to grow. Between 1986 and 1991, the total contract value of foreign investment was US$33.2 billion, an average of US$6.6 billion annually. Actual foreign capital inflows were US$16.7 billion, or US$3.3 billion per year. Compared with the previous period, these figures increased by 142 per cent and 255.3 per cent, respectively. Surprisingly to many observers, in the aftermath of Tiananmen, with foreign loans coming to a halt, most Western countries imposing economic sanctions on China and many Western firms retreating from China, the actual inflows of FDI remained high rather than falling precipitously. This was largely due to the dramatic entry of firms from Asia, most noticeably, from Hong Kong and Taiwan. Taiwanese firms entered into China after the lifting of restrictions on mainland investment by the Taiwanese authorities. Asian firms rapidly increased their share in the Chinese market. The structure of foreign investment changed considerably. The share of productive and export–oriented projects grew rapidly. The areas of investment expanded as well.

By 1988, the legislated investment incentives in China compared favourably to those offered by other Asian countries, although there is considerable evidence of non–legislative disincentives to investing in China. In the early 1990s China was developing what was rapidly becoming one of the most liberal foreign investment environments in the developing world. This paved the way for a new investment boom beginning in 1992.

High–Growth Period: 1992 Onwards

This period has witnessed an unprecedented surge in FDI in China. It began with Deng Xiaoping's much publicised tour to the southern provinces in early 1992 and his call for accelerating economic reform and growth. The timing was very important. The year 1992 was when inflation was finally brought under control through three years of harsh austerity policies. Many reform policies previously suspended due to inflation were once again ready to be implemented. As a result, FDI surged to new high levels, exceeding US$11 billion in 1992 and then almost reaching US$28 billion in 1993. Between 1992 and 1994, the total values of contracted and actually utilised foreign capital were 4.8 and 3.1 times those of the previous 13 years. A new phenomenon during this period is that many multinational companies from industrialised countries had begun investing in China. The number of large–scale capital– and technology–intensive projects had increased rapidly.

There is little doubt that some of these recorded inflows was Chinese capital that had first flowed out and then returned to China to take advantage of the tax incentives provided to foreign–invested firms. However, overlooking this, China not only attracted more foreign investment in 1992 than any other developing country, it was the recipient of almost one–quarter of the total flow of FDI to developing countries (World Bank 1993). With actual investment exceeding US$27 billion in 1993, China remained far and away the largest developing country recipient of FDI and absorbed an even larger share of the total FDI to developing countries.

It should be noted that, unlike in the 1980s, the orientation of foreign investment policy in the 1990s has shifted from coastal regions to inland areas. This is largely because the high concentration of foreign investment in the coastal areas over the previous decade broadened the existing income gap between the East and the West of China, which could potentially jeopardise the long–term stability of the nation. An increasing number of inland provinces and cities were demanding the same policy treatment as that given to coastal open areas. In view of this, the central government began to open more inland cities and regions for foreign investment. The process started from cities along the Yangtze River and along the inland provinces bordering neighbouring countries.

In 1992, the State Council added six port cities along the Yangtze River, 13 border cities and 18 capital cities of inland provinces to the list of 'open cities', which implied that these cities would enjoy the same policy autonomy as the coastal open cities. The six port cities along the Yangtze River are located in five provinces, including Sichuan province which has a population of over 100 million, the largest in China. Yangtze River's Three Gorges economic open area was also established thereafter to invite foreign participation in the Three Gorges project.

China has over 20,000 kilometres of inland borders with 15 countries. Peoples living along both sides of the borders traditionally have close cultural and economic relations. In 1992, 13 inland border cities were opened up for promoting border trade and economic cooperation with neighbouring countries. Fourteen border economic co–operation areas were soon established to attract foreign investment. Foreign capital started to penetrate into China's inland areas.

However, the contracted value of foreign investment peaked in 1993 and slipped in the following years to US$81.4 billion, although the actually received foreign investment continued to rise. Unlike the decline in the early years, the fall in contracted investment after 1993 has resulted mainly from China's domestic economic cycles. As the economy grew strongly during the period 1992–93, inflation pressure began to build again. The government reacted quickly to tighten fiscal and monetary policy in 1993 and 1994. In particular, construction projects in real estate were the first to be cut back. Many foreign investment projects, mainly from Hong Kong and contracted in 1993, targeted China's then underdeveloped but booming real estate market. They were hit hardest by the austerity policy.

The government has become more interested in the quality rather than the quantity of foreign investment. It now discourages foreign investment in property development and in the processing industries that typify the early years of the open–door policy. Approval for investment in property development fell from 39.3 per cent of total FDI in 1993 to 28.7 per cent in 1994. Since most property investment came from Hong Kong, the territory's share of total FDI slipped below 60 per cent for the first time. Multinationals were taking up the slack. The average size of foreign investment projects in China crept up from US$1.7 million in 1994 to nearly US$2.8 million in 1995, and further to US$3.3 million in 1996. This suggests that the share of American, Japanese and European investors, each well under 10 per cent of China's total FDI, is expanding.

To level the playing field for all enterprises, the government has begun in recent years to reduce some of the special treatment offered exclusively to foreign–invested firms. For instance, the tariff exemption on the imports of capital equipment by FIEs was abolished in April 1996. At the same time, the administration of foreign investment projects has been further de–

centralised. Foreign investment projects with a total capital of US$30 million or below can now be approved by provincial authorities, instead of the central government, up from the previous authorisation of US$10 million. Such decentralisation will undoubtedly facilitate further capital investment in China.

The explanation for the continuous growth in FDI in the 1980s and the surge in the early 1990s is not obvious. China had a limited legal structure, implying that property rights were not well defined; its currency was not convertible, and hence would–be investors had to plan on exporting part of their products to have an assured source of hard–currency earnings; and growing corruption made the investment environment increasingly inhospitable, particularly for multinationals. However, China overcame these negative factors by continuously liberalising its foreign investment regime. As a result, China's economy was among the fastest–growing countries in the world, and its economic ties with Asian newly industrialised economies, which were highly constrained in the early years of reform, became increasingly important over time.

CURRENT PATTERNS OF FDI IN CHINA

By the end of 1996, China had approved 283,575 foreign–invested projects. Among them, 173,982 were equity joint ventures, 44,509 cooperative ventures and 67,659 wholly foreign–owned ventures. These projects had a contract value of US$488.1 billion, of which US$198.5 billion had been actually used by the ventures (SSB 1997a).

Foreign capital has flowed into China from 150 countries and regions in the world. Hong Kong and Macau rank the first, accounting for 59 per cent of total foreign capital invested over 1983–95, followed by Taiwan (8.6 per cent), the United States (8.1 per cent) and Japan (7.8 per cent). The major Southeast Asian and West European countries also have considerable shares. For instance, the combined share of South Korea and Singapore exceeded that of Japan in 1996. Since the early 1980s, capital from Hong Kong always accounted for about 53–68 per cent of annual inflow of FDI to China. In recent years, however, some of the world's largest multinational companies have started setting up joint ventures or wholly–owned ventures in China on a large scale. This dramatically increases the FDI share of Western in–dustrialised countries in China. In the first half of 1996, the share of Hong Kong's capital in FDI inflow to China dropped to below 39 per cent for the first time.

The east coastal areas have attracted most foreign capital invested in China. Guangdong is by far the largest recipient, which has retained almost

30 per cent of total cumulative FDI received by all provinces. It is followed by Jiangsu (11.3 per cent), Fujian (10.5 per cent), Shanghai (9.1 per cent) and Shangdong (6.3 per cent). This pattern is very much consistent with the regional development policy priority of the government. Foreign investment has grown rapidly in inland provinces in recent years but their share remains rather small.

The designated open cities and areas with special policy treatment for foreign investors have been continuously expanding since 1978. They now include 354 cities and counties covering 550,000 square kilometres and 330 million people or 27 per cent of the entire Chinese population. Within these open cities and areas, there are various types of economic zones, each of which is designed to attract a particular type of foreign investment projects. They also serve the role of stimulating the economic development of surrounding regions. These zones, established over the past 17 years, include 5 SEZs, 32 economic and technological development zones, 52 hi–tech and industrial areas, 13 bonded areas, 14 frontier economic co–operative areas and 11 tourist and holiday areas. As they provide favourable treatment and better infrastructure, these different zones have become the main focus of foreign investment in recent years.

In the early 1980s, the first wave of foreign investment was concentrated mainly in the tourist industry and in the processing and assembling of labour–intensive manufactures. Since the late 1980s, foreign investment has gradually spread to a wide range of industries: petroleum, coal, transport, telecommunication equipment, metallurgy, machinery, electronics, chemicals, building materials, light industries, textiles, medicine and pharmaceutical, agriculture, real estate, services and tourism. However, the sectoral distribution of FDI is still uneven. Over the period 1979–95, the agricultural sector received only 1.5 per cent of FDI and the service sector gained less than 40 per cent of total FDI while the industrial sector as a whole received nearly 60 per cent of FDI (Table 2.2).

Within the industrial sector, a cumulated total of 314.7 billion yuan of foreign capital (equivalent to US$37.7 billion at the 1995 exchange rate) was actually invested by the end of 1995, according to the latest industrial census (Office of the Third National Industrial Census 1996).[4] Manufacturing industries are the major beneficiaries. Out of 39 industrial sectors, the top ten recipients, all manufacturing, had obtained 62 per cent of foreign capital invested in the industrial sectors (Table 2.3). In the meantime, mining industries as a whole received only 0.32 per cent of total foreign capital invested in the industrial sectors.

As for the services sector, foreign–invested firms are heavily concentrated in four areas: transport and communications, wholesale and retail trade,

Table 2.2   Sectoral distribution of foreign direct investment, 1979–95

Sector	No. of projects (unit)	Share (%)	Contracted (US$100m)	Share (%)
Agriculture	6,270	2.4	59.7	1.5
Industry	196,436	75.9	2,322.3	58.7
Services	56,023	21.7	1,576.6	39.8
Total	258,729	100.0	3,958.6	100.0

Source: MOFERT (1985–95).

Table 2.3   Top ten recipients of foreign investment in industry, 1995

Industry	As % of total FDI
Electronic and telecommunication equipment	9.89
Textile industry	8.19
Nonmetal mineral products	7.29
Electric equipment and machinery	6.01
Electric power, steam and hot water	5.67
Transportation equipment manufacturing	5.32
Raw chemical materials and products	5.16
Metal products	5.08
Garments	5.02
Total	62.05

Source: Office of the Third National Industrial Census (1996).

social services and real estate (Table 2.4). Among the four areas, the social service industry (includes tourist facilities) accounted for nearly half of the total output value of foreign–invested firms in this sector. Foreign investment in this industry mainly went to tourist facilities such as hotels and related services. On average, however, foreign–invested firms had a much lower output share in the service sector than in the industrial sector, only 1.3 per cent according to the recent data from the 1995 first national tertiary sector census. It implies that the service sector is very likely to become a focal point for the next round of foreign investment in China.

Since the early 1990s, some highly restricted service industries have be–gun experiments in opening to foreign investment, which include banking, insurance, civil aviation, freight, commerce and accounting. By mid–1993, for instance, China had six joint–venture banks, three wholly–owned foreign banks, three joint–venture financial companies and one wholly–owned foreign financial company. The insurance market remains highly protected. Only a few foreign insurance companies have been allowed to sell a limited number of their products in the designated cities. It has been reported that the government is about to further liberalise the banking and insurance sectors and invite more foreign companies to compete in China's domestic market.

Table 2.4   Structure of foreign–invested firms in the service sector, 1992

Industry	Share in total FDI output (%)	As % of sector's output
Agricultural services	0.07	0.13
Geological prospecting and water conservancy	0.05	0.07
Transport, storage and communications	12.57	0.92
Wholesale, retail trade and restaurants	22.79	0.84
Financial intermediations and insurance	2.49	0.24
Real estate activities	13.97	4.74
Social services	45.36	9.74
Health care, sporting and social welfare	0.47	0.18
Education, culture and arts	0.57	0.16
Scientific research and polytechnic services	0.87	0.79
Government agencies and social organisations	0.27	0.04
Others	0.52	0.39
Total	100.00	1.32

Source: Office of the first National Tertiary Industry Census (1995).

Foreign investment in retailing was highly restricted prior to 1992. But in the second half of 1992, substantial liberalisation began. The new regu–lations allow Sino–foreign joint ventures in retailing, generally with a 50–50 split in equity shares, in Beijing, Shanghai, Tianjin, Guangzhou, Dalian, Qingdao, and the five SEZs. These joint ventures receive the right to directly import commodities they sell, rather than going though an established state trading company, but imports are not supposed to comprise more than 30 per cent of retail sales. By the end of 1993, agreements had been signed for eight large shopping centres in China. Considering the current outdated commercial systems in many Chinese cities, it is expected that the scope of foreign involvement in the commerce sector will be further expanded.

CONTRIBUTIONS OF FOREIGN–INVESTED FIRMS

By the end of 1994, more than 91 thousand foreign–invested firms were operating in China (Table 2.5) employing 12.6 million workers, 7.5 per cent of total urban employment. In 1995, foreign–invested industrial firms produced 1,071 billion yuan worth of output, or 19.5 per cent of total industrial output. In 1994, foreign–invested firms generated a tax revenue of 39 billion yuan, 8 per cent of total government revenue. In some areas, the revenue generated by foreign–invested firms have become an important source of revenue for local governments. In the general literature, foreign direct investment is believed to have played three major roles in the development process of an economy: as a source of savings and long–term investment, as an agent of technology transfer and a catalyst of restructuring the economy.[5] This section is intended to answer the question as to what roles FDI has played in China.

Table 2.5   Foreign–invested firms, 1991–94

Item	1991	1992	1993	1994	1995
Number of firms (cumulative, 10,000 units)	2.1	3.5	7.2	9.1	n.a.[a]
Number of workers (10,000 persons)	290	490	1,000	1,260	898[b]
Industrial output (Current billion yuan)	124.1	206.6	361.4	652.2	1,071.4
Tax revenue (Current billion yuan)	7.0	10.7	20.6	39.0	n.a.

Notes
[a] n.a.: not available.
[b] Industrial employees only.

Sources: Li et al. (1995, p. 69), SSB (1996, p. 424), Office of the Third National Industrial Census (1997b).

The contribution of foreign capital to China's domestic capital formation has been increasing steadily, especially in recent years. As shown in Table 2.6, total foreign capital inflows (foreign borrowing and direct investment) amounted to a mere 4 per cent of China's total capital investment in 1985. Ten years later, it had risen to 15 per cent. In addition to direct involvement, foreign investment has also contributed to domestic capital formation through mobilising domestic investment, especially in infrastructure. It is estimated that in the early years of the reform period when infrastructure condition was poor, the average domestic funds required for each dollar of

foreign investment was between six and seven yuan. Today, in the established open areas, one dollar of foreign investment still needs at least one
yuan to facilitate its implementation. According to these estimates, the
overall domestic investment associated with FDI has been substantial. The
impact of foreign investment is most noticeable in the coastal regions and
certain industries in which FDI is heavily concentrated.

*Table 2.6   Foreign capital and domestic capital formation in China,
            1985–95 (billion yuan)*

Year	Domestic capital formation		Foreign capital inflow	
	Total	- Fixed assets	Total	- Fixed assets
1985	338.6	264.1	13.6	9.2
1990	644.4	473.2	49.2	28.5
1991	751.7	594.0	40.7	31.9
1992	963.6	831.7	105.9	46.9
1993	1,499.8	1,298.0	224.5	95.4
1994	1,926.1	1,685.6	372.4	176.9
1995	2,387.7	2,030.1	401.9	229.6

Note: Total foreign capital inflow was converted from the US dollar values using annual average
rates of exchange.

Sources: SSB (1997a, pp. 17 and 132, 1997b, p. 19).

The figures in Table 2.6, however, may overestimate the real contribution
of FDI to domestic capital formation. In fact, total foreign capital, entering
China every year, has not all been used as long–term investment in fixed
assets. There is evidence that foreign investment in fixed assets represented
only a portion of total capital inflows in recent years. In 1995, for instance,
foreign–funded fixed asset investment was 230 billion yuan (US$27.7
billion), representing only 57 per cent of total capital inflows over that year.
This figure, if correct, is surprisingly low. One may argue that the remaining
foreign capital was used as working capital. This is not true because, if the
remainder of foreign capital, 172.3 billion yuan, was used in inventory
investment, it would account for nearly half of China's total inventory
investment in that year. It is impossible for half of inventory investment to
be actually funded by foreign capital.[6] The payments for foreign technology
transfer might have consumed some of the remaining foreign–investment
funds, however, a significant portion of annual FDI was still unaccounted
for. It could well have been channelled into other unknown uses, including,
among other things, short–term speculations in China's newly emerging

stock or property markets, or simply have been deposited in a commercial bank for higher interest earnings.

This raises the question as to the importance of FDI as a source of additional savings for China. It is argued that if the domestic saving rate falls short of the investment requirement, foreign capital inflow could serve as an additional source of savings. This argument does not seem applicable to China. Insufficient savings has not been a problem for China in its recent growth because China has one of the world's highest saving rates. The tight monetary policy in the past few years has restricted the expansion of credit and resulted in further building up of investable funds in the banking sector.

Moreover, with an international reserve of US$100 billion, China does not seem to have a foreign exchange shortage problem either. In the last three years, China has been running a current account surplus which, combined with inflows of FDI, has contributed to the rapid build–up of foreign reserves. This has made China a net capital outflow country, instead of a capital inflow country. China does not need foreign capital to supplement domestic savings or investment. It needs foreign capital to bring in modern technologies and managerial know–how for upgrading its domestic industrial structure and transforming its formerly planned economy. To find the real contribution of FDI, one needs to look closely at China's industrial structure.

The impact of FDI on China's industry can be seen from Table 2.7. According to the 1995 national industrial census, the foreign–invested firms altogether produced 19.5 per cent of China's total industrial gross output. In many industries, foreign–invested firms had a much larger share of total output. As shown in Table 2.7, these industries include electronic and telecommunication equipment (60 per cent), leather products (54 per cent), garments (50 per cent), stationery, education and sports goods (50 per cent), instruments, cultural and office machinery (40 per cent), plastic products (33 per cent), other manufacturing (31 per cent) and food manufacturing (30 per cent) and so on. In the meantime, mining and raw industrial material processing industries had much fewer foreign–invested firms which contri–buted much less to their output. The distribution of foreign–invested firms across industries in terms of their output shares largely conforms with the above pattern.

China's policy in relation to foreign investment has been deliberately biased towards export–oriented firms. Through this policy, potential foreign investors are encouraged to seek domestic exporting firms as their partners. As a result, foreign–invested firms have rapidly become major exporters in recent years. In 1988, as shown in Table 2.8, the value of exports from FIEs was US$2.5 billion, accounting for only 5.2 per cent of China's total exports. By 1996, exports from foreign–invested firms reached US$61.5 billion, amounting to over 40 per cent of China's total exports (Table 2.8).

Table 2.7   Structure of foreign–invested industrial firms, 1995

Industry	Share in total FDI output (%)		As % of sectoral output	
Coal mining and processing	2.10	(18)	0.24	(36)
Petroleum and natural gas	2.60	(15)	4.05	(29)
Ferrous metals mining	0.20	(37)	0.21	(37)
Nonferrous metals mining	0.59	(33)	0.66	(34)
Nonmetal minerals mining	0.66	(32)	3.41	(30)
Other minerals mining	0.01	(39)	1.33	(33)
Logging	0.30	(36)	0.01	(39)
Food processing	5.54	(5)	20.45	(16)
Food manufacturing	1.81	(22)	30.24	(8)
Beverage manufacturing	2.10	(17)	23.47	(15)
Tobacco processing	1.83	(21)	0.55	(35)
Textile industry	8.38	(1)	17.90	(19)
Garments	2.68	(14)	50.15	(3)
Leather, furs, down and related products	1.77	(23)	53.63	(2)
Timber processing	0.74	(30)	28.26	(10)
Furniture manufacturing	0.41	(34)	29.90	(9)
Papermaking and paper products	1.85	(20)	17.01	(20)
Printing and record pressing	0.75	(29)	18.01	(18)
Stationery, educational and sports goods	0.68	(31)	50.13	(4)
Petroleum processing and coking products	3.69	(11)	1.43	(32)
Raw chemical materials and products	6.95	(2)	13.18	(23)
Medical and pharmaceutical products	1.75	(24)	19.59	(17)
Chemical fibres	1.47	(25)	13.75	(24)
Rubber products	1.13	(27)	25.04	(12)
Plastic products	2.05	(19)	33.37	(6)
Nonmetal mineral products	5.49	(6)	11.68	(26)
Smelting and pressing of ferrous metals	6.66	(3)	6.28	(28)
Smelting and pressing of nonferrous metals	2.50	(16)	12.63	(25)
Metal products	3.00	(13)	26.62	(11)
Ordinary machinery manufacturing	4.31	(10)	14.19	(21)
Special purpose equipment manufacturing	3.20	(12)	8.86	(27)
Transportation equipment manufacturing	6.01	(4)	24.62	(13)
Electric equipment and machinery	4.72	(7)	24.34	(14)
Electronic and telecommunication equipment	4.61	(8)	59.97	(1)
Instruments, culture and office machinery	0.77	(28)	39.65	(5)
Other manufacturing	1.27	(26)	31.19	(7)
Electric power, steam and hot water	4.44	(9)	13.80	(22)
Gas production and supply	0.14	(38)	3.40	(31)
Tap water production and supply	0.33	(35)	0.16	(38)
Total	100.00		19.50	

Note: Figures in parentheses are the descending ranking orders.

Source: SSB (1996).

Table 2.8   Exports of foreign–invested firms, 1988–96

Year	Exports (US $100m)	Share in total exports (%)	Contribution to export growth (%)[a]
1988	24.6	5.2	18.1
1989	49.2	9.4	48.6
1990	78.1	12.6	30.2
1991	120.5	16.7	43.0
1992	173.6	20.4	40.5
1993	252.4	27.5	115.2
1994	347.1	28.7	32.4
1995	468.8	31.5	43.8
1996	615.1	40.7	638.9

Note: [a] The share of export increase of foreign–invested firms in total export increase.

Sources: Li et al. (1995), SSB (1997a).

The annual increase in FIE exports has usually accounted for 30–40 per cent of export growth since 1988. In some years, China's export growth was entirely driven by foreign–invested firms. In 1993 and 1996, for instance, the increase in FIEs' exports exceeded the total export increase because of the decline in domestic firms' exports.

It should be pointed out, however, that the figures below may overestimate the importance of foreign–invested firms in China's exports. In examining the FIEs' role in China's exports, two types of exports must be dis–tinguished: the domestically produced goods and the goods processed or assembled using imported parts and semi–finished components. The latter contributes much less to domestic value–added because it mainly involves the use of labour and capital in the last stage of the production process. Such exports have increased dramatically in recent years. In 1995, for instance, the value of processed exports was equivalent to 31.5 per cent of China's total exports (General Customs Administration 1996). Table 2.8 may not reflect the true picture about foreign investment firms in China's export production because FIEs' exports are almost exclusively confined to processed products using imported materials or semi–finished inputs. In 1995, as much as 90 per cent of total FIEs' exports, or US$42.1 billion, consisted of products of this kind (Table 2.9). These products could hardly be called 'Chinese' exports, as the processing activities within China add a rather small amount of value to the final products. A more accurate measure of this type of export activities should subtract the value of imported materials and inputs from the value of finished exports. The value of total exports should then include only the value of goods produced through various stages of domestic production and the net revenues of the goods assembled from imported materials at the final stage of production.

Table 2.9   Decomposition of China's total exports, 1995 (US$100 million)

Item	National		Domestic		FIEs	
Total exports	1,487.7	(100%)	1,018.9	(68.5%)	468.8	(31.5%)
Processed exports	737.2	(100%)	316.5	(42.9%)	420.6	(57.1%)
Imports for processing	595.7	(100%)	225.0	(37.8%)	370.6	(62.2%)
Net export revenues	141.5	(100%)	91.5	(64.7%)	50.0	(35.3%)
Exports net of imports for processing	892.0	(100%)	793.9	(89.0%)	98.2	(11.0%)

Source: General Customs Administration (1996).

It is shown in Table 2.9 that the value of exports net of imports for processing in 1995 was US$89.2 billion, of which 89 per cent came from domestic firms and only 11 per cent from foreign–invested firms. The latter figure was much smaller than that estimated from total exports (31.5 per cent). This is because the share of net export revenues in total processed exports for FIEs was only 11.9 per cent, much lower than that for domestic firms, 28.9 per cent. This low share may be justifiable by arguing that FIEs need more imported equipment to set up processing production than their domestic counterparts. However, transfer pricing could also be responsible for such a low revenue rate. None the less, the statistics seem to indicate a rather high cost for FIEs to be engaged in export–processing activities. In contrast, domestic firms seem to be much more profitable in these activities, as is indicated by an extremely favourable export revenue rate.

The involvement of foreign investment in China's export–producing industries would certainly raise productive efficiency and international competitiveness in these industries. However, the linkage effects – especially backward linkage effects – that the foreign investment may have on native industries may be quite limited because of their heavy concentration on processing activities. It also indicates that foreign direct investment in China's manufacturing industries is still in its early stages and mainly involved in the activities making use of China's unlimited supply of low–cost labour.

Are FIEs more export oriented? To answer this question, one needs to compare the ratio of exports to total output for domestic and foreign–invested firms. The value of domestic gross industrial output includes the revenues generated from export–processing activities, which can be estimated by subtracting the imports of goods for export processing from the value of processed exports. According to the 1995 industrial census data, the value of total exports from foreign–invested firms was 386.2 billion yuan. This figure was not comparable with the value of exports for domestic firms, reported in the Census, because the latter excludes the imports for export processing. Using the share of exports (net of imports for processing) in total exports from Table 2.9, one can estimate the value of exports (net of imports for processing) for foreign–invested firms. It was 80.9 billion yuan in 1995 (see Table 2.10). The similar figure for domestic firms was 393 billion yuan for the same year.

Table 2.10   Decomposition of China's industrial output, 1995
             (100 million yuan)

Item	National	Domestic		FIEs	
Gross output	54,946.9	44,232.9	(80.5%)	10,714.0	(19.5%)
Added–value	15,446.1	12,859.7	(83.3%)	2,586.4	(16.7%)
Exports[a]	4,738.9	3,930.2	(82.9%)	808.7	(17.1%)
As % of gross output	8.6	8.9		7.5	
As % of added–value	30.7	30.6		31.3	
Gross output (net of exports)	50,208.0	40,302.7	(80.3%)	9,905.2	(19.7%)

Note: [a] Net of imports for export processing.

Sources: Estimated from General Customs Administration (1996) and Office of the Third National Industrial Census (1996).

Domestic firms produced 83 per cent of China's exports while FIEs produced 17 per cent. The latter share is close to, though slightly higher than, that estimated from the Customs statistics, 11 per cent (see Table 2.9). Based on these estimates, the share of exports in gross output and GDP can be readily derived for both types of firms. As shown in Table 2.10, the ratio of exports to gross output for domestic firms in 1995 was 8.9 per cent, which is higher than foreign–invested firms' 7.5 per cent. The ratio of exports to added–value for domestic firms was 30.6 per cent, which is marginally lower than foreign–invested firms' 31.3 per cent. Contrary to the common perception, foreign–invested firms do not seem to be more export oriented than their domestic counterparts in terms of these measurements.

Although foreign–invested firms contribute, to a certain extent, to Chinese industrial exports, a large and increasing proportion of FIEs' output has actually entered China's domestic markets. In 1995, of 1,071.4 billion yuan worth of goods produced by foreign–invested firms, 92.5 per cent were sold to China's domestic markets. This represents an average share of 19.7 per cent of China's industrial goods market. Domestic sales of FIEs were concentrated in transport equipment, electronic and telecom equipment, food processing, electric equipment and machinery, and textiles. The market shares of FIEs are expected to rise as more and more large multinational corporations enter China. Unlike the early arrivals of small or medium–sized and labour–intensive firms from Hong Kong and Taiwan, the new entrants of large multinationals, equipped with modern technologies, mainly target China's huge and underexploited domestic markets. The main benefits of FIEs currently may come largely from their indirect effects on China's domestic firms. These include spillovers of new technologies, new products and new ways of management as well as the pressures of fierce competition brought along with the entry of FIEs. The presence of FIEs has forced and will continue to press domestic firms to match their performance in an attempt to prevent their market shares from shrinking even further. Such an impact of foreign investment could be much more important over the long run than its role as just a supplement for domestic savings or its direct contribution to national income.

PERFORMANCE OF FOREIGN–INVESTED FIRMS

As shown above, foreign–invested firms have been playing an increasingly important role in the Chinese economy. However, a rigorous assessment of the performance of FIEs is hampered by unavailability of sufficient data on these firms. As the prominence of FIEs is a recent phenomenon, the sys–tematic collection of data on FIEs by the State Statistical Bureau has begun only recently.[7]

This section will provide a preliminary assessment of the performance of FIEs by comparing foreign–invested industrial firms with China's domestic firms. This comparative study is based only on the data from China's industrial sector because this is where most FDI is concentrated and the most recent compatible data on both types of firms can be obtained. Based on the recent publication of 1995 industrial census data, the significance of foreign–invested firms in the Chinese industry can be summarised in Table 2.11.

In 1995, nearly 10 per cent of Chinese industrial firms were foreign invested: either joint ventures, cooperatives, or wholly foreign–owned firms. These firms hired 7.7 per cent of the industrial labour force and possessed 16.9 per cent of total capital assets, including fixed assets and working capital (inventory and financial assets). They produced 19.5 per cent of industrial gross output and 16.7 per cent of industrial added–value. In

Table 2.11   Foreign–invested industrial firms in China, 1995

Indicator	All industrial firms	Foreign–invested firms	
Number of firms (100 units)	5,103.81	495.59	(9.71)
Gross output (100 million yuan)	54,946.86	10,713.97	(19.50)
Added–value (100 million yuan)	15,446.13	2,586.41	(16.74)
Total capital (100 million yuan)	79,233.92	13,348.47	(16.85)
Number of workers (10 thousand persons)	8,575.58	660.53	(7.70)
Value–added tax revenue (100 million yuan)	1,056.68	85.66	(8.11)
Corp tax revenue (100 million yuan)	508.01	53.72	(10.57)

Note: Figures in parentheses are the percentage shares of FIEs in industrial totals.

Source: Office of the Third National Industrial Census (1996).

addition, foreign–invested firms paid 8.9 per cent of total tax revenues from the industrial sector. A striking feature of FIEs emerging from this table is that the shares of employment and tax revenues are substantially lower than that of output or value–added. Table 2.12 provides a more detailed comparison between foreign–invested and domestic industrial firms at the aggregate level. Some of the main observations from the table are highlighted in the following.

- There is a dramatic disparity between the two types of firms in terms of output and inputs. Given an output level, foreign–invested firms tend to employ less labour and more capital than domestic firms. With 23 per cent less labour and 69 per cent more capital assets, an average foreign–invested firm produces 125 per cent more output but only 87 per cent more added–value than an average domestic firm.
- Workers in FIEs are much better equipped and more productive than their domestic counterparts. The average capital–labour ratio in FIEs is 75.3 thousand yuan, more than twice that of domestic firms. This enables a FIE worker to produce 162 thousand yuan worth of output, nearly three times what a worker of a domestic firm could produce.
- The disparity in average capital productivity is less dramatic than in the labour force. The output–fixed capital ratio for FIEs is only 33 per cent

Foreign Direct Investment in the Chinese Economy

Table 2.12   Comparison between foreign–invested and domestic firms: selected indicators

Indicator	Domestic firms	Foreign– invested firms	FIE/ dom.
Output and factors			
Output/Fixed–capital (yuan)	1.62	2.15	(1.33)
Added–value/Fixed–capital (yuan)	0.47	0.52	(1.11)
Fixed–capital/Worker (10,000 yuan)	3.45	7.53	(2.18)
Output/Worker (10,000 yuan)	5.59	16.22	(2.90)
Added–value/Worker (10,000 yuan)	1.62	3.92	(2.42)
Wage/Worker (100 yuan)	49.09	72.00	(1.47)
For Chinese Employees	49.09	68.60	(1.40)
For Foreign Employees	–	289.20	–
Value–added/Gross output (%)	29.07	24.14	(0.83)
Firm size			
Output/Firm (10,000 yuan)	959.87	2,161.86	(2.25)
Added–value/Firm (10,000 yuan)	279.06	521.89	(1.87)
Fixed–capital/Firm (10,000 yuan)	592.62	1,004.43	(1.69)
Workers/Firm (100 person)	1.72	1.33	(0.77)
Tax and profits			
Profits/Total capital (%)	2.19	3.48	(1.59)
Loss–making firm ratio (%)	23.46	39.95	(1.70)
Losses/Profits (%)	75.01	68.06	(0.91)
Corp tax rate (%)	36.80	13.42	(0.36)
Value–added tax rate (%)	15.75	11.84	(0.75)

Source: Office of the Third National Industrial Census (1996).

higher than domestic firms while output–labour ratio is 190 per cent higher. The differences in the labour forces between two types of firms seem to contribute more to the observed higher output level per firm in FIEs.

• The table indicates that foreign–invested firms paid 25 per cent less value–added tax than domestic firms. Even this may still overestimate the real value–added tax rate for FIEs. This is because, under China's export promotion policy, all firms are entitled to claim back the value–added tax they have paid during the process of export production, when their products leave the country. As FIEs are involved in export activities, the real value–added tax rate for FIEs may be much lower than what is suggested in the table. Taking export tax returns into account, foreign–invested firms may actually pay far less value–added tax than their domestic counterparts.

- Foreign–invested industrial firms, on average, appear to be more profitable than their domestic counterparts. However, this cannot be fully attributable to operational efficiency of FIEs over domestic firms. As indicated in Table 2.12, foreign–invested firms paid only one–third of the normal corporate tax, due to the favourable policies towards FDI. It can therefore be estimated that, if FIEs paid corporate tax at the same rate as domestic firms (36.8 per cent), their profit ratio would be reduced by one per cent to 2.5 per cent, which is only marginally (0.3 per cent) higher than that of domestic firms. In this regard, FIEs do not seem to be so much more profitable than domestic firms.

- It is surprising to note that nearly 40 per cent of FIEs were reportedly losing money in 1995. This ratio is much higher than the figure for domestic firms, 23.5 per cent and even higher than that for state–owned enterprises (33.8 per cent). This high loss–making ratio substantially reduced the profitability of FIEs as a whole. The exact causes of this high loss ratio are unknown, but it is suspicious that all of them were genuine loss–makers. The alleged widespread transfer pricing of foreign com-panies may be responsible for at least some of these so–called losses. The real profitability of FIEs could therefore be much higher than the above statistics suggest.

- The production of FIEs appears to be more 'roundabout' than domestic firms, indicated by the relatively low (high) ratio of added–value (intermediate inputs) to gross output value. However, this 'roundabout-ness' may largely result from FIEs' extensive export assembling and processing activities, in which imported instead of domestically produced intermediate goods are involved in the production of the final products. Therefore, the high 'roundaboutness' has not generated sufficient beneficial linkage effects on upstream domestic industries.

The differences between FIEs and domestic firms can further be seen in the compositions of their added–value. Total added–value from the income side can be decomposed into wages, tax payments, profits and depreciation allowance. These components, for the two types of firms, are shown in Table 2.13. In 1995, foreign–invested firms spent proportionally much less on wages and tax payments than domestic firms. As a result, their profit and depreciation shares in total added–value were proportionally much higher. It is also surprising to note that depreciation allowance was extremely high for foreign–invested firms, accounting for more than 43 per cent of their total added–value. This gives an implicit depreciation rate of 18.5 per cent,[8] almost twice the domestic firms' 9.4 per cent. The low depreciation rate of domestic firms could lead to an overuse of fixed capital assets, which may, to some extent, provide an explanation for their low capital productivity and hence less desirable performance.

Table 2.13   Composition of added–value: foreign–invested and domestic firms (100 million yuan)

Indicator	Domestic firms		Foreign–invested firms	
	Level	%	Level	%
Wage and welfare	4,504.4	35.0	618.3	23.9
Tax payments	3,477.9	27.0	445.5	17.2
Profits	1,234.5	9.6	400.4	15.5
Depreciation	3,642.8	28.3	1,122.3	43.4
Added–value	12,859.7	100.0	2,586.4	100.0

Sources: Office of the Third National Industrial Census (1997a, 1997b).

To compare changes in the characteristics of foreign–invested and domestic firms, we estimate the factor elasticities of output and the marginal products of factors for the two types of firms over 1993–95. A simple Cobb–Douglas type of production function is adopted in the estimation,

$$Y = f(K, L) \qquad\qquad (2.1)$$

where Y is output, K and L are capital and labour inputs. In the regression, cross–section data on added–value, fixed capital assets and number of employees from 39 industrial sectors are used (SSB various years). The added values and fixed capital assets are all in current prices. The regressions are conducted separately for each year from 1993 to 1995 to avoid complication of arbitrarily adjusting capital data for intertemporal comparability. Fixed capital assets are used to proximate the input of capital. Two types of fixed capital assets data are reported in Chinese statistics: the original value and the net value. The latter is equivalent to the original value net of cumulative annual depreciation. As there is no easy way to discriminate between either of these two sets of capital data, the regression results on both capital data are reported. The estimated results are reported in Table 2.14.

The performance of the two types of firms can be compared in terms of factor elasticities, average and marginal products (Table 2.15). A number of observations are in order. First, both foreign–invested and domestic firms demonstrate a certain degree of increasing returns to scale in production. More interesting is that the degree of scale economies is increasing for domestic firms while decreasing for FIEs. This may be explained by the relatively small size of the domestic firms in most industries. Second, elasticity of output with respect to capital is generally higher while elasticity with respect to labour is lower in FIEs than in domestic firms. However, the

Table 2.14   OLS regression results for China's industrial firms, 1993–95

Variable	1993		1994		1995	
Foreign–invested firms						
ln FKO	0.65	(6.61)	0.56	(5.40)	0.67	(4.39)
ln LB	0.41	(3.97)	0.49	(4.31)	0.38	(2.30)
Constant	−0.59	(−1.98)	−0.35	(−1.04)	−0.52	(−0.72)
$\bar{R}^2$	0.98		0.97		0.90	
ln FKN	0.64	(6.18)	0.52	(4.97)	0.61	(3.86)
ln LB	0.43	(4.01)	0.54	(4.80)	0.44	(2.60)
Constant	−0.55	(−1.78)	−0.27	(−0.79)	−0.33	(−0.45)
$\bar{R}^2$	0.98		0.97		0.89	
Domestic firms						
ln FKO	0.53	(5.55)	0.56	(4.79)	0.59	(4.73)
ln LB	0.50	(4.50)	0.55	(3.96)	0.49	(3.13)
Constant	−0.65	(−0.73)	−1.77	(−1.52)	−1.33	(−1.00)
$\bar{R}^2$	0.89		0.84		0.80	
ln FKN	0.54	(5.66)	0.56	(4.67)	0.62	(4.47)
ln LB	0.50	(4.56)	0.55	(3.86)	0.49	(3.03)
Constant	−0.56	(−0.65)	−1.69	(1.44)	−1.78	(1.29)
$\bar{R}^2$	0.89		0.84		0.79	

Notes
1. The dependent variable = ln (VA).
2. Number of observations = 39.
3. Figures in parentheses are *t*–ratios.
4. FKO = fixed capital (original value).
5. FKN = fixed capital (net value).
6. LB = labour.

gaps seem to have narrowed by the end of the period as capital elasticity of output increases in domestic firms and labour elasticity in FIEs decreases. These results seem to suggest the existence of a trend of convergence between the two types of industrial firms.

Third, at the beginning of the period, the average and marginal product of both factors are much higher in FIEs than in domestic firms. The superiority of FIEs over domestic firms seems to have eroded as its marginal product of capital declines faster and its marginal product of labour rises slower than that of domestic firms. By the end of the period, for instance, marginal

Table 2.15   Marginal product for foreign–invested and domestic industrial firms, 1993–95

Variable	1993			1994			1995		
	ES	AP	MP	ES	AP	MP	ES	AP	MP
Foreign–invested firms									
Fixed capital (orig)	0.65	0.64	0.42	0.56	0.49	0.28	0.67	0.49	0.33
Labour	0.41	3.31	1.37	0.49	3.40	1.66	0.38	3.84	1.45
Fixed capital (net)	0.64	0.79	0.51	0.52	0.56	0.29	0.61	0.58	0.36
Labour	0.43	3.31	1.44	0.54	3.40	1.84	0.44	3.84	1.69
Domestic firms									
Fixed capital (orig)	0.53	0.49	0.26	0.56	0.43	0.24	0.59	0.42	0.25
Labour	0.50	1.48	0.74	0.55	1.67	0.92	0.49	1.89	0.92
Fixed capital (net)	0.54	0.69	0.37	0.56	0.60	0.34	0.62	0.60	0.37
Labour	0.50	1.48	0.74	0.55	1.67	0.92	0.49	1.89	0.93

Notes
1. ES: elasticity at mean.
2. AP (average product) and MP (marginal product) of capital are measured in yuan.
3. AP and MP of labour are measured in 10,000 yuan.

Source: Table 2.14.

product of capital in FIEs has even dropped to below the level of its domestic counterpart, if capital is measured as the net value of fixed capital assets.

Two possible explanations may be offered for this observed trend of convergence in the industrial sector. On the one hand, the rapid decline of the marginal product of capital in FIEs could be attributed to the dramatic increase in foreign capital inflows to Chinese industries over such a short period. On the other hand, the marginal product of capital in domestic firms has been quite stable over the same period while the marginal product of labour has increased much faster than that in FIEs. The presence of FIEs has certainly contributed to this rapid increase in the marginal product of labour in domestic firms. The comparison has revealed that foreign–invested firms on average have higher productivity and more efficiency, but the gap between foreign–invested firms and domestic firms has narrowed over recent years.

CONCLUDING REMARKS

This chapter has reviewed the formation of China's foreign investment policy and the process of establishing a legal framework for foreign investment over the past 18 years. The rapid inflows of foreign capital since the beginning of 1990s can be attributed to this liberal foreign investment policy, the improved infrastructure, as well as China's huge and rapidly growing domestic market. The chapter has also identified the major contributions of foreign investment to China's recent economic growth and compared the performance of foreign–invested firms and domestic firms.

Although rapid inflows of foreign capital increase its share in domestic capital formation, the main contribution of foreign investment to the Chinese economy has not been that of increasing domestic savings and investable funds. The contribution of foreign capital in fixed asset investment has so far been moderate. The main role of foreign investment in China has been its direct involvement in current production in the form of foreign invested firms. The presence of FIEs helps to re–structure domestic industries, re–organise capital and labour within factories, bring new ways of management, improve upon the quality of existing products and extend export markets. Foreign investment has now penetrated into a wide range of Chinese industries. Foreign–invested firms have produced an increasing proportion of China's manufactured products. They also dominate China's major industrial exports, especially the exports of processed and assembled products.

The presence of foreign–invested firms has set the standard for domestic firms to follow or imitate. It has also forced the domestic firms to join the competition, which has changed the way domestic firms are operated and, therefore, indirectly increased their productivity and efficiency. This seems to be confirmed by an emerging trend of convergence in factor productivity between foreign–invested and domestic firms.

Foreign–invested firms are now a major player in many sectors of the Chinese economy. However, their contribution to the creation of employ–ment and tax revenues has not been as significant as it should be. Tax concessions provided for FIEs are certainly responsible for these results. As foreign–invested firms have already established large market shares in many industries, it is time for those concessions to be removed and a level playing field to be created for domestic firms to compete on an equal footing with foreign–invested firms.

It has been shown in this chapter that only a small proportion of China's annual foreign capital has actually been used in fixed asset investment. This may suggest some inefficiency in the use of foreign capital. China needs foreign capital for upgrading its industrial structure, which will involve introducing modern technologies and capital equipment. The possible leak of FDI funds to short–term speculations contributes to the volatility of China's emerging, but still vulnerable, financial and property markets. This may confirm the concern of Chinese authorities about the impact of foreign capital on domestic money supply and eventually inflation. There is an urgent need for the government to monitor closely the use of foreign private investment funds and make sure that as much of this capital as possible is being used to form domestic capital, especially fixed capital assets.

At the moment, foreign–invested firms are heavily involved in export manufacturing. However, most manufactured exports from FIEs are simple assembled and processed products with high imported components. This is not unusual at the early stage of export–led economic growth. However, to explore fully the benefits of export–led growth strategies, much more effort is required to increase the domestic component in China's manufactured exports. This will allow the linkage effects of manufactured exports to be extended to other related domestic industries. More foreign capital is needed in those heavy industries that produce industrial raw materials and intermediate products. These industries currently receive disproportionately less foreign investment. FDI will help them upgrade their obsolete equipment and raise the standard of their products to enable them to compete with imported goods.

The requirement of balancing foreign exchange accounts used to be a major constraint on the growth of foreign investment in China. This constraint has eased considerably in recent years as the Chinese currency has been made partially convertible on the current account. It is inevitable, however, that as China moves towards a full currency convertible regime, more and more FIEs' products will find their way to domestic markets. This will intensify already fierce competition between FIEs and domestic firms for domestic market shares. To prepare for the inevitable, an open and fair environment should be established so that domestic firms can compete with foreign–invested firms under the same set of rules.

From the foreign investors' perspective, Chinese markets become in–creasingly tough. As more capital flows in, the marginal return has declined. China's domestic firms are also catching up quickly. New investors must prepare to bring in more advanced technologies or new products to be able to stay ahead of their domestic or foreign competitors.

In line with the state industrial policy, foreign capital is to be directed to a number of priority industries, particularly infrastructure, primary production, technology–oriented projects, and projects in the services sector. The government still grants these firms preferential terms in relation to tax, domestic market share and land use. Under a policy called '(using) market in exchange for technology', China is willing to further open its domestic market to those investors who will bring in advanced technologies. The government will continue to offer favourable terms to manufacturing enterprises that can supply the products that China lacks or products for the export market.

In the light of the last decade's experience, the government is now more cautious about the quality of foreign investment. Local authorities in the east coastal regions have already been more selective in approving investment projects because the advantage in low–cost labour is diminishing rapidly as per capita income increases. Hi–tech and export–oriented projects are still welcome in coastal areas, but labour–intensive manufacturing projects may have to go much further inland to find attractive locations. In fact, an increasing number of inland regions are now offering similar incentives for foreign investors. The only disadvantage in inland areas, compared with the coast, is their relatively poor infrastructure, transport and communication systems. From a long–term point of view, however, these problems will be solved by economic development itself.

Looking ahead, it is most likely that the growth of FDI in China will continue, though perhaps at a less spectacular pace than in the past few years. The FDI growth will be sustained by strong growth momentum; further economic reforms, including the perfection of foreign investment policy; locational advantages in labour– and resource–intensive industries, particularly in the inland regions; and the high demand for foreign capital in newly opened industries, especially in the services sector and infrastructure. However, how to make full use of the invested foreign capital will remain a challenge for China's policy makers in the years ahead.

NOTES

1. Foreign capital in this chapter refers to capital outside mainland China, including not only that from foreign countries but also from Hong Kong, Macau and Taiwan.
2. The Yangtze River Delta covers an area of 100,000 square kilometres. It is home to 14 cities including Shanghai, Nanjing, Hangzhou, Suzhou, Wuxi and Changzhou, each of which has a population of over one million, and with an aggregate population of 70 million. The Pearl River Delta comprises nine cities including Guangzhou, Zhuhai, Fuoshan and Dongguan. Its area is greater than Taiwan and it accounts for 70 per cent of Guangdong's GDP.
3. Pudong faces downtown Shanghai across the Huangpu River. It encompasses 350 square kilometres, 11 times the total completed area of 14 coastal economic development zones. According to the plan, Pudong New Area would be a self–contained city with its own airport, subway and ring roads with five independent complex sub–areas specialising in hi–tech manufacturing, education and research, financial and trade, as well as export processing.
4. The statistics on China's industry hereafter refer to all industrial enterprises at or above the township level, unless otherwise indicated.
5. For a survey, see Lloyd (1996).
6. In fact, the same figure was even higher in previous years, 64 per cent for 1993 and 81 per cent for 1994.

7. None the less, some attempts have been made to use available data to empirically estimate the impact of FDI and FIEs on China's domestic economy. See, for instance, Shan (1996), Sun (1996) and Wei (1996).
8. It is defined here as the ratio of depreciation allowance to the original value of fixed capital assets.

REFERENCES

General Customs Administration, various years. *Yearbook of customs statistics of the PRC*, General Customs Office, Beijing.

Lardy, N., 1994. *China in the world economy*, Institute for International Economics, Washington, DC.

Li, L.Q., Zeng, P.Y., He, C.L. and Wu, Y. (eds.), 1995. *China's utilisation of foreign capital* (*Zhongguo liyong waizi jichu zhishi*), China Foreign Economic and Trade Publishing House, Beijing.

Lloyd, P., 1996. 'The role of foreign investment in the success of Asian industrialization', *Journal of Asian Economics*, **7(3)**, 407–33.

Ministry of Foreign Economic Relations and Trade of China (MOFERT). *Almanac of China's foreign economic relations and trade*, annual since 1984, Bejing.

Office of the First National Tertiary Industry Census, 1995. *Statistics of the first census on the tertiary industry in China 1991–1992* (*Zhongguo shouci disan chanye pucha ziliao*), Vol. 1, China Statistical Publishing House, Beijing.

Office of the Third National Industrial Census, 1996. *Summary data of the 1995 third national industrial census of the PRC* (*Zhonghua renmin gonghe guo 1995 nian disanci quanguo gongye pucha ziliao zhaiyao*), China Statistical Publishing House, Beijing.

Office of the Third National Industrial Census, 1997a. *Data of the 1995 third national industrial census of the PRC: total enterprises* (*Zhonghua renmin gonghe guo 1995 nian disanci quanguo gongye pucha ziliao: zonghe, qiye juan*), China Statistical Publishing House, Beijing.

Office of the Third National Industrial Census, 1997b. *Data of the 1995 third national industrial census of the PRC: state–owned, foreign invested, and village and township enterprises* (*Zhonghua renmin gonghe guo 1995 nian disanci quanguo gongye pucha ziliao: guoyou, sanzi, xiangzheng juan*), China Statistical Publishing House, Beijing.

Shan, J., 1996. 'Foreign capital, domestic savings and growth: the case of China', *Working Paper*, **7/96**, Department of Applied Economics, Victoria University of Technology.

SSB (State Statistical Bureau), various years. *Annual report of industrial statistics* (*Gongye tongji nianbao*), China Statistical Publishing House, Beijing.

SSB (State Statistical Bureau), 1996. *Statistical yearbook of China 1996* (*Zhongguo tongji nianjian*), China Statistical Publishing House, Beijing.

SSB (State Statistical Bureau), 1997a. *A statistical survey of China 1997* (*Zhongguo tongji zhaiyao*), China Statistical Publishing House, Beijing.

SSB (State Statistical Bureau), 1997b. *China statistical yearbook on investment in fixed assets 1950–1995* (*Zhongguo gudin zichan touzi tongji nianjian*), China Statistical Publishing House, Beijing.

Sun, H.S., 1996. 'Macroeconomic impact of direct foreign investment in China 1979–93', *Working Paper*, **232**, Department of Economics, University of Sydney, June.

Wei, S.J., 1996. 'Foreign direct investment in China: sources and consequences', in T. Ito and A. Krueger (eds), *Financial deregulation and integration in East Asia*, University of Chicago Press, Chicago and London, 77–101.

World Bank, 1993. *World debit tables: external finance for developing countries*, Washington, DC.

3. Foreign Capital Stock and Its Determinants

Leonard K. Cheng and Yum K. Kwan

INTRODUCTION

Cross–border investment by multinational firms is one of the most salient features of today's global economy. An important question for policy makers is what are the factors that attract foreign direct investment (FDI), as many countries see attracting FDI as an important element in their strategy for economic development. In this chapter, we attempt to answer this question with reference to the Chinese experience.

Reflecting the US leadership in both inward and outward FDI, the existing studies have focused on the geographical distribution of FDI in the US as well as the location of US direct investment in other countries.[1] As a result of its open–door policy, China has emerged as a major recipient of FDI since the early 1990s. Several papers have attempted to uncover the factors behind the geographical distribution of FDI in China (for example, Chen 1994, Cheng and Zhao 1995, Head and Ries 1994, Roselle, Ying and Barlow undated).

The usual approach to estimating the effect of potential determinants of FDI is to regress the chosen dependent variable, such as the probability of locating FDI in a location or the amount of investment located in a location, on a set of independent variables which on theoretical grounds might affect the profitability of investment. These variables typically reflect local market potential, cost of production, cost of transport, taxes, and the treatment of foreign investors. This chapter distinguishes itself from the existing studies by explicitly recognising the facts that (a) investment flow takes time to adjust towards the target stock of FDI, and (b) the target stock itself changes with the environment. More specifically, we apply Chow's (1967) partial adjustment model to analyse the Chinese FDI data from 1986 to 1995.

A partial adjustment model of FDI is specified in the next section. This is followed by a review of the statistical analyses of the location of FDI in the literature and surveys of investors in China and Hong Kong. Subsequently, the data and estimation procedures are described, and the estimation results are reported. The final section compares our estimation results with the existing findings in the literature and makes some concluding remarks.

A PARTIAL ADJUSTMENT MODEL

Let Y_{it} be the stock of FDI in region i at time t and $Y_{it}*$ the corresponding equilibrium or desired stock. Following Chow (1967), we assume that the flow of investment serves to adjust Y_{it} towards $Y_{it}*$ according to the following process:

$$\frac{d \ln Y_{it}}{dt} = \alpha(\ln Y_{it}* - \ln Y_{it}), \quad 0 < \alpha < 1. \tag{3.1}$$

Equation (3.1) says that the percentage change of the FDI stock is proportional to the gap between $\ln Y_{it}$ and $\ln Y_{it}*$. We focus our analysis on capital stock, as opposed to investment flow, because the profitability of new investment depends on the marginal productivity of the existing stock. Other things being equal, a larger existing stock would make additional investment less profitable due to the law of diminishing returns. Also, investment takes time to realise, so the actual capital stock can only adjust gradually towards the desired stock.

Because $d\ln Y_{it} = dY_{it}/Y_{it}$, the equation says that the rate of change of the FDI stock (that is, the flow of FDI in the absence of depreciation) is proportional to the existing stock, holding the gap constant, and vice versa. Under this specification, the accumulation of the stock is assumed to generate a self–reinforcing effect that attracts further investment, but such effects diminish as the stock approaches the equilibrium level. That the quantity of existing stock asserts a positive influence on the flow of FDI can be rationalised as a result of agglomeration effects – positive externalities generated by localisation of industry – as emphasized by Head and Ries (1994) and Head, Ries and Swenson (1995) in their study of FDI location in China and the US, respectively.

In practice, (3.1) is replaced by its discrete version (where lower–case letters stand for logarithmic values, for example, $y_{it} = \ln Y_{it}$),

$$y_{it} - y_{it-1} = \alpha(y_{it}* - y_{it-1}) \tag{3.2}$$

or

$$y_{it} = (1-\alpha)y_{it-1} + \alpha y_{it}* \tag{3.3}$$

For the adjustment process described by equation (3.3) to be stable (that is, non–explosive) and non–fluctuating, $(1 - \alpha)$ must be a positive fraction. To estimate the above equation, we need to specify the determinants of $y_{it}*$. Theoretically, the location choice of FDI is determined by relative profitability. If a location is chosen as the destination of FDI, then from the investor's point of view, it must be more profitable to produce in that location than in others, given the location choice of other investors. If the goods are produced for exports, the costs of producing the goods and the costs and reliability of transporting them to the world market are most crucial. If the goods and services are produced for the local market, then local demand factors would also matter.

In both cases, government policies such as preferential tax treatment, market access, and the time and effort needed to gain government approval and so on, would have an impact on a location's attractiveness to foreign investors. A general empirical observation is that preferential tax treatment as an inducement for FDI is more important for export–oriented investment than for investment that is aimed at the local market, and the opposite is true for policies on market access.[2] Consistent with these theoretical considerations and empirical observations, statistical analyses of the location choice of FDI in the US and of US direct investment in other countries have pointed to the importance of three sets of variables:[3]

1. Access to national and regional markets.
2. Local labour market conditions, including wages, quality of workers, and the degree of unionisation; infrastructures; manufacturing agglomeration and density.
3. Preferential policy towards FDI.

Rozelle, Ying and Barlow (undated) study the impact of a number of investment policy variables on FDI in 128 cities (excluding the special economic zones) in 1986. The other explanatory variables are 'gross industrial output' and 'distance to Hong Kong'. They have found that (a) 'the distance from Hong Kong is inversely related to investment activity' and (b) 'policies which facilitate the process of doing business have a more significant effect on foreign investment than certain income tax–reducing or promotional measures'.

Hong Kong has been the largest source of FDI in China by far. Thus, it would be useful to know which factors are considered important by investors from Hong Kong. Such information has been contained in two surveys conducted by the Hong Kong Federation of Industries (1991, 1993). In the first survey, geographical proximity to Hong Kong was considered a crucial factor for investing in the Pearl River Delta by 96.7 per cent of over 1,200 respondents. The second survey, with a total of close to 800 respondents, discovered that 'regardless of the type of industry, the distance from Hong Kong seemed to be one of the most important factors for the choice of factory locations in China'.

In a survey of about 1,000 'foreign' investors (including those from Hong Kong, Macau, and Taiwan) conducted by the China Statistical Bureau in early 1994,[4] 81.9 per cent of the respondents indicated that labour supply was an important attraction, and over half of them regarded it as the most important factor. Over half of the investors said they were attracted by the domestic market, and 56 per cent said preferential tax treatment was an important factor.

On the basis of the existing statistical analyses of the location of FDI and results from surveys of foreign investors in China and Hong Kong, we postulate that the desired stock of FDI in region i in period t, $y_{it}*$, is a function of region i's location, infrastructure, labour quality, wage rate, per capita regional income, per capita GDP, and policies designed to attract FDI. Given the importance of FDI originating from Hong Kong, our location variable is the straight line distance to Hong Kong from a region's capital (*DHK*). This variable captures not only the relative ease of moving goods to the world market, but also the ethnic and cultural distance between a region and the Hong Kong investors. Our choice of infrastructure variable is the length of roads per unit of land mass (*HY*).

A region's real wage cost is denoted by *WAGE*, and the percentage of the population with at least junior secondary school education (*PPSJ*) is used as a proxy for labour quality.[5] The choice of the education variable *PPSJ* is motivated by the consideration that a middle–school education is relevant to FDI in China given that many of the industries receiving FDI do not require highly skilled workers. A region's per capita real income (*PCRI*) is included to capture the attractiveness of the regional market while per capita *GNP* is used to capture the state of the national economy. The use of *PCRI* to capture the regional market and of *HY* to capture infrastructure follows Coughlin, Terza and Vachira (1991).

The policy variables include the number of special economic zones (*SEZ*),[6] open coastal cities (*OCC*), economic and technological development zones (*ETDZ*), and open coastal areas (*OCA*). *SEZ* and *OCC* were the two most important policy designations in attracting FDI to China, but they were confined to a small subset of regions along the coast. To a large extent, *ETDZ* is an extension of the *OCC*. In contrast with these three policy variables, *OCA* were introduced later, far more numerous, and geographically most dispersed.[7] In terms of what each policy designation was able to offer, *SEZ* would be ranked at the top, to be followed by *OCC* and *ETDZ*, and *OCA* would be at the bottom.

To avoid simultaneity problems and to allow for time lags, lagged income, wage and policy variables are used in the analysis. We also construct a number of alternative variables for sensitivity analysis. Relative wage cost (*RWAGE*) (that is, a region's wage cost divided by average wage cost across regions) measures a region's wage cost relative to all the other regions. Relative per capita real income (*RPCRI*), relative education (*RPPSJ*), and relative infrastructure (*RHY*) are similarly defined. Given the positive correlation of the policy variables, we also consider their sum as an aggregate policy variable, $ZONE = OCC + ETDZ + OCA$ (the correlation among these three policy variables is quite high).[8] Given that the absolute size of *OCA* is much larger than that of the other three policy variables, *OCA* and *ZONE* are highly positively correlated.[9]

Collecting the above–mentioned explanatory variables in a vector x_{it}, we write the equilibrium stock as

$$y_{it}* = \pi' x_{it} \tag{3.4}$$

where π is a vector of parameters. Substituting (3.4) into (3.3) and appending random disturbances, our empirical model can be written as

$$y_{it} = (1 - \alpha)y_{it-1} + \beta' x_{it} + \varepsilon_i + u_{it} \tag{3.5}$$
$$i = 1, 2, ..., N, \qquad t = 1, 2, ..., T.$$

where $\beta = \alpha \pi$, ε_i captures the (unobserved) region–specific effects, and u_{it} is assumed to be independently and identically distributed for all i and t.

DATA AND ESTIMATION PROCEDURE

According to the preceding descriptions, a list of variables can be defined as follows:

Y_t	natural log of cumulative real realised FDI at the end of year t.
PPSJ	natural log of the percentage of population six years or older with junior secondary school education or above.
RPPSJ	natural log of the ratio of antilog (*PPSJ*) and its national average.
HY	natural log of (kilometres of roads/square kilometres of land mass).
RHY	natural log of the ratio of antilog (*HYI*) and its national average.
WAGE	natural log of region i's real wage.
RWAGE	natural log of (region i's real wage/average of the regions' real wages).
PCRI	natural log of per capita real regional income.
RPCRI	natural log of (region i's per capita real income/average of the regions' per capita real income).
GNP	natural log of China's real per capita GNP.
ETDZ	natural log of (number of *ETDZ* + 1), where '1' is added to allow for zero *ETDZ* in many regions.
OCA	natural log of (number of *OCA* + 1), where '1' is added to allow for zero *OCA* in many regions.

OCC	natural log of (number of *OCC* + 1), where '1' is added to allow for zero *OCC* in many regions.
SEZ	natural log of (number of *SEZ* + 1), where '1' is added to allow for zero SEZ in many regions.
ZONE	natural log of (number of *ETDZ* + number of *OCC* + number of *OCA* +1).

The FDI data are obtained from Ministry of Foreign Trade and Economic Corporations (MOFTEC) and most of the other data are from various issues of *China Statistical Yearbook*. The deflator for FDI is the US producer price index of capital equipment published by the US Bureau of Labor Statistics. The deflator for per capita real income is the consumer price index of each region. The 1993 figure for the length of the railway in Tianjin given in *China Statistical Yearbook* is not consistent with data of the previous year. The length of the railway in 1993 is considerably shorter than that in 1992. Therefore, the figure from the *Tianjing Statistical Yearbook* is adopted instead. In addition, the 1994 figure is not available, but it is assumed equal to that of 1993. Data about the regions' education were available only as a result of censuses (entire population or sampling), namely, in 1982, 1987, 1990 and 1993. The 1982 data were found in the *1986 Almanac of China's Population*. The 1987, 1990 and 1993 data were found in *China Population Statistical Yearbook* 1988, 1990 and 1994, respectively. Data for all other years were generated by linear intrapolation and extrapolation. *PPSJ* is the percentage of the population aged six or above with at least a junior secondary school education. Regional income data are only available up to 1992; figures for 1993–95 are interpolated from the corresponding regional GDP data which replace the national income data starting from 1993. We first estimate a fixed effect model, $\ln(RI_{it}) = \alpha_i + \beta \ln(GDP_{it}) + \varepsilon_{it}$, using data for the interim period 1990–92 during which both RI and GDP are available. RI figures for 1993–95 are then interpolated from the estimated equation using the available GDP data.

Data

In our sample, a region is either a province, or a centrally administered municipality, or an autonomous region. Regional data for realised FDI from 1979 to 1982 are available only as the total amount over the four–year period. Annual realised FDI data at the regional level are available beginning in 1983. The stock of FDI in year *t* is defined as the amount of cumulative FDI from 1979 to the end of the year (China's open–door policy began in 1979). While FDI stock figures were available beginning 1982, most regions started to have positive stocks only in 1983 and some did not have a positive stock as late as 1985.[10] Since FDI stock lagged one year is needed as a pre–determined variable, the dependent variable starts from 1986 and ends in 1995. Thus, the panel data used in the following econometric analysis cover 29 regions over a ten–year period. Xizang (Tibet), the thirtieth region, had no FDI at all throughout the entire period and is thus excluded. In addition, all real variables are measured in 1990 prices.

Estimation Procedure

Equation (3.5) is a panel data dynamic regression model with a lagged dependent variable on the right–hand side. It is known that in this case the usual fixed effect least square dummy variable (*LSDV*) estimator is biased at the order of $1/T$ (Anderson and Hsiao 1981, 1982, and Hsiao 1986). In particular, the estimate of the coefficient of the lagged dependent variable is biased downwards. The other problem with the fixed effect model is that, in our application, the explanatory variables include two time–invariant variables (*DHK* and *OCC*) and two other variables that are nearly time–invariant (*SEZ* and *ETDZ*). In view of the fixed effect dummy variables the time–invariant variables result in singularity, thus rendering none of the corresponding parameters identifiable.

We thus adopt a random effect specification in which the region–specific effect is treated as part of a composite error term, $v_{it} = \varepsilon_i + u_{it}$, and the two error–components, ε_i and u_{it}, are assumed to satisfy all standard assumptions and are mutually independent. Such a composite error, however, creates heteroscedasticity which renders the ordinary least square estimator inefficient and, in the current context of a dynamic model, also biased and inconsistent. We estimate the model by the generalised least square method, which is consistent and fully efficient. The relevant formulae are standard and can be found in Hsiao (1986).

ESTIMATION RESULTS

The estimation results of equation (3.5) are given in the first column of Table 3.1. All of the explanatory variables except *ETDZ* have the expected sign. The labour quality variable, *PPSJ*, the location variable *DHK*, and all of the four policy variables are statistically insignificant. Since the policy variables are rather highly correlated, we include only one variable at a time and then tried *ZONE*. When that is done, the coefficients for both *ZONE* and *OCA* become significant, which is to be expected due to the extremely positive correlation between *OCA* and *ZONE*. The coefficient for *DHK* also becomes significant in these two and other cases, which could be due to the removal of *SEZ* as an independent variable as *SEZ* and *DHK* are quite negatively correlated.[11] For some reason, the coefficient for *HY* becomes insignificant when that for *DHK* becomes significant.

Table 3.1   *Estimation results (dependent variable: natural log of cumulative real realised FDI, sample period: 1986–95)*

Constant	−5.465	−4.658	−4.918	−4.695	−4.497	−4.627
	(−4.99)**	(−4.76)**	(−4.90)**	(−4.78)**	(−4.49)**	(−4.71)**
$y_{t-1}(1-\alpha)$	0.895	0.900	0.898	0.903	0.903	0.900
	(57.20)*	(58.28)**	(56.61)*	(58.75)*	(58.23)	(58.15)*
RPPSJ	0.042	0.086	0.036	0.067	0.063	0.082
	(0.46)	(0.93)	(0.40)	(0.73)	(0.66)	(0.89)
HY	0.058	0.039	0.054	0.040	0.041	0.040
	(2.27)*	(1.56)	(2.10)*	(1.62)	(1.61)	(1.59)
WAGE	−0.557	−0.488	−0.521	−0.491	−0.485	−0.500
	(−3.96)**	(−3.47)**	(−3.62)**	(−3.48)**	(−3.40)**	(−3.52)**
PCRI	0.297	0.259	0.301	0.273	0.280	0.266
	(3.65)**	(3.30)**	(3.99)**	(3.48)**		(3.40)**
GNP	1.100	0.988	1.018	0.994	0.965	0.991
	(7.52)**	(7.43)**	(7.41)**	(7.41)**	(7.19)**	(7.43)**
SEZ	0.157		0.121			
	(1.77)		(1.46)			
OCC	0.087			0.066		
	(0.916)			(1.55)		
ETDZ	−0.120				0.037	
	(−1.552)				(0.88)	
OCA	0.030					0.027
	(1.189)					(2.01)*
ZONE		0.028				
		(2.07)*				
DHK	−0.018	−0.078	−0.049	−0.080	−0.087	−0.078
	(−0.39)	(−2.14)*	(−1.08)	(−2.20)*	(−2.39)*	(−2.14)*
Exclude	8 – 11, 13	12, 13	8, 13	9, 13	10, 13	11, 13
p–value of *F*-test	0.015	0.006	0.017	0.015	0.033	0.006

Notes

t–statistics are in parentheses.

*   Significant at the 5% level.

**   Significant at the 1% level.

The last two rows report *F*–test results for the joint null hypotheses of excluding the policy variables and *DHK*. 'Exclude' indicates the row numbers of the variables to be excluded. '*p*–value' is the marginal significance level of the *F*–test; a small value signifies rejection of the null hypothesis.

The coefficient for y_{t-1} was remarkably stable. It was almost 0.9, indicating a strong self–reinforcing effect of past values of y_t on its current value. The coefficient for *WAGE* was also quite stable around 0.5, indicating a one per cent increase in a region's wage costs would reduce its FDI by about half a percent.

The coefficient of *PCRI* is in the range of 0.25–0.3, whereas the coefficient of *GNP* is very close to unity. This last result suggests that, other things being equal, regional FDI is proportional to China's per capita GNP.

The estimation results of a variant of equation (3.5) obtained by replacing the variables *PPSJ*, *HY*, *WAGE* and *PCRI* by their relative counterparts *RPPSJ*, *RHY*, *RWAGE*, and *RPCRI*, respectively, are given in Table 3.2. The signs of the coefficients are identical to those in Table 3.1, and the pattern of significance is almost identical. Despite the substitution of the above four variables by their relative counterparts, the estimates of $(1 - \alpha)$ remain unchanged. However, the coefficient of *GNP* has fallen from unity to the range of 0.77–0.87.

It is well known that until recently, China's policy towards FDI was largely location based, that is, it spread its preferential FDI policies from Guangdong and Fujian (in the form of four SEZ), to the coastal cities (in the form of 14 OCC), and then to the coastal regions (in the form of over 30 ETDZ in the OCC and elsewhere and subsequently hundreds of OCA),[12] so it would not come as a surprise to observe the policy variables are negatively related to *DHK* (which is most negatively related to *SEZ*). To purge the multicollinearity problem caused by the inclusion of *DHK*, we have re–estimated equation (3.5) and its relative variant by dropping the variable. The results are presented in Tables 3.3 and 3.4. A comparison with Table 3.1 reveals that there were two major effects of dropping *DHK*. First, the variable *HY* has become highly significant. Second, the policy variable *OCC* has become significant when it is entered as the only policy variable, but *SEZ* is highly significant with or without other policy variables. A comparison of Table 3.4 with Table 3.2 reveals that dropping *DHK* from the variant model has exactly the same effects in the original model.

Thus, Tables 3.3 and 3.4 have confirmed the apparently important role of the *SEZ* and *OCC* in attracting FDI. Their impact can be marred, however, by the inclusion of collinear variables such as *DHK*. It thus seems that earlier findings of the importance of *DHK* as a determinant of FDI might be capturing the effect of the policy variables (for instance, Roselle, Ying and Barlow undated, and Cheng and Zhao 1995).

CONCLUDING REMARKS

Using a conditional logit model and a sample of 931 foreign ventures not originating from Hong Kong, Macau or Taiwan in 54 Chinese cities over the

Table 3.2   *Estimation results, option 1 (dependent variable: natural log of cumulative real realised FDI, sample period: 1986–95)*

Constant	−5.857 (−5.67)**	−4.953 (−5.87)**	−5.296 (−5.87)**	−5.008 (−5.88)**	−4.706 (−5.48)**	−4.938 (−5.84)**
y_{t-1} $(1-\alpha)$	0.899 (56.70)*	0.905 (58.75)**	0.903 (56.99)**	0.908 (59.14)**	0.909 (59.00)*	0.905 (58.52)**
RPPSJ	0.116 (1.22)	0.153 (1.62)	0.091 (0.99)	0.126 (1.35)	0.125 (1.31)	0.153 (1.60)
HY	0.064 (2.47)*	0.047 (1.91)	0.063 (2.45)*	0.049 (1.98)*	0.049 (1.96)	0.048 (1.93)
WAGE	−0.421 (−2.91)**	−0.350 (−2.44)*	−0.385 (−2.62)**	−0.355 (−2.47)*	−0.348 (−2.41)*	−0.361 (−2.50)*
PCRI	0.210 (2.46)*	0.171 (2.09)*	0.224 (2.86)**	0.190 (2.34)*	0.190 (2.20)*	0.177 (2.16)*
GNP	0.871 (6.43)**	0.797 (6.47)**	0.822 (6.58)**	0.807 (6.52)**	0.773 (6.12)**	0.796 (6.44)**
SEZ	0.142 (1.57)		0.117 (1.42)			
OCC	0.068 (0.70)			0.073 (1.73)		
ETDZ	−0.102 (−1.30)				0.049 (1.17)	
OCA	0.035 (1.33)					0.031 (2.26)*
ZONE		0.031 (2.32)*				
DHK	−0.013 (−0.27)	−0.064 (−1.77)	−0.038 (−0.84)	−0.066 (−1.82)	−0.073 (−2.00)*	−0.065 (−1.77)
Exclude	8 – 11, 13	12, 13	8, 13	9, 13	10, 13	11, 13
p–value of *F*–test	0.026	0.007	0.038	0.023	0.052	0.008

Notes
t–statistics are in parentheses.
* Significant at the 5% level.
** Significant at the 1% level.
The last two rows report *F*–test results for the joint null hypotheses of excluding the policy variables and *DHK*. 'Exclude' indicates the row numbers of the variables to be excluded. '*p*–value' is the marginal significance level of the *F*–test; a small value signifies rejection of the null hypothesis.

Table 3.3   Estimation results, option 2 (dependent variable: natural log of
cumulative real realised FDI, sample period: 1986–95)

Constant	−5.439	−4.113	−4.772	−4.156	−3.830	−4.067
	(−5.05)**	(−4.34)**	(−4.82)**	(−4.35)**	(−3.96)**	(−4.28)**
$y_{t-1}(1-\alpha)$	0.897	0.920	0.905	0.924	0.927	0.921
	(59.85)**	(72.34)**	(61.11)**	(73.67)**	(74.22)**	(72.53)**
PPSJ	0.029	0.024	0.005	0.003	0.008	0.021
	(0.35)	(0.28)	(0.06)	(0.04)	(0.09)	(0.24)
HY	0.064	0.065	0.070	0.067	0.070	0.066
	(3.14)**	(3.15)**	(3.39)**	(3.24)**	(3.36)**	(3.19)**
WAGE	−0.556	−0.420	−0.509	−0.423	−0.408	−0.433
	(−4.03)**	(−3.15)**	(−3.63)**	(−3.14)**	(−3.02)**	(−3.22)**
PCRI	0.287	0.186	0.269	0.198	0.196	0.193
	(3.69)**	(2.66)**	(3.89)**	(2.84)**	(2.61)**	(2.77)**
GNP	1.094	0.872	0.987	0.880	0.829	0.875
	(7.54)**	(7.12)**	(7.36)**	(7.08)**	(6.77)**	(7.13)**
SEZ	0.177		0.172			
	(2.68)**		(2.69)**			
OCC	0.099			0.080		
	(1.10)			(1.97)*		
ETDZ	−0.129				0.048	
	(−1.76)				(1.18)	
OCA	0.029					0.031
	(1.16)					(2.42)*
ZONE		0.032				
		(2.46)*				

Notes
t–statistics are in parentheses.
*   Significant at the 5% level.
** Significant at the 1% level.

Table 3.4 *Estimation results, option 3 (dependent variable: natural log of cumulative real realised FDI, sample period: 1986–95)*

Constant	−5.896	−4.774	−5.346	−4.841	−4.455	−4.747
	(−5.98)**	(−5.70)**	(−6.03)**	(−5.72)**	(−5.24)**	(−5.66)**
$y_{t-1}(1-\alpha)$	0.901	0.921	0.909	0.924	0.928	0.921
	(58.83)**	(71.63)**	(60.93)**	(72.72)**	(73.88)**	(71.79)**
PPSJ	0.105	0.103	0.066	0.075	0.067	0.102
	(1.18)	(1.16)	(0.77)	(0.85)	(0.76)	(1.14)
HY	0.068	0.069	0.075	0.072	0.074	0.070
	(3.29)**	(3.32)**	(3.64)**	(3.43)**	(3.53)**	(3.37)**
WAGE	−0.423	−0.294	−0.379	−0.298	−0.283	−0.307
	(−2.96)**	(−2.15)*	(−2.64)**	(−2.16)*	(−2.07)*	(−2.23)*
PCRI	0.205	0.112	0.201	0.129	0.120	0.117
	(2.49)*	(2.53)*	(2.79)**	(1.77)	(1.54)	(1.61)
GNP	0.864	0.708	0.791	0.717	0.666	0.705
	(6.42)**	(6.21)**	(6.55)**	(6.23)**	(5.73)**	(6.17)**
SEZ	0.157		0.158			
	(2.33)*		(2.45)*			
OCC	0.076			0.086		
	(0.84)			(2.09)*		
ETDZ	−0.108				0.059	
	(−1.45)				(1.45)	
OCA	0.034					0.034
	(1.31)					(2.59)**
ZONE		0.035				
		(2.65)**				

Notes
t–statistics are in parentheses.
*   Significant at the 5% level.
** Significant at the 1% level.

period 1984–91, Head and Ries (1994) study the existence of agglomeration effects from foreign firms and the domestic industrial sector along with other regressors including policies towards FDI, infrastructure, industrial wages and industrial productivity.[13] They have found evidence for agglomeration effects, and positive effects for FDI policies and infrastructure (but not for the airport dummy). Like Head and Ries, we have found strong and consistent agglomeration effects. Like them we have also found positive effects of good infrastructure, but the effects are not always significant unless *DHK* is dropped.

Chen (1994) examines the significance of five potential determinants of regional distribution of FDI in China from 1987 to 1991, namely, market, wage, industrial efficiency, R&D intensity and infrastructure.[14] He has found that (a) 'market only affects FDI in the middle region(s)', (b) 'wages do not affect FDI', and (c) 'FDI may not necessarily locate near innovative Chinese industries'. In our study, however, we have found that both national and regional markets are consistently significant, and wage costs have a significantly negative effect in all cases. The last result is in stark contrast with Chen (1994) and Head and Ries's (1994) findings that the effect of wages is negligible.

The effect of preferential policies and distance from Hong Kong deserve a more careful explanation. The coefficient of *DHK* has the expected negative sign in all cases, thus confirming Rozelle, Ying and Barlow's finding that 'the distance from Hong Kong is inversely related to investment activity' but it is significant in some cases but not in others. Moreover, without exception, it is insignificant whenever *SEZ* enters as an additional independent variable.

Until recently China's FDI policy has been location based and it initially started in regions close to Hong Kong, therefore, the policy variables are negatively related to *DHK* although some are more closely related than others. Thus, it could well be capturing the effect of the policy variables. Our regression results without this variable in Tables 3.3 and 3.4 have given support to such a hypothesis. And the *F*-tests for the joint significance of *DHK* and the policy variables reported in Tables 3.1 and 3.2 show very clearly the collinearity effect. Without exception, the *F*-tests are all highly significant despite the variables being individually insignificant in most cases. Thus, our conclusion is that *DHK* should not be used as an independent variable along with the FDI policy variables.

The policy variables themselves are also positively correlated, and the correlation among *OCC*, *ETDZ* and *OCA* is particularly strong. When they are entered separately as independent variables, with or without *DHK*, none are significant. Thus, it seems that their sum *ZONE* would be a more proper independent variable to include.

In the absence of *DHK*, *SEZ* is by far the most significant variable (in terms of the *t*-value and size of the coefficient) either when it enters as the only policy variables or with the other three policy variables. The importance of *SEZ* is widely recognized, and it is also supported by our statistical analysis, provided that a proxy variable such as *DHK* is not included to take away its significance.

The education variable PPSJ does not have any significant impact on FDI, as first found by Cheng and Zhao (1995). This is perhaps not surprising, because as China started its open–door policy, FDI was attracted not to areas with higher education attainment, but to South China, due to preferential policy and its geographical proximity to Hong Kong.

NOTES

1. For example, Coughlin, Terza and Vachira (1991), Friedman, Gerlowski and Silberman (1992), Head, Ries and Swenson (1995), Wheeler and Mody (1992), and Woodward (1992).
2. OECD (1992, p.81) states that 'one factor influencing the role played by investment incentives is whether the foreign investment is intended to replace imports by local production or is geared to production for export. In the former case, it is likely that the effect of incentives will be relatively limited. The existence of a specific and often protected market is often the major determinant of the investment, as market protection is a powerful incentive. In the second case, on the other hand, incentives are probably more important.'
3. See the references cited in note 1.
4. The results of the survey of were reported in *Ming Pao*, a Chinese language newspaper in Hong Kong, on 28 March 1994.
5. Woodward (1992) used the 'mean year of school completed by population over 25' as an education variable. Our education variables are the percentages of the population aged six and over who have attained at least a particular educational level.
6. Hainan became a province and an SEZ in 1988. Shanghai's Pudong New Zone, treated as an SEZ for the purpose of classification of policy designations, was established in 1990. The SEZ variable for all other regions remained constant over the entire period, that is, 3 for Guangdong, 1 for Fujian, and 0 for all other regions.
7. Even cities not very close to the coast, such as Zinan, the capital city of Shandong, were designated as *OCA*. For a description of the evolution of China's policy towards FDI, see Cheng (1994).
8. The coefficient of correlation between *OCC* and *ETDZ* is 0.84. That between *ETDZ* and *OCA* is 0.806, and that between *OCC* and *OCA* is 0.847. The coefficients of correlation between SEZ and the other three policy variables, in contrast, are only between 0.3 and 0.4.
9. The coefficient of correlation between *OCA* and *ZONE* is 0.967.
10. Regions whose positive initial stock did not begin in 1983 include Jiling (1985), Anhui (1984), Yunnan (1984), Qinghai (1984), and Ningxia (1984), where the year in parenthesis indicates the year when FDI stock first became positive.
11. The coefficient of correlation between *SEZ* and *DHK* is –0.7.
12. See Cheng (1994) for a detailed description of the evolution of the policy.
13. The size of the domestic industrial sector is measured by either the number of domestic industrial enterprises or the value of domestic industrial output. Policies are captured by two dummy variables depending on whether a city was one of the economic zones before or after 1986. Infrastructure is measured by the number of deep–water berths, a dummy variable for railroad, and another dummy variable for airport.
14. Market is defined as per capita income divided by employment in manufacturing. Wage is the industrial wage rate. Industrial efficiency is before tax profits divided by industrial output. R&D intensity is R&D employees divided by population. And infrastructure is miles of railroad divided by total area of land mass.

REFERENCES

Anderson, T.W. and Hsiao, C., 1981. 'Estimation of dynamic models with error components', *Journal of American Statistical Association*, **76**, 598–606.

Anderson, T.W. and Hsiao, C., 1982. 'Formulation and estimation of dynamic models using panel data', *Journal of Econometrics*, **18**, 47–82.

Chen, C.H., 1994. 'The locational choice of foreign direct investment in mainland China: an empirical study' (in Chinese), *Economic Papers*, **150**, Chung–Hua Institution for Economic Research, Taipei.

Cheng, L.K., 1994. *Foreign direct investment in China*, Organisation for Economic Co–Operation and Development Report COM/DAFFE/IME/TD (94) 129.

Cheng, L.K. and Zhao, H.Y., 1995. 'Geographical patterns of foreign direct investment in China: location, factor endowments, and policy incentives', Mimeo, Department of Economics, Hong Kong University of Science and Technology, Clear Water Bay, Hong Kong.

Chow, G.C., 1967. 'Technological change and the demand for computers', *American Economic Review*, **57**, 1117–30.

Coughlin, C., Terza, J.V. and Vachira, 1991. 'State characteristics and the location of foreign direct investment within the United States', *Review of Economics and Statistics*, **73**, 675–83.

Friedman, J., Gerlowski, D.A. and Silberman, J., 1992. 'What attracts foreign multinational corporations? evidence from branch plant location in the United States', *Regional Science*, **32**, 403–18.

Head, K. and Ries, J., 1994. 'Inter–city competition for foreign investment: static and dynamic effects of China's incentive areas', Mimeo, Faculty of Commerce, University of British Columbia.

Head, K., Ries, J. and Swenson, D., 1995. 'Agglomeration benefits and location choice: evidence from Japanese manufacturing investment in the United States', *Journal of International Economics*, **38**, 223–47.

Hong Kong Federation of Industries, 1991. *Hong Kong's industrial investment in the Pearl River Delta*, Hong Kong.

Hong Kong Federation of Industries, 1993. *Investing in China*, Hong Kong.

Hsiao, C., 1986. *Analysis of panel data*, Cambridge University Press, Cambridge, New York.

Organisation for Economic Co–operation and Development (OECD), 1992. *The OECD declaration and decisions on international investment and multinational enterprises: 1991 Review*, Paris.

Rozelle, S., Ying, Y. and Barlow, M., undated. 'Targeting transaction costs: an evaluation of investment incentive policies in China's foreign trade zones', Mimeo, Food Research Institute, Stanford University.

Wheeler, D. and Mody, A., 1992. 'International investment location decisions: the case of US firms', *Journal of International Economics*, **33**, 57–76.

Woodward, D.P., 1992. 'Locational determinants of Japanese manufacturing start–ups in the United States', *Southern Economic Journal*, **58**, 690–708.

4. The Performance of FDI

Yanrui Wu

Within the new growth framework, foreign direct investment (FDI) is treated as one of the factor inputs along with labour and (domestic) capital. It is argued that FDI is one of the main forces driving economic growth in the less–developed countries. In particular, It has long been recognised that FDI is a major source of technology and know–how to developing countries (Balasubramanyan, Salisu and Sapsford 1996). FDI distinguishes itself from other forms of investment by its ability to transfer not only production know–how but also other technical, managerial and marketing skills. It also brings tremendous externalities into the host countries, namely, promoting competition, technical progress through investment in R&D, and through specialisation.

However, the experience of the developed economies shows that whether foreign capital is productive depends on some initial conditions in the hosting economies. It is particularly argued that the Marshall Plan worked for Europe after the Second World War because the European countries receiving aid possessed the necessary structural, institutional, and attitudinal conditions, for example, well–integrated commodity and money markets, highly developed transport facilities, a well–trained and educated workforce, and an efficient government bureaucracy. These pre–conditions helped convert new capital effectively into higher levels of output in Europe.

Since the inception of economic reform in 1978, China has experienced two decades of rapid growth in foreign direct investment. This growth was particularly impressive in the first half of the 1990s. As a result, FDI as a share of total investment has increased rapidly during the past fifteen years. Immediately, one may ask how efficiently FDI has been utilised in the Chinese economy, given the poor infrastructure and an economic system in transition. The current chapter presents an analysis on this issue. In particular, it focuses on comparing FDI performance among the Chinese regions. The rest of the chapter begins with a brief review of foreign investment in China. Some conceptual issues about performance measurement are then examined. This is followed by empirical estimations and interpretations of the results. Finally, some summary remarks are presented in the conclusion.

FOREIGN INVESTMENT IN CHINA: A REVIEW

Foreign investment has very much been a recent event in the People's Republic of China. The first regulatory document relating to foreign investment was released in July 1979. In the same year, foreign investment was, for the first time, recorded in the official statistical source. Only a small amount was invested in the initial five years (1979–83), with an average annual growth rate of 34 per cent. During the period 1984–91, more foreign capital was injected into the Chinese economy, with a growth rate of 20 per cent annually. It was in 1992, with the initiative of developing Pudong Region in Shanghai and Deng Xiaoping's tour of southern China, that foreign funds started pouring into China. Foreign investment in China grew from US$4.4 billion in 1991 to US$42.4 billion in 1996, with an average annual rate of growth of 32 per cent (Figure 4.1).

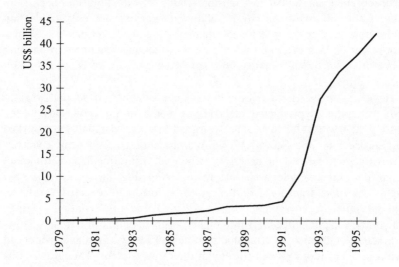

Sources: Statistical Yearbook of China, various issues.

Figure 4.1   Foreign direct investment in China, 1979–96

China's foreign investment is characterised by several distinct features. First, there are considerable variations across the regions. Guangdong, due to its proximity to Hong Kong, has for the past two decades been the largest recipient of China's foreign investment (Table 4.1). The ten coastal regions together have attracted the bulk of China's FDI. Although Guangdong still dominates other Chinese provinces, its position has been challenged by

Table 4.1   FDI shares in Chinese regions (%)

Regions	1983	1990	1995	1996
Beijing	5.03	7.94	2.88	3.69
Tianjin	0.71	2.39	4.05	5.11
Hebei	0.17	1.13	1.46	1.97
Liaoning	0.44	7.12	3.80	4.12
Shanghai	1.68	5.08	7.71	9.35
Jiangsu	0.82	4.05	13.83	12.37
Zhejiang	0.19	1.39	3.35	3.61
Fujian	2.26	8.32	10.78	9.69
Shandong	0.44	4.32	7.17	6.25
Guangdong	38.98	41.86	27.34	27.90
Others	49.28	16.40	17.63	15.94
China	100	100	100	100

Sources: Statistical Yearbook of China, 1984, 1991 and 1997.

Shanghai and other coastal provinces since the early 1990s. Thus, competition for foreign capital has become intense in the 1990s. The second characteristic of China's foreign investment is that Hong Kong and Taiwan have been the major providers of capital (Table 4.2). Apart from the United States, Asian countries have provided the bulk of China's foreign investment.

China's success in attracting foreign investment has given rise to many questions. For instance, has FDI been utilised efficiently in China? What role has FDI played in China's recent growth? Can other countries draw lessons from the Chinese experience? Several studies addressing these questions have so far been reported. Two pioneering studies by Kueh (1992) and Lardy (1995) looked at some broad issues of foreign investment in the reforming Chinese economy.[1] More recent studies, however, have focused on specific topics. For example, Chen et al. (1995) found that FDI was positively associated with China's economic growth. They also investigated the effect of FDI on regional disparity and income distribution. Another two recent studies by Chen (1996) and Sun (1996) examined regional factors affecting FDI flows and industrial linkage effects of FDI, respectively. The issue of FDI performance is important but ignored in the literature. The

Table 4.2   Sources of China's FDI by country (%)

Country	1990	1996
Hong Kong	53.91	49.49
Taiwan	6.38	8.26
Japan	14.44	8.76
Singapore	1.45	5.33
Korea		3.57
United Sates	13.08	8.17
Germany	1.84	1.23
Britain	0.38	3.09
Italy	0.12	0.40
Australia	0.71	0.46
France	0.60	1.01
Sub–total	92.91	89.78
China	100	100

Sources: Statistical Yearbook of China, 1992 and 1997.

present chapter attempts to fill this gap. It is the first of a series of studies that the author has undertaken to examine how efficiently FDI as a factor input is utilised in China.

MEASURING FDI PERFORMANCE: AN INPUT–DISTANCE FUNCTION APPROACH

Following the new growth theory, FDI is assumed to be a factor input and its performance can then be examined in the framework of production functions. Various methods have so far been developed to measure the performance of factor inputs. The approach employed in this study falls into the broad category of the stochastic frontier method which is related to the concept of input–oriented technical efficiency first proposed by Farrell (1957) and popularised by Aigner, Lovell and Schmidt (1977), and Meeusen and van den Broeck (1977).[2] The important difference between the traditional production function method and the production frontier technique is that, given outputs, the latter allows for production above the cost frontier, or below the best–practice output, given inputs. The ratio of the actual input used (observed output) over the minimal input requirement (potential output) then gives an indicator of the performance of the factor input considered.

According to Shephard (1953), an input distance function can be defined as follows

$$D(Y, X) = \max \{\theta: X/\theta \in L(Y)\} \qquad (4.1)$$

where $L(Y)$ is the input requirement set, that is,

$$L(Y) = \{X: X \text{ can produce } Y\} \qquad (4.2)$$

and Y is the output vector which can be produced using input vector X. The distance function, $D(Y, X)$, is non–decreasing, positively linearly homo–geneous and concave in X, and non–increasing in Y. It will take a value which is greater than or equal to unity depending whether the input vector, X, is located above or on the inner boundary of the input set. Thus, the input distance function seeks the greatest possible radial shrinkage of the observed input bundle X which still allows production of the observed output bundle Y. It gives an indicator of factor performance by comparing the largest feasible contraction of an input with the observed use of the input. In addition, the value of the input distance function is also the reciprocal of the input–oriented measure of technical efficiency (Farrell 1957). This measure captures deviations from the best–practice frontier.

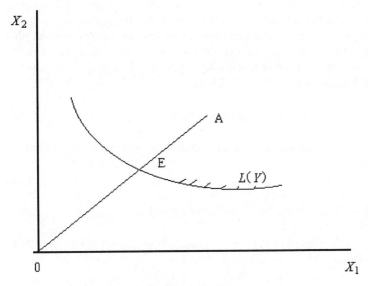

Figure 4.2   Input–oriented technical efficiency

Figure 4.2 presents a graphic illustration of input–oriented technical efficiency. Following Grosskopf and Hayes (1993), consider the observed input bundle at A, which produces the same level of output at E (that is, the technically efficient production point). The technical efficiency at A is then defined as the ratio of 0E over 0A, that is, the ratio of minimal to observed resource use. Obviously, technical efficiency is the reciprocal of the distance function at A and the distance function $D(Y, X) = 0A/0E$ is greater than or equal to unity for all feasible input bundles. The difference between technical efficiency and unity gives an indicator of technical inefficiency that measures the proportion by which inputs can be saved while the same level of output can be produced.

Given production technology $f(\bullet)$, the statistical formulation of the input–distance function (4.2) can be expressed as

$$D(Y, X) = f(X, Y, \rho)\ e^{v} \tag{4.3}$$

where ρ is a vector of parameters to be estimated and v is the random disturbance term intended to capture the effects of measurement error and statistical noise and is assumed to be independently and identically distributed as $N(0, \sigma_v^2)$.

The basic problem with the estimation of equation (4.3) is that the left–hand side of the distance function, $D(Y, X)$, is not observable. Furthermore, if production occurs on the frontier, the distance function has a value of unity and hence the dependent variable is invariant. In logarithmic form, the left–hand side of the distance function will be zero for all observations (that is, $\ln D(Y, X) = \ln 1 = 0$). However, this problem can be avoided when the property that the distance function is homogeneous of degree one in inputs is imposed (Fare and Primont 1995). That is,

$$D\ (Y, \kappa X) = \kappa\ D(Y, X) \tag{4.4}$$

Thus, if one of the inputs such as X_0 is chosen and assume $\kappa = 1/X_0$, then

$$D(Y, X/X_0) = D(Y, X)\ /X_0 \tag{4.5}$$

For the logarithmic form, (4.5) can be converted into

$$\ln\ [D(Y, X)\ /\ X_0] = \ln D(Y, X/X_0) = \ln f(Y, X/X_0) + v \tag{4.6}$$

That is,

$$-\ln\ (X_0) = \ln f(Y, X/X_0) + v - \ln D(Y, X) \tag{4.7}$$

Replace the unobservable ln $D(Y, X)$ by u in (4.7) to obtain a stochastic input distance function

$$- \ln (X_0) = \ln f(Y, X/X_0) + v - u \qquad (4.8)$$

where u is non–negative and assumed to have a normal distribution with zero mean and variance σ_u^2. Based on the conditional distribution of u given $\varepsilon = v - u$, the input distances would be predicted as

$$D = E[e^u | \varepsilon] \qquad (4.9)$$

Technical efficiency can then be estimated using the property that the distance function is the reciprocal of the Farrell input–oriented measure of technical efficiency. Equations (4.8) and (4.9) can be estimated by the maximum likelihood method (Coelli and Perelman 1996).

EMPIRICAL ESTIMATION AND RESULTS

Given the above presentation, the empirical model can be expressed as

$$- \ln(FDI) = \alpha_0 + \alpha_1 \ln(L / FDI) + \beta_k \ln(K / FDI) + \gamma \ln(GDP) + v - u$$

and

$$u = \delta_0 + \delta_1 t + \varpi \qquad (4.10)$$

where *FDI*, *L*, *K* and *GDP* represent foreign capital stock, employment, domestic capital stock and gross domestic product, respectively, and ϖ is defined by the truncation of the normal distribution with zero mean and variance σ_u^2 such that the point of truncation is $(-\delta_0 - \delta_1 t)$, that is, $\varpi \geq -\delta_0 - \delta_1 t$, and thus, u's are non–negative and obtained by truncation at zero of the normal distribution with mean $(\delta_0 + \delta_1 t)$ and variances, σ_u^2.

This empirical specification is applied to a data sample covering China's ten coastal regions, Beijing, Tianjin, Hebei, Liaoning, Shanghai, Jiangsu, Zhejiang, Fujian, Shandong and Guangdong. The statistics are drawn from various issues of China's *Statistical Yearbook*. Employment is represented by the total number of workers employed instead of man–hours, due to the lack of data on the latter. Both domestic and foreign capital stocks are estimated by assuming a rate of depreciation of 5 per cent, and using the following structure of capital formation

$$K_t = (1-\gamma)K_{t-1} + I_t \tag{4.11}$$

where γ is the rate of depreciation and I_t investment in the tth year.

Foreign capital stock is estimated by assuming that 1978 foreign capital was zero. The data of net domestic capital stock are estimated from gross investment data in each year. For this purpose, the capital stock in the first period is assumed to be the sum of all past investments and a rate of 5 per cent is allowed for capital depreciation. Symbolically,

$$K_1 = \int_{-\infty}^{1} I_t dt = \frac{I_0 e^{\theta}}{\theta} \tag{4.12}$$

where $I_t = I_0 e^{\theta t}$, and θ and I_0 are estimated by linear regressions using the investment series (1981–95).

Regional GDP is drawn from the provincial statistical yearbooks (Wu 1997). Both output and capital stock data are measured in 1980 constant prices. The price deflator is estimated from GDP data which are available in both current and constant prices. The estimation results reported in Table 4.3 are derived by using the computer program, FRONTIER 4.1 (Coelli 1992, Battese and Coelli 1995). It is clear that the estimates of all coefficients are significant and of appropriate sign. The negative sign of the time trend implies that the efficiency of *FDI* improves over time.

Table 4.3   Estimation results

	Coefficient	*t*–ratio
Constant	–0.239	–2.514
ln (*L/FDI*)	0.277	18.028
ln (*K/FDI*)	0.674	34.034
ln (*GDP*)	–0.905	–51.926
sigma–squared	0.032	5.057
gamma	0.824	12.954
Intercept	1.148	17.258
t	–0.173	–11.153

Source: Author's own estimates.

Given these estimates, the performance indicators can then be derived and are reported in Figure 4.3. According to this chart, the indicators of FDI performance have moved following an inverted–V shape. It seems that all regions have gone through a learning process lasting for about ten years. The turning points occurred during the period of 1989–91. In the early 1990s, FDI performance has become stable and converged across the ten regions. It is interesting to note that performance has been most volatile in Guangdong, the largest host of China's FDI. Other provinces might have benefited from the experience of Guangdong and have hence performed better.

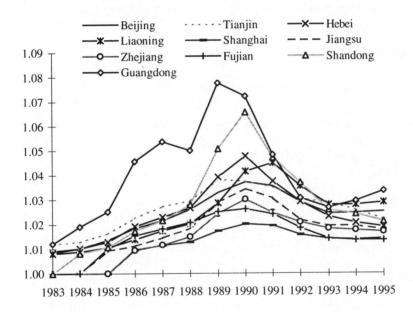

Source: Author's own estimates.

Figure 4.3   FDI performance in selected Chinese regions, 1983–95

SUMMARY REMARKS

In the light of the new growth framework, this chapter has investigated the performance of China's FDI as a factor input. It is found that FDI performance has gone through an inverted V–shape learning process in the past fifteen years. By 1995, all regions have shown relatively efficient use of foreign capital, that is, less than 3 per cent of overutilisation of FDI. This trend of convergence might be determined by some common factors such as the development of infrastructure, growth of the non–state sector and economic reform. According to official statistical records, over the past decade, all regions considered have shown consistent changes in per capita income, the role of the non–state sector and infrastructure development (road and telephones).[3] Per capita FDI among the regions has also recorded a similar growth pattern. A detailed investigation of the effect of these factors is beyond the scope of the present chapter and will be carried out by the author in the near future. In addition, the assumption of 'radial shrinkage' of observed inputs in the technique employed could be removed should the price information on all factor inputs be available and reliable. This limitation indicates scope for more rigorous exercises.

NOTES

1. Other general studies include Wang (1995) and Lan (1996).
2. Comprehensive surveys of efficiency measurement techniques are documented in Fried, Lovell and Schmidt (1993) and Lovell (1996).
3. Because of the limit of space, graphic illustration is omitted.

REFERENCES

Aigner, D. J., Lovell, C.A.K. and Schmidt, P., 1977. 'Formulation and estimation of stochastic frontier production function models', *Journal of Econometrics*, **6**, 21–37.

Balasubramanyan, V.N., Salisu, M. and Sapsford, D., 1996. 'Foreign direct investment and growth in EP and IS countries', *Economic Journal*, **106**, 92–105.

Battese, G. and Coelli, T., 1995. 'A model for technical inefficiency effects in a stochastic frontier production function', *Empirical Economics*, **20**, 325–32.

Chen, C–H., 1996. 'Regional determinants of foreign direct investment in mainland China', *Journal of Economic Studies*, **23**, 18–30.

Chen, C., Chang, L. and Zhang, Y., 1995. 'The role of foreign direct investment in China's post–1978 economic development', *World Development*, **23**, 691–703.

Coelli, T.J., 1992. 'A computer program for frontier production function estimation: FRONTIER, version 2.0', *Economics Letters*, **39**, 29–32.

Coelli, T. and Perelman, S., 1996. 'Efficiency measurement, multiple–output technologies and distance functions: with application to European railways', *Working Papers*, CREPP 96/05, Universite de Liege.

Fare, R. and Primont, D., 1995, *Multi–output production and duality: theory and applications*, Kluwer Academic Publishers, Boston.

Farrell, M.J., 1957. 'The measurement of productive efficiency', *Journal of the Royal Statistical Society*, Series A, General **120**, 253–82.

Fried, H., Lovell, C.A.K. and Schmidt, S. (eds), 1993. *The measurement of productive efficiency*, Oxford University Press, Oxford.

Grosskopf, S. and Hayes, K., 1993. 'Local public sector bureaucrats and their input choices', *Journal of Urban Economics*, **33**, 151–66.

Kueh, Y.Y., 1992. 'Foreign investment and economic change in China', *The China Quarterly*, **131**, 637–90.

Lan, P., 1996. *Technology transfer to China through foreign direct investment*, Avebury, Aldershot.

Lardy, N.R., 1995. 'The role of foreign trade and investment in China's economic transformation', *The China Quarterly*, **144**, 1065–82.

Lovell, C.A.K., 1996. 'Applying efficiency measurement techniques to the measurement of productivity change', *Journal of Productivity Analysis*, **7**, 329–40.

Meeusen, W. and van den Broeck, J., 1977. 'Efficiency estimation from Cobb–Douglas production functions with composed error', *International Economic Review*, **18**, 435–44.

Shephard, R.W., 1953. *Cost and production functions*, Princeton University Press, Princeton.

Sun, H., 1996. 'Direct foreign investment and linkage effects: the experience of China', *Asian Economies*, **25**, 5–27.

Wang, Z.Q., 1995. *Foreign investment and economic development in Hungary and China*, Avebury, Aldershot.

Wu, Y., 1997. 'Productivity and efficiency: evidence from the Chinese regional economies', *Discussion Paper*, **97.18**, Department of Economics, University of Western Australia.

PART II

Foreign Direct Investment, Trade and Economic
Growth

Exploitation, Investment, Trade and Economic Growth

P33
F21 079 (China)

5. The Impact of FDI and Trade

Chunlai Chen

INTRODUCTION

Since the early 1980s, together with the fast growth and huge amount of FDI inflows, China's international trade has grown very rapidly from US$38.14 billion in 1980 to US$280.85 billion in 1995 with an annual growth rate of over 14 per cent. As a result, China's share of world total trade has increased from 0.94 per cent in 1980 to 2.86 per cent in 1994, ranking it the eleventh–largest trading country in the world.

What are the sources of China's rapid trade expansion since the early 1980s? Many studies have addressed this question. In general three main sources contributing to China's rapid trade expansion have been identified. They are (a) the results of market–oriented economic reforms and open–door policies in general and the trade liberalisation in particular (Lardy 1992), (b) the fast growth of township and village enterprises (TVEs) associated with the remarkable export expansion since the early 1980s and particularly after 1984 (Findlay, Watson and Wu 1994), and (c) the massive inflows of FDI associated with the fast trade growth of foreign–funded enterprises (FFEs), whose trade share reached 39.1 per cent of China's total trade in 1995.

Among the three main sources contributing to the rapid increase of China's international trade expansion, the first two have been extensively studied. However, the third source, the inflow of FDI, has not been analysed much up to now. There are a number of questions relating to the impact of FDI on the rapid expansion of China's foreign trade which are worth both theoretical analysis and empirical investigation.

In the FDI literature, the nature of FDI in terms of the multinational enterprises' (MNEs) principal market for their products can be classified into two broad categories. One is domestic market–oriented FDI which takes the host country's domestic markets as the main market for its products. Another is international market–oriented, or export–oriented, FDI which takes the international market as the main market for its products.

In practice, export–oriented FDI has been playing an important role in the process of export–led industrialisation in many developing countries. Affiliates of MNEs, as part of the parent company's global network, have marketing channels in place, possess experience and expertise in the many complex facets of product development and international marketing, and are well placed to take advantage of inter–country differences in the costs of production. In view of these considerations, attracting export–oriented FDI has become an integral element of policy reforms aimed towards export–led industrialisation in many developing countries. The successful examples, which are often cited, are the newly industrialising economies (NIEs).

Since the 1980s, both FDI inflows into China and the international trade of China have witnessed a tremendous increase. Is this a coincidence or is there a special relationship between FDI and trade? This chapter is designed to investigate empirically the impact of FDI on trade, based on the evidence from China. We seek to answer the questions: what is the role of FDI in China's trade expansion, what is the impact of FDI on the differences in China's provincial trade, and what is the impact of FDI on China's bilateral trade with its trade partners?

The chapter is structured as follows. The development of the theories of the relationship between FDI and trade is reviewed first. Then China's international trade expansion since the 1980s is described. Subsequently this chapter investigates the role of FDI in China's international trade by directly examining the contribution of FFEs to China's trade growth both at the national level and at the provincial level. This is followed by analyses of the impact of FDI on trade, based on the evidence first from China's provincial trade flows and then from China's bilateral trade flows. The final section summarises the main findings.

THE RELATIONSHIP BETWEEN FDI AND TRADE: A BRIEF REVIEW

Traditionally, the theories of FDI and international trade have been developed separately. FDI theory tries to explain why firms invest in particular countries, and uses the notions of ownership, internalisation and location advantages as determinants of investment choices. Trade theory, developed much earlier, has put emphasis on why countries trade with each other and has developed the principle of comparative advantage as the determinant of trade patterns. However, during the past 30 years, several attempts have been made by international trade theorists to integrate the theories of FDI and trade.

Vernon (1966) developed the product–cycle model to explain the sequence from domestic production of a new product to its export and then foreign production by the US MNEs in the post–second World War period. In the product–cycle model which deals with a single product, FDI has been viewed as replacing trade. As Dunning (1993, p.71) pointed out:

> It did not explain, nor purport to explain, resource based, efficiency seeking or strategic asset acquiring FDI. Vernon offered a theory which was partial in that it addressed itself to only some of the issues surrounding MNE activity. On the other hand, the product cycle was the first dynamic interpretation of the determinants of, and relationship between, international trade and foreign production.

Kojima (1973, 1985) from a macroeconomic point of view and by comparing American and Japanese FDI pointed out that Japanese FDI is primarily trade oriented and responds to the dictates of the principle of comparative advantage. In contrast, US FDI is conducted mainly within an oligopolistic market structure, is anti–trade oriented and operates to the long–term disadvantage of both the source and host countries. In general, Kojima's macroeconomic approach predicts that export–oriented FDI occurs when the source country invests in those industries in which the host country has a comparative advantage. Therefore, export–oriented FDI is characterised as being welfare improving and trade creating since it can promote both host and source countries' exports. It has been pointed out that Kojima's neo–classical framework is unable to capture the role of firm–specific advantages in determining FDI flows (Dunning 1988) and, moreover, it fails to explain much of the modern trade. This means that it cannot explain the kind of trade flows that are based less on the distribution of factor endowments and more on the need to exploit the economies of scale, product differentiation and other manifestations of market failure (Dunning 1993, p. 90).

Since the early 1980s a small number of international economists have constructed models by combining ownership advantages and location advantages to integrate FDI into trade theories. In these models, the activities of firms are divided into two categories. The first consists of headquarters activities, which involve engineering, managerial and financial services, as well as services of reputation, trademarks and so forth, which can be transferred at no cost even to distant production facilities. This set of activities is often simply indicated as research and development. The second consists of the actual production process, which can be further divided into intermediate goods production and final goods production. Under the assumptions of zero transport costs of headquarters services and increasing returns to scale of the actual production process, firms can geographically separate production facilities from headquarters, but they concentrate pro–

duction facilities in one location in order to reap associated scale economies. These models have focused mainly on either vertical or horizontal FDI, where the first consists of the geographical separation of different stages of the value–added chain and the second consists of the duplication of the entire production process, except for headquarters activities, in several countries.

Helpman (1984) and Helpman and Krugman (1985) constructed models to integrate vertical FDI into international trade theory, explained in terms of factor proportion asymmetries between countries. The models demon–strate the possibility of FDI reversing trade patterns when countries are very different in terms of relative factor endowments. FDI generates com–plementary trade flows of finished goods from foreign affiliates to parent companies or to the home country and intra–firm transfers of intangible headquarters services from parent companies to foreign affiliates. If pro–duction is divided into upstream and downstream production, the FDI–trade relationship can be developed further with the emergence of intra–firm parent–to–affiliate exports of intermediate inputs. The models require large differences in countries' relative factor endowments for FDI to take place and a principal implication is that MNEs are more important between countries the greater the difference between them. They apply best to the relationship of vertical FDI and trade between developed and developing countries.

Markusen (1984), Brainard (1992), Horstmann and Markusen (1992), Markusen (1995), and Markusen and Venables (1995) have produced models to integrate horizontal FDI into international trade theory. There are three key elements in the models, namely firm–level activities like research and development that are joint inputs across plants, plant–level scale of economies, transport costs, geographical and cultural distance costs and all kinds of impediments to trade between countries. According to the models, the higher the value of firm–level fixed costs and tariffs and transport costs relative to plant–level scale economies, the more likely is the presence of MNEs. These models based on the trade–off between proximity and concentration postulate a substitution relationship between FDI and trade. A further development of the theory to allow for separation of upstream and downstream production predicts exports of intermediate goods from parent companies to their foreign affiliates when firms decide to invest in downstream affiliates. This version thus introduces an element of comp–lementarity between FDI and international trade (Brainard 1992). A second elaboration of the theory introduces asymmetries between countries in terms of market size, factor endowments and technological efficiency. This version thus makes it possible for national and multinational firms and, therefore, FDI and trade to exist simultaneously (Markusen and Venables 1995). Moreover, multinationals are more likely to exist in equilibrium when the countries are large and when the countries have similar relative factor endowments. This implies that MNEs are of greater importance between countries that are relatively similar in size, per capita income, and relative factor endowments (Markusen 1995). Therefore, the models apply best to the relationship of horizontal FDI and trade between developed countries.

Although these recent models have made a considerable contribution to the theoretical study of the relationship between FDI and trade by integrating FDI into international trade theories, it has been argued that, because the models are constrained by a simple two–country general equilibrium framework, they cannot significantly represent real MNEs' behaviour and empirical FDI and trade relationships (United Nations 1996). Moreover, the models do not take into account, for instance, the role of governments in reshaping countries' comparative advantages and in influencing trade patterns, the importance of macroeconomic factors such as structural unemployment or growth, and market imperfections such as information asymmetry and limitations on knowledge computational capabilities of decision makers (Dunning 1995). Therefore, more empirical studies of the relationship between FDI and trade not only are necessary but also will throw light on the future improvements of the theoretical models integrating FDI and trade.

INTERNATIONAL TRADE EXPANSION SINCE 1980

What has been China's trade performance in the last 16 years? We answer this question by examining three aspects: aggregate trade growth, share in the world trade and the degree of openness or trade dependence.

One of the greatest achievements of China's open–door policy is the remarkable increase of China's international trade both in exports and in imports. Since the early 1980s, China's international trade has increased tremendously. Table 5.1 presents China's international trade performance during the 16 years from 1980 to 1995. The table and figure indicate that in that time China's international trade has increased significantly. The total trade volume increased from US$38.14 billion in 1980 to US$280.85 billion in 1995 with an annual growth rate of 14.24 per cent. The export volume increased from US$18.12 billion in 1980 to US$148.77 billion in 1995 with an annual growth rate of 15.07 per cent, and the import volume increased from US$20.02 billion in 1980 to US$132.08 billion in 1995 with an annual growth rate of 13.40 per cent.

Table 5.2 presents China's trade share in total world trade. During the last 15 years, with the rapid growth of international trade, China's share in

Table 5.1   China's international trade performance (1980–95)

Year	Total trade ($US million)	Exports ($US million)	Imports ($US million)
1980	38,140	18,120	20,020
1981	44,020	22,010	22,010
1982	41,600	22,320	19,280
1983	43,610	22,220	21,390
1984	53,550	26,140	27,410
1985	69,600	27,350	42,250
1986	73,840	30,940	42,900
1987	82,650	39,440	43,210
1988	102,800	47,520	55,280
1989	111,680	52,540	59,140
1990	115,440	62,090	53,350
1991	135,630	71,840	63,790
1992	165,530	84,940	80,590
1993	195,710	91,760	103,950
1994	236,730	121,040	115,690
1995	280,850	148,770	132,080
Annual growth rate (%)	14.24	15.07	13.40

Sources
1. Data for 1980–94 are from the Editorial Board of the Almanac of China's Foreign Economic Relations and Trade (1995), *Zhongguo Duiwai Jingji Maoyi Nianjian 1995/96* [Almanac of China's Economic Relations and Trade 1995/96], Zhongguo Shehui Chubanshe, Beijing, p.403.
2. Data for 1995 are from the State Statistical Bureau (1996), *Zhongguo Tongji Nianjian 1996* [China Statistical Yearbook 1996], Zhongguo Tongji Chubanshe, Beijing, p.580.

Table 5.2   China's trade share in the world trade (1980–94)

Year	China as % of total world trade	China as % of total world exports	China as % of total world imports
1980	0.944	0.910	0.977
1981	1.098	1.116	1.081
1982	1.114	1.224	1.015
1983	1.183	1.229	1.139
1984	1.378	1.374	1.382
1985	1.762	1.421	2.085
1986	1.702	1.454	1.941
1987	1.631	1.586	1.675
1988	1.791	1.681	1.898
1989	1.800	1.726	1.871
1990	1.648	1.806	1.496
1991	1.947	2.100	1.800
1992	2.218	2.323	2.118
1993	2.663	2.526	2.797
1994	2.858	2.965	2.753
Annual growth rate (%)	8.234	8.803	7.680

Sources: Calculated from the various issues of the Editorial Board of the Almanac of China's Foreign Economic Relations and Trade, *Zhongguo Duiwai Jingji Maoyi Nianjian*, [Almanac of China's Economic Relations and Trade], Zhongguo Shehui Chubanshe, Beijing.

total world trade has increased remarkably, from less than 1 per cent (0.9 per cent) in 1980 to 2.9 per cent in 1994, with an annual growth rate of 8.2 per cent, which makes China the eleventh–largest trading country in the world. Decomposing the total trade share, exports grew steadily and rapidly, with an annual growth rate of 8.8 per cent. Imports experienced relatively large fluctuations with an annual growth rate of 7.7 per cent.

Table 5.3 presents China's trade to GNP ratio, which is also a measure of openness or trade dependence. As the data show, China's openness or trade dependence increased significantly from 12.8 per cent in 1980 to 41 per cent in 1995, with an annual growth rate of over 8 per cent. Such a big jump within only 16 years, for a large country, is very rare.

However, there are some arguments about how open China is. As Findlay and Watson (1996) point out, there is considerable uncertainty over the measurement of China's openness to trade since both sides of the equation of openness are open to interpretation and debate. They cite several studies of China's openness to demonstrate their arguments. For example, as Lardy (1992) has pointed out, in China's case the calculations of the ratio are difficult since the conversion of the domestic data into US dollar terms is problematic. In general, official exchange rates tend to understate the purchasing power of the domestic currency and thus to overstate the degree of openness expressed by the ratio. Using the official data, Lardy shows a ratio of over 26 per cent in 1989 and cites Chinese sources with estimates of up to 33 per cent. Lardy (1994), however, challenges this assessment and cites competing analyses of China's GNP based on purchasing power parity which indicate a substantially lower ratio of around 10 per cent in 1988. Subsequently, he updated this method to 1990 and finds a trade to GNP ratio in that year of a little over 9 per cent (using an estimate of real per capita income of about US$1,100 in 1990). Other studies based on the same method produced very similar estimates of China's openness. For example, the Asia Pacific Economics Group (1995) estimated an openness of over 13 per cent in 1994 by using real per capita income of US$1,543 in that year. Consequently, Findlay and Watson (1996) argue that when the figures are adjusted, China begins to look like many other large countries, a little more open than India and a little less than the United States. Therefore, when we talk about China's openness, special caution should be taken because of the data problems discussed above.

In general, the above analysis shows that in the last 16 years China has achieved remarkable progress in improving its trade performance and has greatly integrated itself into the world economy. However, the question is what have been the sources for China's rapid trade expansion since the early 1980s? As we have briefly mentioned in the preceding section, three main sources have been identified by previous studies. First is the results of market–oriented economic reforms and trade liberalisation; second is the rapid growth of TVEs; and third is the massive inflows of FDI associated with the fast trade growth of FFEs. Our interest here is to investigate the impact of FDI on China's trade growth. Therefore, in the next section we shall examine the direct contribution of FFEs to China's trade growth.

Table 5.3   China's trade to GNP ratio (1980–95)

Year	Total trade as % of GNP	Exports as % of GNP	Imports as % of GNP
1980	12.75	6.07	6.68
1981	15.41	7.71	7.71
1982	14.85	7.97	6.88
1983	14.81	7.55	7.26
1984	17.25	8.34	8.91
1985	24.15	9.45	14.70
1986	26.61	11.16	15.45
1987	27.29	13.01	14.28
1988	27.17	12.56	14.61
1989	25.99	12.23	13.76
1990	31.42	16.87	14.55
1991	35.71	18.91	16.80
1992	37.95	19.47	18.49
1993	35.96	16.86	19.10
1994	43.80	22.40	21.40
1995	41.03	21.74	19.29
Annual growth rate (%)	8.11	8.88	7.33

Sources: Calculated from the State Statistical Bureau (1995), *Zhongguo Duiwai Jingji Tongji Nianjian 1994* [China Foreign Economic Statistical Yearbook 1994], Zhongguo Tongji Chubanshe, Beijing, and the State Statistical Bureau (1996), *Zhongguo Tongji Nianjian 1996* [China Statistical Yearbook 1996], Zhongguo Tongji Chubanshe, Beijing.

THE ROLE OF FFES IN CHINA'S TRADE EXPANSION

The Contribution of FFEs to Trade Growth

The most direct way to measure the impact of FDI on China's trade growth is to examine the trade performance of FFEs. Table 5.4 presents the trade volume and shares of FFEs in China from 1980 to 1995. As the table indicates, in terms of trade volume, FFEs' trade has increased very rapidly from US$43 million in 1980 to US$109,818 million in 1995, with an annual growth rate of 68.71 per cent. This rapid trade growth of FFEs has reflected the FFEs' rapid export and import growth, whose annual average growth rates reached 78.32 per cent and 65.13 per cent, respectively, from 1980 to 1995.

Table 5.4   Trade and shares of FFEs in China (1980–95)

Year	FFEs' total (US$ million)			FFEs as % of China's total		
	Total trade	Exports	Imports	Total trade	Exports	Imports
1980	43	8	34	0.11	0.05	0.17
1981	143	32	111	0.33	0.15	0.50
1982	329	53	276	0.79	0.24	1.43
1983	618	330	288	1.42	1.49	1.35
1984	468	69	399	0.87	0.26	1.46
1985	2,361	297	2,064	3.39	1.09	4.89
1986	3,012	582	2,430	4.08	1.88	5.67
1987	4,330	1,208	3,122	5.24	3.06	7.23
1988	8,203	2,456	5,747	7.98	5.17	10.40
1989	13,709	4,913	8,796	12.28	9.35	14.87
1990	20,120	7,814	12,306	17.43	12.58	23.07
1991	28,954	12,047	16,907	21.35	16.77	26.50
1992	43,726	17,356	26,370	26.42	20.43	32.72
1993	67,070	25,237	41,833	34.27	27.51	40.24
1994	87,647	34,713	52,934	37.03	28.68	45.76
1995	109,818	46,876	62,942	39.10	31.51	47.66
Annual average growth rate	68.71%	78.32%	65.13%	47.93%	53.63%	45.61%

Sources
1. Data for 1980–93 are from the State Statistical Bureau (1995), *Zhongguo Duiwai Jingji Tongji Nianjian 1994* [China Foreign Economic Statistical Yearbook 1994], Zhongguo Tongji Chubanshe, Beijing, p.164.
2. Data for 1994–95 are from the State Statistical Bureau (1996), *Zhongguo Tongji Nianjian 1996* [China Statistical Yearbook 1996], Zhongguo Tongji Chubanshe, Beijing, p.596.

Another way to look at the contribution of FFEs to China's trade growth is to examine the shares of FFEs' trade in China's total trade (Table 5.4). From 1980 to 1984 FFEs' shares in China's total trade as well as in exports and imports were almost negligible, averaging less than one per cent. However, after 1984 the trade share of FFEs began to increase gradually, reaching 12.3 per cent in 1989. Since 1990 the trade shares of FFEs have experienced unprecedented growth, reaching 39.1 per cent of China's total trade and 31.5 per cent and 47.7 per cent of China's total exports and imports, respectively, in 1995.

The Issues in FFEs' Trade Balance

However, together with the rapid trade growth, FFEs have also involved serious trade balance issues. Table 5.4 clearly shows that, except in 1983, FFEs have been running trade deficits continuously since 1980, and the size of the deficits grew rapidly. Since all FFEs in China are supposed to balance their own foreign exchange expenditure and income, the continuous and increasingly large trade deficit implies a critical issue for FFEs in China.

If we decompose FFEs' total imports into those which are part of FFEs' investments and those which are goods and materials for FFEs' production, the picture of the FFEs' trade balance would change dramatically. According to China's official statistics, the equipment imported by FFEs as part of their investments are reported both as FDI and as FFEs' imports. As Table 5.5 shows, this type of import, according to the available data of 1992 to

Table 5.5 Decomposing of FFEs' imports and the adjusted FFEs' trade balance

Year	FFEs' total imports (US$ million)	Equipment imported as investments (US$ million)	Equipment imports as % of FFEs' total imports	FFEs' imports of goods and materials (US$ million)	Adjusted FFEs' trade balance (US$ million)
1992	26,370	8,018	30.41	18,352	−996
1993	41,833	16,613	39.71	25,220	17
1994	52,934	20,300	38.35	32,634	2,079
1995	62,948	18,740	29.77	44,208	2,668

Sources: Calculated from the State Statistical Bureau (1995), *Zhongguo Duiwai Jingji Tongji Nianjian 1994* [China Foreign Economic Statistical Yearbook 1994], Zhongguo Tongji Chubanshe, Beijing, and the Ministry of Foreign Trade and Economic Cooperation (1996), *Foreign Economic Statistical Bulletin*, April 1996.

1995, accounted for 30 per cent of FFEs' total imports in 1992, 40 per cent in 1993, 38 per cent in 1994, and 30 per cent in 1995. If we deduct this from FFEs' total imports, then the trade balance of FFEs would be in surplus in 1993 to 1995.

According to China's regulations on FFEs and on foreign exchange control, all FFEs in China are required to balance their own foreign exchange. The regulations are implemented through requiring FFEs to open a renminbi (RMB) deposit account and a separate foreign exchange deposit account with either the Bank of China or another bank approved by the State Administration for Exchange Control (SAEC). All foreign exchange receipts and disbursements must flow through the foreign exchange account. Before December 1996, since the RMB was not convertible on either the current or capital account into foreign exchange, this rule effectively required FFEs to generate all foreign exchange needed for the remittance of dividends, expenditures and other distributions. However, there are some options for FFEs to fuel their foreign exchange bank accounts. These options include: domestic sales of sophisticated products; foreign exchange adjustment; reinvestment of RMB profits; domestic products export; government assistance; mortgage RMB on foreign exchange; import substitution; and foreign exchange swaps. These options have greatly improved the situation of foreign exchange management of FDI firms. However, balancing foreign exchange will continue to be a problem until the RMB becomes convertible. As a result, in December 1996, the Chinese government announced that the RMB would be convertible on current accounts from the start of December 1996. This includes all payments for international goods and services trade, repayments of loans and profit remittance. This significant policy change in foreign exchange management will not only assist China's international traders but also facilitate foreign investors in their business operations in China.

The Correlation between Provincial Trade and FFEs' Trade

Although China as a whole has achieved great progress in its international trade expansion, the trade performance among China's provinces has been very unbalanced. As Table 5.6 shows, in terms of individual provinces, Guangdong's trade performance has been the best, averaging more than 30 per cent of China's total trade from 1991 to 1993 and growing rapidly as well. Following Guangdong, Shanghai, Fujian, Jiangsu and Liaoning are among the top five largest trade provinces in China. In terms of regions, the eastern region overwhelmingly dominated China's trade, accounting for nearly 80 per cent of China's total trade.

Table 5.6   The shares of provincial trade in China's total trade and the
shares of FFEs' trade in provincial total trade (%)

Province	Provincial trade over China's total trade			FFEs' trade over provincial total trade		
	1991	1992	1993	1991	1992	1993
Beijing	2.53	2.23	2.24	43.13	56.74	51.24
Tianjin	2.64	2.37	2.01	23.95	32.64	61.26
Hebei	2.63	2.11	1.70	9.78	16.16	27.65
Shanxi	0.77	0.71	0.63	12.56	13.80	18.24
Inner Mongolia	0.78	0.93	0.87	6.89	7.04	8.91
Liaoning	8.79	7.64	6.13	17.31	23.25	32.71
Jilin	1.71	1.94	2.16	2.71	7.91	13.73
Heilongjiang	2.60	2.83	2.22	3.72	5.14	10.06
Shanghai	10.50	9.75	9.20	25.09	34.06	46.05
Jiangsu	5.88	6.25	6.31	27.70	39.78	52.67
Zhejiang	4.50	4.65	4.45	14.43	20.09	33.15
Anhui	1.11	1.10	0.93	7.08	11.13	21.15
Fujian	5.66	6.57	7.16	67.65	67.39	61.44
Jiangxi	0.92	0.90	0.81	12.12	17.15	33.24
Shandong	6.05	5.85	5.40	12.70	21.19	35.66
Henan	1.55	1.56	1.26	3.82	8.77	19.14
Hubei	1.79	1.69	1.85	10.88	17.05	26.47
Hunan	1.80	2.08	1.71	4.48	7.50	12.60
Guangdong	28.98	29.58	34.06	79.54	83.56	72.81
Guangxi	1.31	1.63	1.49	13.14	12.85	25.48
Hainan	1.76	1.69	1.87	19.49	22.57	24.24
Sichuan	2.24	2.20	2.12	8.24	10.92	16.60
Guizhou	0.32	0.34	0.26	6.85	13.33	14.71
Yunnan	0.99	0.96	0.88	3.01	4.92	7.79
Shaanxi	1.00	1.06	1.09	11.11	8.92	14.32
Gansu	0.36	0.42	0.35	1.73	5.19	11.77
Qinghai	0.10	0.10	0.09	1.31	2.21	0.67
Ningxia	0.13	0.13	0.10	8.66	2.88	6.79
Xinjiang	0.60	0.75	0.66	6.15	6.28	6.23
By Regions						
Coastal Region	78.69	78.08	79.78	45.09	52.00	56.03
Central Region	17.03	17.24	15.91	11.99	16.01	22.26
West Region	4.28	4.68	4.31	6.36	6.97	10.00

Sources: Calculated from the State Statistical Bureau (1995), *Zhongguo Duiwai Jingji Tongji Nianjian 1994* [China Foreign Economic Statistical Yearbook 1994], Zhongguo Tongji Chubanshe, Beijing, and the various issues of the Editorial Board of the Almanac of China's Foreign Economic Relations and Trade, *Zhongguo Duiwai Jingji Maoyi Nianjian* [Almanac of China's Economic Relations and Trade], Zhongguo Shehui Chubanshe, Beijing.

It is very interesting to note that the provinces which have higher shares in China's total trade also have higher shares of FFEs' trade in provincial total trade. For example, in 1993 for the top five largest trade provinces, the shares of FFEs' trade in their provincial total trade were 73 per cent in Guangdong, 46 per cent in Shanghai, 61 per cent in Fujian, 53 per cent in Jiangsu and 33 per cent in Liaoning, respectively. In terms of regions, the share of FFEs' trade in the eastern region has exceeded more than half of the region's total trade since 1992.

Figure 5.1 presents the provincial shares in China's total trade and the FFEs' shares in each province's total trade. The figure clearly demonstrates the positive relationship between provincial trade shares in China's total trade and the FFEs' trade shares in each province's total trade.

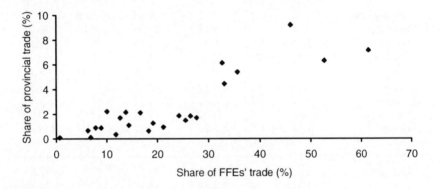

Source: Refer to Table 5.6.

Figure 5.1   The relationship between provincial shares in China's total trade and FFEs' shares in provincial trade (1993)

Both Table 5.6 and Figure 5.1 suggest that there may exist a positive correlation between the shares of provincial trade in China's total trade and the shares of FFEs' trade in provincial total trade. To examine this relationship further, a Spearman's rank correlation test across provinces for the years of 1991 to 1993 was conducted. The test results are presented in Table 5.7. The Spearman's rank tests show that the null hypothesis of no correlation between these two variables is rejected for all three years at the 99 per cent significance level. The test results revealed that there was a positive correlation between the provincial trade shares in China's total trade and the FFEs' trade shares in provincial total trade. These results imply that the provinces which have higher shares of FFE trade in their provincial total trade will have higher trade shares in China's total trade. In other words, the higher trade share of a province in China's total trade is associated with or directly related to the higher trade share of FFEs in its provincial total trade.

Table 5.7   Spearman's rank correlation test between the shares of provincial trade in China's total trade and the shares of FFEs' trade in provincial total trade

Year	Calculated Spearman's rank Correlation coefficient (r_s)	Critical value of Spearman's rank correlation coefficient (r_0) ($n = 29$, $\alpha = 0.01$)	Null hypothesis of 'no correlation'
1991	0.668473***	0.440	$r_s > r_0$, reject null hypothesis
1992	0.721182***	0.440	$r_s > r_0$, reject null hypothesis
1993	0.736456***	0.440	$r_s > r_0$, reject null hypothesis

Note: *** Indicates 99% significant level of Spearman's rank coefficient (one–tailed test).

However, to investigate the impact of FDI on trade, we cannot just rest our conclusion on correlations. Therefore, in the next section we move beyond correlations and employ more comprehensive econometric models to investigate the relationship between FDI and trade.

FDI and Trade: an Empirical Investigation

What is the relationship between FDI and trade? The theories reviewed in the preceding sections predict either a substitute or complementary relationship between FDI and trade. However, some empirical studies have revealed a positive relationship between FDI and trade (United Nations 1993, 1996; World Bank 1994; Petri 1995). Our analyses above also revealed that FDI has a positive impact on trade in the case of China. This positive relationship between FDI and trade suggests that FDI and trade in China are primarily complementary rather than substitutes in bridging the differences in factor endowments between China and its foreign investors and trade partners. To investigate the relationship between FDI and trade further, we conducted the following empirical tests based on the evidence from the impact of FDI on China's provincial trade and from the impact of FDI on China's bilateral trade.

To test the relationship between FDI and trade, our hypothesis is that FDI has a positive effect on trade flows since FDI and trade are complementary. There are two ways to test our hypothesis: one is based on the product level and the other is based on the aggregate level. In this study, because of data constraints, we adopt the second method and use the aggregate data both from the provincial level and from China's bilateral level to test the relationship between FDI and trade.

In both of the empirical investigations, our framework of analysis is based on the gravity model of international trade. There are many of factors influencing the magnitudes of international trade. However, based on the spirit of the gravity model of international trade, the size and the geographical distance of countries are the most important factors de–termining the magnitudes of bilateral trade as well as countries' overall trade (Frankel and Romer, 1996). In this study, in addition to the common variables specified by the gravity model, we deliberately add FDI as an explanatory variable.[1] We want to see, in addition to the other variables, whether FDI has any impact on China's provincial trade and China's bilateral trade flows, and if so, what is the direction of the impact.

THE IMPACT OF FDI ON TRADE: EVIDENCE FROM CHINA'S PROVINCIAL TRADE

Specification of the Variables

Based on the spirit of the gravity model of international trade, we include the following variables in the estimation of the model of China's provincial aggregate trade flows with the rest of the world.

1. Provincial aggregate trade. Provincial aggregate trade (T) is the dependent variable in this study. It is the sum of exports and imports of each province with the rest of the world in a year at 1980 constant US dollar price. In this study we do not consider inter–provincial trade among China's provinces.
2. Size of province. The size of the province is measured by the total population (POP) at the year end. Using population as the size of a country is practised in many studies. The population variable not only reflects the size of an economy but also reflects the level of resource endowment. In addition, in the case of China, since the number of state–owned enterprises (SOEs) in each province is different, the value–

added of SOEs is calculated as part of provincial GDP, but the trade of SOEs may go through another channel and may not be calculated as part of the provincial trade. Therefore, the population is a more consistent variable as compared with GDP in estimating the effect of provincial size on its trade. According to the gravity model, we expect that the provincial population has a positive effect on provincial aggregate trade with the rest of the world.

3. Per capita income of province. The per capita income (*PY*) is measured by per capita national income of each province at 1980 constant Renminbi price. The effect of per capita income on provincial aggregate trade is expected to be positive.

4. Relative distance of province. The relative distance, a linkage variable, is measured by the index of remoteness (*RMT*) which is the weighted average distance of each province with respect to all countries in the world. Taking account of the transport and information cost associated with the relative distance, the expected effect of remoteness on provincial aggregate trade flows with the rest of the world is negative.

5. Foreign direct investment. Foreign direct investment (*FDI*) is another linkage variable. The data for (*FDI*) are the total investment stock of FFEs at the year end in each province at 1980 constant US dollar price. The reason for using the total investment stock of FFEs instead of using the inflows of FDI is based mainly on the following considerations. First, there is a time lag between the inflows of FDI and the effects generated by that inflow on trade. Second, FDI has accumulated effects on trade, which means that all the FDI historically invested has effects on current trade. Therefore, to avoid these problems we use the total investment stock of FFEs in each province to estimate the effects of FDI on trade. The total investment stock of FFEs not only reflects the current production capacity of FFEs, which has direct effects on current trade flows, but also captures the effects of all historically invested FDI on current trade flows. In this study the total investment stock of FFEs is expected to have a positive effect on the provincial trade flows.

Regression Results and Explanations

We establish the following equation to test the impact of FDI on provincial aggregate trade flows:

$$\ln T_i = \beta_0 + \beta_1 \ln POP_i + \beta_2 \ln PY_i + \beta_3 \ln RMT_i + \beta_4 \ln FDI_i + \varepsilon_i \qquad (5.1)$$

Where ε_i is the stochastic disturbance, the βs are the regression parameters to be estimated and the variables are defined as in Table 5.8. The estimated coefficients of $\ln POP$, $\ln PY$, $\ln RMT$, and $\ln FDI$ variables will be elasticity.

Table 5.8   List of variables of provincial aggregate trade equation

Variable name	Specification of variables	Source
T_i	Total trade flows (exports plus imports) of province i. Millions of US dollars at 1980 price.	Various issues of the *Almanac of China's Economic Relations and Trade.*
POP_i	Total population of province *i*. Ten thousand people.	Various issues of *China Statistical Yearbook.*
PY_i	Per capita income of province *i*. Renminbi yuan per capita at 1980 price.	Same as above.
RMT_i	Weighted average distance of province *i* from the rest of the world.	Countries' and world GDPs are from various issues of the *World Development Report* and the distances are measured from the map in the *Almanac of China's Economic Relations and Trade.*
FDI_i	Total investment stock of FFEs in province *i*. Millions of US dollars at 1980 price.	*China Foreign Economic Statistics 1979–91* and *China Foreign Economic Statistical Yearbook 1994.*

Using ordinary least squares (OLS) cross–section regression analysis with White's heteroscedasticity–consistent covariance matrix correction for un-known form of heteroscedasticity (White 1980), the relationship between provincial trade flows and the suggested explanatory variables is in-vestigated across provinces for the four separate years of 1987, 1989, 1991 and 1993. There are 29 provinces in the sample excluding Tibet. The regression results are reported in Table 5.9.

Table 5.9 Regression results of provincial trade equations

Variable	Model 87	Model 89	Model 91	Model 93
Constant	2.2893	3.5538	5.6949	6.5689
	(0.5357)	(0.8067)	(1.877)	(1.355)
LnPOP	0.75293	0.61607	0.43061	0.32038
	(8.211)***	(8.621)***	(7.425)***	(3.152)***
LnPY	1.1390	0.98541	0.56037	0.54441
	(6.941)***	(7.682)***	(4.182)***	(3.417)***
LnRMT	−2.2562	−2.1502	−1.8926	−1.9094
	(−3.295)***	(−2.498)**	(−3.313)***	(−2.086)**
LnFDI	0.14028	0.19670	0.36531	0.32208
	(2.016)**	(2.323)**	(4.790)***	(2.166)**
Adjusted R^2	0.91	0.91	0.94	0.91
DF	24	24	24	24
F–statistics	72.37	71.94	107.68	71.97

Notes
Adjusted White's heteroscedasticity–consistent *t*–statistics in brackets.
** Statistically significant at 0.05 level.
*** Statistically significant at 0.01 level.

Before we draw any conclusion from the regression results, we apply some diagnostic tests to justify the adequacy of our estimated model for the description of the variations of provincial trade flows with the rest of the world. The results of diagnostic tests for Model 89 and Model 93 are provided in Table 5.10. In general, the log–linear form equation of the provincial trade flows performs quite well against a number of diagnostic tests. Therefore, we accept this model as an adequate representation of the provincial trade flows with the rest of the world.

Based on the diagnostic tests for our estimated model, we are now in a position to draw some inference from the regression. The regressions performed very well. All the models with the suggested independent variables offer very good explanations of the variance in China's provincial aggregate trade flows with the rest of the world. In general, provincial trade

Table 5.10   Diagnostic tests for Model 89 and Model 93 heteroscedasticity

Tests	Test statistics	95% Critical value	Test statistics	95% Critical value
		Model 89		Model 93
B–P–G	$X^2(4) = 5.727$	9.48773	$X^2(4) = 3.140$	9.48773
ARCH	$X^2(1) = 0.006$	3.84146	$X^2(1) = 0.074$	3.84146
Harvey	$X^2(4) = 2.265$	9.48773	$X^2(4) = 1.332$	9.48773
Glejser	$X^2(4) = 4.524$	9.48773	$X^2(4) = 1.970$	9.48773

Functional form

Ramsey RESET specification tests using Powers of $\hat{Y}$	Test statistics	95% Critical value	Test statistics	95% Critical value
		Model 89		Model 93
RESET (2)	$F(1,23) = 0.91287$	4.28	$F(1,23) = 1.0893$	4.28
RESET (3)	$F(2,22) = 0.76463$	3.44	$F(2,22) = 1.0822$	3.44
RESET (4)	$F(3,21) = 0.76870$	3.07	$F(3,21) = 0.8831$	3.07

Normality

Normality tests	Test statistics	95% Critical value	Test statistics	95% Critical value
		Model 89		Model 93
Goodness–of–fit test	$X^2(3) = 7.0171$	7.81473	$X^2(3) = 5.0926$	7.81473
Jarque–Bera test	$X^2(2) = 0.6405$	5.99146	$X^2(2) = 1.4141$	5.99146

is positively related to provincial population size and per capita income, and negatively related to provincial remoteness from the rest of the world. The effect of FDI on provincial trade is positive and statistically significant for all regressions in the four years of 1987, 1989, 1991 and 1993. The interesting finding is that the coefficients of FDI for the four years have been increasing over time, which suggests that the effect of FDI on provincial trade has become more and more important from the late 1980s to the early 1990s. The estimated coefficients of FDI indicate that a one per cent increase in provincial FDI stock would have resulted in a less than 0.20 per cent increase in provincial total trade in the late 1980s. However, in the early 1990s a one per cent increase in provincial FDI stock will result in more than 0.30 per cent increase in provincial total trade. This finding is consistent with the facts that the trade shares of FFEs both in China's provincial trade and in China's total trade have been increasing over time since the late 1980s and particularly during the early 1990s.

Thus the regression results have revealed the positive impact of FDI on trade from the evidence of China's provincial trade. However, the results based on the evidence of China's provincial aggregate trade only revealed that FDI has a positive impact on promoting the trade of China's host provinces. What is the impact of FDI on bilateral trade? We investigate and answer this question in the following section.

THE IMPACT OF FDI ON TRADE: EVIDENCE FROM CHINA'S BILATERAL TRADE

In the preceding section we revealed empirically the positive impact of FDI on promoting trade in China's host provinces. In this section we shall investigate the impact of FDI on bilateral trade flows based on evidence of the bilateral trade between China and its trade partners in the world.

Specification of the Variables

According to the essence of the gravity model of international trade, the two most important factors explaining bilateral trade flows are the geographical distance between the two countries and their economic size. In this study we also add FDI to the gravity model. The goal is to see how much of the bilateral trade flows between China and its trade partners can be explained by the factors common to bilateral trade throughout the world, and how much is contributed by the effect of FDI.

1. Bilateral trade. Bilateral trade (BT) is the dependent variable which is the total merchandise trade volume, exports plus imports, between China and each of its trade partners in a year in 1987 constant US dollars.
2. Size of economy. According to the gravity model of international trade, the volume of trade between two countries is very much determined by their economic size. In this study we use GDP as the economic size and enter GDPs in product form in the regression model. The practice of entering GDPs in product form is empirically well established in bilateral trade regression (Frankel 1994; Wei and Frankel 1994). GDPs are presented in 1987 constant US dollars, and are expected to have a positive effect on bilateral trade flows.
3. Geographical distance. Also based on the spirit of the gravity model, the geographical distance with its associated transport cost is a very important factor in determining the volume of bilateral trade flows. The distance variable is expected to have a negative effect on bilateral trade. The data on distance between China and each of its trade partners are generated by directly measuring from the map.
4. Foreign direct investment. Data for FDI are the accumulated capital stock invested by each of China's trade partners at the year end, in 1987 constant US dollars. The reason for the use of FDI stock instead of FDI flows as the explanatory variable is the same as discussed in the preceding section. We expect the higher the FDI stock in China from a particular country, the higher the bilateral trade flows between China and that particular trade partner.

Regression Results and Explanations

The following equation is estimated to test the impact of FDI on bilateral trade flows between China and each of its trade partners.

$$\ln BT_{C,j} = \beta_0 + \beta_1 \ln GDPs_{C,j} + \beta_2 \ln DIST_{C,j} + \beta_3 \ln FDI_{C,j} + \varepsilon_j \qquad (5.2)$$

Where ε_j is the stochastic disturbance, the βs are the regression parameters to be estimated, and the variables are defined as in Table 5.11. The estimated coefficients of $\ln GDPs$, $\ln DIST$, and $\ln FDI$ variables will be elasticity.

Also using OLS cross–section regression analysis with White's hetero–scedasticity–consistent covariance matrix correction for unknown form of heteroscedasticity, the relationship between bilateral trade flows and the suggested explanatory variables is investigated across countries for the four separate years of 1990, 1991, 1992 and 1993. There are 101 of China's trade partners in the sample. The regression results are reported in Table 5.12.

Table 5.11   List of variables of China's bilateral trade regression equation

Variable name	Specification of variables	Source
BT_{*j}	Sum of export and import between China and country j. Millions of US dollars at 1987 price.	*China Foreign Economic Statistical Yearbook 1994.*
$GDPs_{*j}$	Product of GDPs of China and country j. Millions of US dollars at 1987 price.	Various issues of the *World Development Report.*
$DIST_{*j}$	Distance between China and country j.	Measured from the map in the *Almanac of China's Economic Relations and Trade.*
FDI_{*j}	Accumulated FDI stock invested by country j in China. Millions of US dollars at 1987 price.	Calculated from the various issues of the *Almanac of China's Economic Relations and Trade.*

Table 5.12   Regression results of China's bilateral trade equations

Variable	Model 90	Model 91	Model 92	Model 93
Constant	−3.8764	−3.5071	−4.4414	−4.7951
	(−2.794)**	(−2.616)**	(−2.986)***	(−4.027)***
Ln*GDPs*	0.6917	0.6696	0.6885	0.7150
	(10.36)***	(10.68)***	(10.07)***	(11.34)***
Ln*DIST*	−0.7846	−0.7572	−0.6531	−0.6633
	(−8.025)***	(−7.643)***	(−4.815)***	(−6.649)***
Ln*FDI*	0.1161	0.1246	0.1008	0.1151
	(3.466)***	(3.838)***	(2.845)***	(2.936)***
Adjusted R^2	0.83	0.82	0.78	0.86
DF	97	97	97	97
F–statistics	158.48	154.01	121.52	208.08

Notes
Adjusted White's heteroscedasticity–consistent *t*–statistics in brackets.
** Statistically significant at 0.05 level.
*** Statistically significant at 0.01 level.

As in the previous section, to justify the adequacy of our estimated model for the description of the variations of China's bilateral trade flows with each of its trade partners, we apply some diagnostic tests in our estimated model. The results of diagnostic tests for Model 91 and Model 93 are provided in Table 5.13. In general, the log–linear form equation of China's bilateral trade flows with each of its trade partners performs quite well against a number of diagnostic tests. Therefore, we accept this model as an adequate representation of China's bilateral trade flows with each of its trade partners.

Based on the diagnostic tests, we can now draw the inference from the regression. In all the regressions the independent variables have the expected signs and are statistically significant. As in previous studies using the gravity model in explaining international bilateral trade flows, a country's size and geographical distance are also the most important two variables in our regressions. However, in our study, the added variable *FDI* is a positive and statistically significant factor in explaining the bilateral trade flows between China and its trade partners. The regression results show that the higher the FDI stock invested by China's trade partners, the higher the bilateral trade flows will be between China and its trade partners. The estimated coefficients of *FDI* are relatively stable at the range of 0.10 to 0.12 for the four years from 1990 to 1993, which indicates that a one per cent increase in FDI stock will result in about a 0.11 per cent increase in bilateral trade flows between China and its trade partners in the early 1990s.

Main Findings

Our investigation of the impact of FDI on trade, based on the evidence, both from China's provincial total trade flows with the rest of the world and from China's bilateral trade flows with its trade partners, have revealed several interesting findings. In general three main findings are worth mentioning.

First, the key finding of this study is that FDI has a positive impact both on promoting China's host province total trade flows with the rest of the world and on increasing the bilateral trade flows between China and its trade partners. Therefore, the regression results have proved that the relationship between FDI and trade, in the case of China, is mainly complementary. This finding is consistent with the real situation that FDI in China is concentrated mainly in labour–intensive and export–oriented manufacturing activities.

Second, the positive impact of FDI on promoting China's provincial trade flows has been increasing over time from the late 1980s to the early 1990s. This finding is consistent with the fact that the trade shares of FFEs both in

Table 5.13   Diagnostic tests for Model 91 and Model 93 heteroscedasticity

Tests	Test statistics	95% Critical value	Test statistics	95% Critical value
	Model 91		Model 93	
B–P–G	$X^2 (3) = 6.871$	7.81473	$X^2 (3) = 5.459$	7.81473
ARCH	$X^2 (1) = 1.186$	3.84146	$X^2 (1) = 0.261$	3.84146
Harvey	$X^2 (3) = 3.988$	7.81473	$X^2 (3) = 4.217$	7.81473
Glejser	$X^2 (3) = 8.142$**	7.81473	$X^2 (3) = 7.325$	7.81473

Functional form

Ramsey RESET Specification tests using	Test statistics	95% Critical value	Test statistics	95% Critical value
Powers of $\hat{Y}$	Model 91		Model 93	
RESET (2)	$F(1,96) = 0.31069$	3.96	$F(1,96) = 0.00252$	3.96
RESET (3)	$F(2,95) = 0.70374$	3.11	$F(2,95) = 0.01683$	3.11
RESET (4)	$F(3,94) = 0.59345$	2.71	$F(3,94) = 0.01199$	2.71

Normality

Normality tests	Test statistics	95% Critical value	Test statistics	95% Critical value
	Model 91		Model 93	
Goodness–of–fit test	$X^2 (4) = 5.8728$	9.48773	$X^2 (4) = 7.1634$	9.48773
Jarque–Bera test	$X^2 (2) = 0.4117$	5.99146	$X^2 (2) = 1.1171$	5.99146

Note: ** Statistically significant at 0.05 level.

the provincial trade and in China's total trade have been increasing very rapidly, particularly in the early 1990s. This implies that FDI will play an ever–more important role in China's trade expansion.

Third, comparing the impact of FDI on China's provincial trade flows and on China's bilateral trade flows in the early 1990s, the impact of FDI on China's provincial trade flows was larger than that on China's bilateral trade flows. This is because the impact of FDI on China's provincial trade flows is the total effect of FDI on trade, while the impact of FDI on China's bilateral trade flows is only part of the effect of FDI on trade. A considerable portion of trade generated by FDI may go to the third countries rather than between China and the FDI source countries. This situation is especially important for the NIEs, since their FDI in China is mainly international market export oriented and particularly towards the developed countries' markets.

CONCLUSION

In this chapter we examined China's outstanding trade performance in the last 16 years and correspondingly investigated the relationship between FDI and trade and the impact of FDI on trade from the evidence of China. In general we found a positive relationship between FDI and trade and a positive impact of FDI on trade, both empirically from China's provincial trade and from China's bilateral trade. More precisely the following main findings are worth mentioning.

First, in the last 16 years, China's international trade has experienced an unprecedented growth. However, China's achievements in its fast in–ternational trade expansion have a number of causes. The market–oriented economic reforms and trade liberalisation, the remarkable development of TVEs, and the massive inflows of FDI during the last 16 years have all contributed greatly to the success of China's international trade growth. Apart from the other two main factors, FDI's contribution to China's trade growth has been very impressive. From 1980 to 1995, the share of FDI–related trade in China's total trade increased from 0.11 per cent to 39.1 per cent with an annual growth rate of 48 per cent. As a result, FDI has become one of the most important contributors to China's international trade growth, and its importance is increasing over time.

Second, because of the unbalanced distribution of FDI among China's provinces, the contribution of FDI to provincial trade among provinces is also different. However, the interesting finding is that provinces with higher trade shares in China's total trade are also the provinces with higher trade shares of FFEs in their provincial trade. In other words, provinces which have higher trade shares of FFEs in their provincial trade are the leading trade provinces in China. This finding revealed a very important positive relationship between FDI and trade in the case of China.

Third, to move beyond the correlations between FDI and trade, the empirical regression analyses revealed that FDI has positive and statistically significant impacts both on China's provincial total trade flows and on China's bilateral trade flows. The regression results have proved that the relationship between FDI and trade is mainly complementary in the case of China. This important finding is consistent with the fact that FDI in China is concentrated mainly in labour–intensive and export–oriented manu–facturing activities.

Fourth, since the above findings are derived from the evidence of China, they may not be applied to other countries. However, if we take into account the source–country and host–country specific characteristics, we also can generalise some basic implications from the above findings. First, in terms of the source countries and their investment patterns, as has been discussed in the previous chapters, the major source countries investing in China are the developing countries, particularly the NIEs. As determined by their own ownership advantages, their investments are concentrated mainly in labour–intensive activities and tend to be more export oriented. Second, in terms of host–country characteristics, China is well endowed with abundant labour and has a comparative advantage in labour–intensive activities. Therefore, the labour–intensive and export–oriented investment patterns of the developing source countries are well matched with China's resource endowments and comparative advantages. Ultimately, under these conditions FDI has a positive impact on trade. Therefore, we may generalise that FDI would have a positive impact on trade if developing source countries invest in a country which is well endowed with abundant labour and has a comparative advantage in labour–intensive activities.

NOTE

1. Adding some additional variables in the gravity model of international trade is used in a number of studies. Among others, for example, Frankel (1994), Wei and Frankel (1994), Frankel and Romer (1996).

REFERENCES

Asia Pacific Economics Group (APEG), 1995. *Asia Pacific profiles*, APEG, Canberra, Australia.

Brainard, S., 1992. 'A simple theory of multinational corporations and trade with a trade–off between proximity and concentration', *NBER Working Paper Series*, **4269**.

Dunning, J., 1988. 'The eclectic paradigm of international production: a restatement and some possible extensions', *Journal of International Business Studies*, **19**, 1–32.

Dunning, J., 1993. *Multinational enterprises and the global economy*, Addison–Wesley, Wokingham, England.

Dunning, J., 1995. 'What's wrong – and right – with trade theory?', *International Trade Journal*, **9(2)**, 163–202.

Findlay, C. and Watson, A., 1996. 'Economic growth and trade dependency in China', *Chinese Economy Research Unit Working Paper*, **96/5**, University of Adelaide.

Findlay, C., Watson, A. and Wu, H. (eds), 1994. *Rural enterprises in China*, Macmillan, London.

Frankel, J., 1994. 'Is Japan creating a yen bloc in East Asia and the Pacific?', in J. Frankel and M. Kahler (eds), *Regionalism and rivalry: Japan and the U.S. in Pacific Asia*, University of Chicago Press, Chicago.

Frankel, J. and Romer, D., 1996. 'Trade and growth: an empirical investigation', *NBER Working Paper Series*, **5476**.

Helpman, E., 1984. 'A simple theory of international trade with multinational corporations', *Journal of Political Economy*, **92**, 451–71.

Helpman, E. and Krugman, P., 1985. *Market structure and foreign trade*, MIT Press, Cambridge, Massachusetts.

Horstmann, I. and Markusen, J., 1992. 'Endogenous market structures in international trade', *Journal of International Economics*, **32**, 109–29.

Kojima, K., 1973. 'A macroeconomic approach to foreign direct investment', *Hitotsubashi Journal of Economics*, **14**, 1–21.

Kojima, K., 1985. 'Japanese and American direct investment in Asia: a comparative analysis', *Hitotsubashi Journal of Economics*, **26**, 1–35.

Lardy, N., 1992. *Foreign trade and economic reform in China 1978–1990*, Cambridge University Press, Cambridge.

Lardy, N., 1994. *China in the world economy*, Institute for International Economics, Washington, DC.

Markusen, J., 1984. 'Multinational, multi–plant economies, and the gains from trade', *Journal of International Economics*, **16**, 169–89.

Markusen, J., 1995. 'The boundaries of multinational enterprises and the theory of international trade', *Journal of Economic Perspectives*, **9(2)**, 169–89.

Markusen, J. and Venables, A., 1995. 'Multinational firms and the new trade theory', *NBER Working Paper Series*, **5036**.

Petri, P., 1995. 'The interdependence of trade and investment in the Pacific', in E. Chen and P. Drysdale (eds), *Corporate links and foreign direct investment in Asia and the Pacific*, Harper Educational Publishers, Australia.

State Statistical Bureau, 1986–1996. *China statistical yearbook 1986–1996*, Zhongguo Tongji Chubanshe, Beijing.

United Nations, 1993. *World investment report 1993: transnational corporations and integrated international production*, United Nations publication, United Nations, New York and Geneva.

United Nations, 1996. *World investment report 1996: investment, trade and international policy arrangements*, United Nations publication, United Nations, New York and Geneva.

Vernon, R., 1966. 'International investment and international trade in the product cycle', *Quarterly Journal of Economics*, **80**, 190–207.

Wei, S. and Frankel, J., 1994. 'A "Greater China" trade bloc?', *China Economic Review*, **5(2)**, 179–190.

White, H., 1980. 'A heteroscedastic consistent covariance matrix estimator and a direct test for heteroscedasticity', *Econometrica*, **50**, 1–25.

World Bank, 1994. *Building on the Uruguay round: East Asian leadership in liberalisation*, World Bank, Washington, DC.

6.   FDI, Trade and Transfer Pricing

Haishun Sun

INTRODUCTION

FDI and foreign trade are two important determinants for a country's economic growth. It is agreed among economists that, as a transfer of a package of capital, technology and management skills from the home country to the host country, FDI tends to contribute to capital formation, technology transfer and productivity growth in the host country. However, the impact of FDI on foreign trade remains debatable. The key issue is whether FDI creates or replaces for foreign trade. At the macro level, Kojima (1973, 1975 and 1982) classifies FDI into two categories: trade–creating and trade–substituting. The first type of FDI creates more trade opportunities between the home and host countries, and therefore, complements foreign trade, whereas the second type of FDI replaces foreign trade or destroys trade conditions. At the micro–level, the role of multinational corporations (MNCs) in international trade, especially the effects of the intra–firm trade of MNCs on the trade balance of the host country, are also less unanimous among academics and policy makers.

This chapter aims to present a study of the impact of FDI on foreign trade in the case of China, using both the macro and micro approaches. The next section discusses the macro and micro approaches which have been developed for the study of the relationship between FDI and foreign trade. Empirical evidence about the influence of FDI on the foreign trade of China is then presented. This is followed by an examination of the role of FDI in China's exports and imports and FDI's influence on the trade balance, and hence an empirical test for Kojima's hypothesis about FDI 'trade–creation' and 'trade–replacement'. Subsequently, this chapter investigates the factors contributing to FDI–induced trade deficits, in particular, the transfer pricing manipulated by MNCs. Then the chapter analyses the motivations and possibility for MNCs to practise transfer pricing in China and presents an empirical examination using indirect evidence. The final section draws conclusions and policy implications.

THEORETICAL BACKGROUND

What role the international trade theory has given to international capital movements, especially FDI, has remained a less–explored issue to date. This is certainly relevant to studying the implications of the multinational corporations for trade theory. The key issues are how international investment affects trade, and what role multinational corporations may play in international trade. These issues can be studied at both the macro and micro levels.

At the macroeconomic level, multinational corporations have changed factor endowments, which is the basis of international trade. First, MNCs have increased international capital mobility through direct investment in different countries. This is expected to change the factor proportion (capital–labour ratio) in the home and host countries. Although it may be true that sometimes a company may establish a subsidiary in a particular country using capital drawn from the host country's domestic market, the basic direction of capital flows from capital–abundant country to capital–shortage country will remain virtually the same. Second, FDI involves the transfer of technology, management know–how and entrepreneurial spirit, and labour training. In essence, this is the transfer of a particular form of capital – human capital. This will definitely affect both the quantity and quality of factors and their combinations in relevant countries, resulting in changes in factor productivity and comparative advantage between products. Such a dynamic change in comparative advantage, as labelled by Kojima (1973, 1975), will inevitably affect international trade both in structure and in direction. At the microeconomic level, a significant part of international trade is carried by and within multinational corporations. Intra–firm trade and transfer pricing manipulated by MNCs have considerably changed the pattern and structure of international trade and also effectively influenced the distribution of income and trade gains in relevant countries. To date there is still the lack of a broadly accepted theory in which the international trade theories are well incorporated with international investment theories. The difficulty is how international direct investment and international trade are related. This issue can be tackled at the macro and micro levels.

Foreign Investment Substitutes for or Complements to Trade: Macro Approach

The traditional theory of international trade, as represented by the Heckscher–Ohlin–Samuelson (H–O–S) model, emphasises the differences in factor endowments between different countries. According to the theory, differences in resource endowments and factor proportions are the determinants of international trade. A country should specialise in the production of the good which intensively uses its abundant factor of production. By producing and exporting its comparatively advantaged product, the country will benefit from international trade. All trade partner countries will be better off from a net trade gain. It is a central proposition of the H–O–S model that factor movements are, at least to some extent, a substitute for trade, and vice versa. Ohlin (1933) stressed that trade on its own would *tend* to equalise factor prices; and factor movements would tend to bring closer the factor prices in the two countries. Due to the existence of transport costs, trade tariffs and differences in production functions, trade and factor movements are not perfect substitutes.

Based on Ohlin's work, Mundell (1957) has explored the special case where trade and factor movements are perfect substitutes. Under the restrictive assumptions of zero transport costs, identical production functions for each good in the two countries, and different factor intensities being required by different products, he argued that free trade tends to result in commodity price equalisation and, even when factors are immobile, in a tendency towards factor–price equalisation in different countries. It is equally true that perfect mobility of factors results in factor–price equalisation and, even when commodity movements cannot take place, in a tendency towards commodity–price equalisation. He proposed that an increase in trade impediments stimulates factor movements and that an increase in restrictions to factor movements stimulates trade. Thus, trade and factor movements are substitutes and replacements for each other. If tariff and other trade impediments are then removed, there is no inducement for any trade.

In his analysis, Mundell dealt with international capital flows as a typical form of international movements of a homogeneous factor of production. He argued that under the condition of perfect capital mobility, all trade will cease since the basis of trade – differences in factor proportions between countries – will no longer exit. This suggests that when capital is perfectly mobile, one can no longer apply the simple H–O–S factor–endowment approach, arguing that the country that is relatively well endowed with capital must export capital–intensive goods. This is because the capital–abundant country may export its capital instead, to the point where it ceases to be relatively well endowed with capital (Corden 1974). Therefore, international capital movements would eliminate commodity movements. Obviously, Mundell's conclusion is just the logical result of two extreme cases, as soon as the restrictive assumptions are relaxed, the conclusion will disappear.

In contrast to Mundell's complete substitute model, Purvis (1972) proposed a model where international capital flows are complements to commodity trade. He defines complements as follows: 'A sufficient condition for complementary is that the initial capital outflow generates an excess demand for imports and an excess supply of exportables at constant term of trade'. If foreign investment creates and/or expands the opportunity to import one product and to export the other product, it is complementary to product trade. On the other hand, if initial capital outflow reduces or eliminates the opportunity to import one product and to export the other product, it will substitute for product trade and is thus trade–destroying.

In particular, his argument focuses on the effect of different production functions between country A (capital–abundant, investing country) and country B (labour–abundant, host country). Assuming that country B has comparatively higher capital productivity in product Y (capital–intensive goods) than in product X (labour–intensive goods) as compared with the same relationship in country A. After capital movements from country A to country B, the output of product Y increased in country B is expected to be more than the output of the product decreased in country A, resulting in a net increase in the output of product Y in the two countries taken together. This represents a net gain from capital movements. As for product X, after capital movements, the output decreases in country B and increases in country A. This is because capital flows from country A to country B tend to pull up the labour costs in country B, and exert pressure on wages in country A, likely resulting in a relative decrease in labour cost in country A. The condition for capital movements to be complements to product trade is that the overall output value of the two goods in the two countries taken together must increase, otherwise trade would be partly eliminated and welfare for the two countries will not rise. However, Purvis's argument does not clarify a crucial element of how and why the production functions differ between the two countries, or under what conditions foreign investment complements and promotes product trade.

Kojima (1973, 1975 and 1982) further developed the Mundell and Purvis models, and specifies the conditions for foreign investment to be complementary to or substituting for commodity trade. He played a pioneering role in developing a systematic macroeconomic approach to foreign direct investment, and in incorporating FDI into international trade theory. As a starting point, he distinguishes FDI from international money capital movements. FDI is, in essence, the transmission to the 'host' country of a 'package' of capital, managerial skills and technology (Johnson 1973). FDI not only transfers capital, but also transplants superior production technology through training of labour, transfer of management and marketing know–how, from advanced industrial countries to less–developed countries. As a result of technology transfers, superior production functions can be transferred from investing countries to the host country. In addition, through the activities of subsidiaries and joint ventures in particular industries, foreign investing companies can spread over the industries in the host country and play a role as tutor, training local labourers, engineers and managers, ultimately improving the productivity of local firms.

In what type of industries can FDI easily transfer technology and improve the production functions in the host country, and eventually create more trade opportunities? Kojima argued that if FDI flows into industries in which the host country has a comparative advantage, it tends to improve the productivity of the host economy and therefore stimulates more exports. This is because, as he argues, the smaller the technological gap between the investing and host countries, the easier it is to transfer technology and improve productivity in the latter. In terms of developing host countries, FDI flowing into labour–intensive industries are largely trade–creating. FDI flowing into capital–intensive industries, where the host country is comparatively disadvantaged, is trade–replacing, or trade–destroying as such types of investment are essentially import–substituted, resulting in a decrease in trade between the investing and host countries. On the part of the investing country, if outward investments come from its comparatively disadvantaged industries, for example, labour–intensive or resources–oriented investments, they tend to be trade–creating; if outward investments come from its comparatively advanced industries, they tend to be trade–replacing since such investments do not fit the host country's comparative advantage, and eventually reduce the total output of the two countries and their trade volume.

Some authors (for example, Arndt 1974, Geroski 1979, Mason 1980, Buckley 1983, Lee 1984 and Dunning 1985) cast doubt on the validity of Kojima's hypothesis. They argue that international investments made by multinational corporations may be diversified in various industries including capital/technology intensive and labour–intensive industries, depending on firms' competitive advantage in the host country's market, with net impact on foreign trade being uncertain. In addition, Kojima's theory may fail to explain the 'double–way' international investments between industrialised countries (for example, between the US and Europe), although it may be applied to international investments flowing from industrialised countries to developing countries.

Intra–firm Trade of MNCs: Micro Approach

A multinational corporation (MNC) is an enterprise that owns and controls value–adding activities in two or more countries. These activities can include production, marketing and research and development (Casson and Pearce 1988). The activities of MNCs have an important impact on international trade. First, international direct investments made by MNCs reallocate economic resources globally and the capacities of production, according to relative costs of production in different countries. This is expected to bring about a dynamic change in comparative advantages in relevant countries, thus leading to changes in the structure and pattern of international trade. Second, global activities of production, marketing and R&D by MNCs build world–wide linkages, which in turn facilitate transfer of technologies and quicker flows of information. This tends to stimulate the flow of commodities. Third, horizontal and vertical integration developed by MNCs' international production activities require and promote international circulation of components, parts and other intermediate products between different countries. This would certainly increase the volume of international trade. Fourth, FDI, especially joint ventures with local firms, can sig–

nificantly improve the host country's access to international markets. In addition, through industrial linkages especially backward linkages, foreign subsidiaries buy locally made intermediate inputs such as parts and components for production of exportables. This will induce exports from domestic firms to increase. The induced exports by FDI can be a considerable part of total exports from the host country. Finally, intra–firm trade within MNCs becomes increasingly important in international trade. It is estimated that at least 25 per cent of international trade is carried out by MNCs through intra–firm trade (United Nations 1992). In addition to direct intra–firm trade, a substantial volume of trade is likely to be conducted by and between units of large MNCs.

Intra–firm trade within MNC networks is crucial to a full understanding of the effects of MNCs on international trade, as the growth of intra–firm trade not only increases the volume of international trade, but also changes the pattern of international trade and the distribution of income and gain from trade. Unlike trade between independent parties – so–called 'arm's–length trade', intra–firm trade is controlled by the same company. To avoid taxation, tariff and business risks, MNCs manipulate transfer pricing for intra–firm trade. Through overinvoicing or underinvoicing exports or imports, MNCs shift profits out of host countries and minimise business risks. As a result, host countries, especially developing host countries, suffer from income loss. Furthermore, manipulative transfer pricing is likely to result in a worsening balance of trade in a developing host country, as exports are underpriced and imports are overpriced by MNCs. Since domestic firms in developing countries lack expertise and marketing networks, MNCs not only directly control intra–firm trade between their units in different countries, but largely control the foreign trade of local firms. Therefore, the coverage of transfer prices not only includes the direct exports and imports of their subsidiaries, but also, to some extent, the trade of domestic firms. The propensity and latitude for an MNC to pursue transfer pricing are dependent on taxation, tariffs, economic policies and business risks in relevant countries. A detailed discussion of the issues will be presented later.

FDI AND FOREIGN TRADE IN CHINA: AN EMPIRICAL INVESTIGATION

Based on the above theoretical discussion, conclusions can be drawn that FDI may play an important role in the foreign trade of the host country by creating more trade opportunities. It is also possible that FDI may partly replace international trade, depending on how FDI changes the existing comparative advantages in the home and host countries. If FDI fits to and strengthens the host country's comparative advantage (comparative disad–vantage for the home country), it would increase foreign trade. Many empirical studies (for example, Hone 1974, Helleiner 1973, Rana 1985) on the impact of FDI on the host country's foreign trade, have been carried out in recent decades, and have found that FDI contributed to the export growth of the host country. In this section, we present an empirical investigation about this issue in the case of China.

Since China began opening to the outside world in 1979, its exports have grown rapidly. During the period from 1980 to 1995, Chinese exports increased by 15.1 per cent annually. As a result, the degree of the openness of the Chinese economy, which can be measured as the sum of exports (X) and imports (M) as a share of GDP, that is, (X + M)/GDP, rose from 15.4 per cent in 1981 to 26.6 per cent[1] in 1995 (SSB 1996, p.580 and p.42). Among the factors promoting the export growth, FDI has played an exceptional role. Foreign–invested enterprises (FIEs) have been the most active players in the export expansion drive. During the period from 1981 to 1995, exports by FIEs grew at an annual rate of 63.3 per cent, with the value of exports increasing from US$32 million to US$468,80 million. Consequently, the share of FIEs in the total exports of China increased sharply from 0.1 per cent in 1981 to 31.5 per cent in 1995 (see Table 6.1). The rapid expansion of FIEs' exports led to a phenomenal growth in China's exports.

In the coastal region, the contribution of FIEs to exports is even more significant. As shown in Table 6.1, FIEs provided nearly half of the total exports of Guangdong Province. In 1995, the share of FIEs in total provincial exports reached 43.6 per cent. For the period from 1986 to 1995, the exports of FIEs in Guangdong increased by US$25,370 million, representing 44.3 per cent of the total increase in the provincial exports. This indicates that FIEs have played a leading role in promoting Guangdong's exports. Due to the FIEs' driving force, Guangdong's exports experienced an exceptional boom in the past ten years. During the period from 1986 to 1995, Guangdong's exports grew at an annual rate of 30.1 per cent. This is significantly higher than the national average growth rate of 17.0 per cent. Similarly, in other coastal provinces, FIEs also contributed considerably to exports. For instance, in Fujian and Tianjin, FIEs provided 43.7 per cent and 44.8 per cent of the total exports, respectively, in 1995.[2] In Shanghai, FIEs provided 30 per cent of the total exports in the same year. Therefore, the impact of FDI on the exports of China (especially in the coastal region) has become critically important.

In terms of category of commodities, FIEs' exports are concentrated in labour–intensive products including textiles, garments, shoes and other fabric products, food, beverages and wine, handicraft articles, toys, TV receivers and sound equipment, clocks and watches, bicycles and parts, plastic articles, household electrical products, sports goods, general metalware, office supplies, and other light manufactured goods. In 1993, these commodities

Table 6.1   FIEs' effect on the foreign trade of China and Guangdong province (US$100 million)

	China									Guangdong								
	Exports			Imports			Trade balance			Exports			Imports			Trade balance	
	Total	FIEs	%	Total	FIEs	%	Total	FIEs		Total	FIEs	%	Total	FIEs	%	Total	FIEs
1980	181.2	0.1		200.2	0.3	0.2	-19.0	-0.3		22.1			3.6			18.5	
1981	220.1	0.3	0.1	220.2	1.1	0.5	-0.1	-0.8		24.2			6.7			17.5	
1982	223.2	0.5	0.2	192.9	2.8	1.4	30.3	-2.3		22.7			8.0			14.7	
1983	222.3	3.3	1.5	213.9	2.9	1.3	8.4	0.4		24.0			9.4			14.6	
1984	261.4	0.7	0.3	274.1	4.0	1.5	-12.7	-3.3		25.2	0.7	2.9	12.1			13.1	
1985	273.5	3.0	1.1	422.5	20.6	4.9	-149.0	-17.6		29.5	2.2	7.3	24.3	3.4	11.9	5.2	-1.2
1986	309.4	5.8	1.9	429.0	24.3	5.7	-119.6	-18.5		42.5	3.9	9.2	25.6	8.5	32.3	16.9	-4.6
1987	394.4	12.1	3.1	432.2	31.2	7.2	-37.8	-19.1		54.4	6.2	11.4	36.2	8.0	22.0	18.2	-1.8
1988	475.2	24.6	5.2	522.8	57.5	11.0	-47.6	-32.9		74.8	12.0	16.1	51.1	11.3	22.1	23.7	0.7
1989	525.4	49.1	9.4	591.4	88.0	14.9	-66.0	-38.9		81.7	22.8	30.2	48.3	19.5	40.4	33.4	3.3
1990	620.9	78.1	12.6	533.5	123.1	23.1	87.4	-45.0		105.6	37.2	37.6	57.5	33.0	57.4	48.1	4.2
1991	719.1	120.5	16.8	637.9	169.1	26.5	81.2	-48.6		136.9	53.3	41.6	85.1	45.1	53.0	51.8	8.2
1992	850.0	173.6	20.4	806.1	263.9	32.8	43.9	-90.3		184.4	81.6	44.3	111.8	60.2	53.8	72.6	21.4
1993	917.6	252.4	27.5	1,039.5	418.3	40.2	-121.9	-165.9		376.0	143.7	38.2	431.2	198.0	45.9	-55.2	-54.3
1994	1,210.1	347.1	28.7	1,156.1	529.3	45.8	54.0	-18.2		532.7	198.4	37.2	477.9	253.6	53.1	54.8	-55.2
1995	1,487.7	468.8	31.5	1,320.8	629.4	47.7	166.9	-160.6		590.5	257.6	43.6	494.8	274.4	55.5	95.7	-16.8

Note: The figures in this table are based on China's Customs Statistics.

Sources: The national figures for period of 1980–93 are calculated from *China's Foreign Economic Statistics 1979–1991* and 1994, published by the State Statistical Bureau (SSB) of China, and the figures for 1994 and 1995 for both China and Guangdong Province are from Statistical Yearbook of China 1996, pp. 582–96. The figures for Guangdong province for the period of 1980–92 are from *Guangdong Sheng Duiwai Jingji Guanxi Tongji Zilao (Statistical Materials of Foreign Economic Relations of Guangdong Province), 1987–1992*, compiled by the Statistical Bureau of Guangdong Province.

Table 6.2 FIEs' contribution to the exports of China by commodity (unit: US$ million)

Commodities	1988			1990			1992			1993		
	FIEs	Total	%	FIEs	Total	%	FIEs	Total	%	FIEs	Total	%
Total	1,746	40,640	4.3	6,021	62,091	9.7	15,591	84,940	18.4	23,390	91,763	25.5
Food, beverage and wine	151	3,602	4.2	304	4,327	7.0	780	5,654	13.8	1,344	6,152	21.9
Textile fibres and fabric	350	7,431	4.7	825	6,235	13.2	2,031	10,465	19.4	2,979	12,242	24.0
Garments, shoes and other fabrics	240	4,270	5.6	1,359	6,498	20.9	3,583	12,385	28.9	5,696	17,656	32.0
Household electrical appliances	57	509	11.1	247	873	28.2	563	1,728	32.6	803	3,179	25.3
TV receivers and sound equipment	270	744	36.3	712	1,550	45.9	1,018	1,887	53.9	982	1,836	53.5
Machinery and equipment	23	997	2.3	134	1,877	7.1	349	2,592	13.5	702	2,839	25.0
Bicycles and spare parts	4	148	2.4	116	308	37.6	184	554	33.3	229	537	42.7
Plastic articles	59	280	20.9	213	447	47.6	526	823	63.9	847	1,490	56.9
Handicraft articles	69	736	9.3	224	899	24.9	708	1,689	41.9	1,021	2,084	49.1
Toys	55	268	20.7	134	314	42.8	351	660	53.1	535	1,512	35.4
Chemicals	55	1,795	3.1	138	2,627	5.3	351	3,746	9.4	590	3,854	15.0
Transport equipment	4	475	0.8	50	857	5.9	349	1,545	22.6	551	1,843	30.0
Clocks and watches	37	131	28.3	122	299	40.9	162	295	55.0	226	421	53.6
Metallic products	62	2,201	2.8	172	2,421	7.1	395	3,685	10.7	639	3,998	16.0
Tools and instruments	81	553	14.7	383	1,422	26.9	1,394	2,603	53.5	1,818	3,440	53.0

Sports goods	2	171	1.2	124	345	36.1	464	838	55.3	750	1,234	60.8
Office supplies	16	38	43.3	35	67	52.2	57	103	55.1	74	135	55.1
General metalware	12	161	7.2	45	245	18.3	141	553	25.4	239	742	32.2
Other	200	16,130	1.24	684	30,481	2.3	2,187	33,134	6.6	3,359	26,570	13.0

Note: The figures of FIEs' exports and China's total exports in this table are based on MOFTEC's statistics, which are sometimes not identical to the statistics published by the Customs.

Sources: The FIEs' exports data are from *Zhongguo Duiwai Maoyi Tongji Nianbao (Annual Statistical Report of China's Foreign Trade) 1988, 1990, 1992 and 1993*; The data on the national total exports are from *Almanac of China's Foreign Economic Relations and Trade, 1990, 1992, 1994* (by MOFTEC).

represented 81.6 per cent of the total exports of FIEs (calculated from Table 6.2). As seen in Table 6.2, FIEs have become the dominant exporter for a number of labour–intensive products, which are the primary commodities exported from China. For example, in 1993 FIEs provided over half of the total value of some of China's major exports, such as TV and sound equipment (53.5 per cent), clocks and watches (53.6 per cent), plastic products (56.9 per cent), office supplies (55.1 per cent), sports goods (60.8 per cent) and industrial tools and instruments (53.0 per cent). In some capital/technology–intensive products, FIEs have provided an increasing volume of the exports. These products include machinery and equipment, transport equipment, and chemical products. In 1993, FIEs accounted for 25.0 per cent, 30.0 per cent and 15.0 per cent, respectively, of these three categories of exports. However, these exports accounted for a small share of the total exports of FIEs, less than 20 per cent.

The structure of exports by FIEs in the case of China, as demonstrated above, provides empirical support for Kojima's hypothesis that if foreign investments flow into industries in which the host country has comparative advantage, they tend to be trade–creating, and thus strengthen exports from the host country. Due to the abundant labour resource and low wages, China has comparative advantage in labour–intensive industries. By investing in these industries, foreign companies can combine their advantages in capital, technologies, and management and marketing skills with Chinese labour resources, creating new competitive advantage in international markets. In addition, foreign investments in the comparatively advantaged industries of China improve the efficiency of resource allocation at the macro level, as a large number of workers would otherwise be unemployed or underemployed if foreign investment flowed into capital/technology–intensive industries. At the micro level, foreign investments in Chinese comparatively advantaged industries are likely to increase the productivity of factors (labour and capital) since factor proportion has been changed (capital/labour ratio rises) by foreign investments in China. This would also create a net gain for investing countries as labour–intensive industries are their comparatively disadvantaged industries. Capital outflows from these industries tend to increase the return to capital for existing firms in these industries. Decreases in supply of these products in the investing country's domestic market tend to stimulate imports from the developing host country. Therefore, further trade opportunities are created by FDIs of this type.

Another type of FDI in China is domestic–market oriented. China's domestic market is large, with 1.2 billion consumers and is also fast developing with the booming economy. It attracts many multinational corporations to invest in China, targeting the domestic market both for consumer goods and producer goods with a wide range of capital/technology content. This type of investment is, in essence, trade–substituting as the products and services produced by foreign–invested enterprises are sold in the domestic market as substitutes for imports. Therefore, this type of FDI tends to worsen the trade balance of China because intermediate inputs used in FIEs are largely imported from overseas, especially from MNCs' home countries, and their products are sold in the Chinese domestic market.

As displayed in Table 6.1, over the period from 1981 to 1995, the foreign trade of FIEs was not balanced. During these 15 years, the imports of FIEs constantly exceeded their exports. Only once (in 1983), were FIEs' exports slightly larger than their imports. As a result, the trade deficit of FIEs has experienced chronic growth, from US$26 million in 1980 to US$16,060 million in 1995. As shown in Table 6.1, prior to 1989 the FIEs' trade deficit exacerbated the existing trade deficit of China. It was an important factor behind the large trade deficits of China for that period. In the most recent six years (1990–95), the increased trade deficits of FIEs have largely offset the trade surplus created by the Chinese domestic sector, hence resulting in either a smaller trade surplus or a larger trade deficit in the trade account of China. Therefore, the direct impact of FIEs on China's balance of foreign trade as a whole has been negative.

A proper assessment of the net impact of FIEs' trade deficit on the Chinese economy requires an analysis of the reasons for the trade deficits and the composition of FIEs' imports. By definition, FIEs' trade deficits result from more imports compared to exports. There are three factors contributing to FIEs' trade deficits. First, FIEs import machinery and equipment as investment goods. When FIEs are established, foreign investors normally provide some (or all) machinery and equipment as an important proportion of their investment equity. The importation of these capital goods accounted for a sizeable proportion of FIEs' total imports in the past few years. For instance, in 1993, 39.5 per cent of FIEs' imports were machinery and equipment as investment goods.[3] If this portion of imports excluded from FIEs' total imports, FIEs' foreign trade has been balanced or has had a slight surplus since 1990. Therefore, the trade deficit is no longer a major problem with FIEs in a real sense because the importation of investment goods, especially advanced machinery and equipment, assists fixed capital investment in China, and is expected to promote economic growth in the long run.

Second, FIEs import the inputs of production including raw materials, spare parts, components and other intermediate products. In general, FIEs have a relatively higher propensity to use imported inputs than local firms. In many cases, they rely heavily on imported raw materials and intermediate inputs. For those FIEs whose products are oriented to the domestic market, this is the major reason for their trade deficits. Trade deficits of this sort could affect the host economy in two ways. On the one hand, according to Keynesian income determination theory, trade deficits represent a net leakage of aggregate demand from the importing country, thereby negatively affecting the economic growth of the country. Therefore, it can be argued that FIEs' trade deficits are likely to have a negative impact on the economic growth of China. On the other hand, if FIEs' products, especially capital goods, can be used as substitutes for imported products, China would benefit from the saving of foreign exchange.

Third, transfer pricing manipulated by foreign investors (MNCs) for FIEs' exports and imports is a major reason for the persistent and increasing trade deficits of FIEs. The foreign trade of many FIEs, including both joint ventures and foreign wholly–owned subsidiaries, is largely controlled by MNCs. Therefore, intra–firm trade within MNC networks dominate the exports and imports of FIEs, and is thus subject to transfer pricing. By using transfer prices, foreign investors undervalue FIEs' exports and overvalue the imports so as to transfer profits out of China, resulting in FIEs' trade deficits and income loss for China. To what extent the transfer prices affect the trade balance of FIEs depends on the difference between the transfer prices and the open market prices for their exports and imports. This issue will be investigated in detail in the following section.

The three factors discussed above simultaneously contribute to the trade deficits of FIEs. The impact of each factor on the economy is different from one other. It can surely be argued that the trade deficit associated with the importation of investment goods is expected to affect Chinese capital formation and economic growth positively. However, the trade deficit caused by transfer pricing and disproportionate input imports relative to product exports, would negatively influence the Chinese economy. Therefore, the net impact of FIEs' trade deficits on the economy depends on the extent to which each factor affects the total trade deficit.

From a developmental point of view, the impact of FDI on the host country's net exports can be divided into two stages. In the first stage (for example, the first 15 years) it would be negative, but in the second stage it would turn positive. This is because in the initial stage, FIEs rely heavily on imported inputs including equipment, intermediate products and raw materials. The low quality and unstable supply of these inputs by local firms or the lack of knowledge about local supply are the major reasons for a lower local content in the total inputs used in FIEs. However, as the quality and supply system of these inputs produced by local firms improve, the local content of inputs used in FIEs will inevitably rise. As a result, the ratio of imported inputs to total inputs will decline. The input localisation policy pursued by the Chinese government also promotes this trend. Therefore, the effect of FDI on the net exports of China is expected to become positive in the near future.

TRANSFER PRICING AND FIES' TRADE

Transfer pricing by MNCs has received considerable attention from academics, host–country governments and international organisations (for example, the UN). A number of studies concerning MNCs' transfer pricing behaviour have been undertaken. Transfer prices are the prices that MNCs set for intra–firm exports and imports across national boundaries (Lecraw 1985, Gray 1993). The transfer prices set by MNCs for the transactions between their related units are different from the arm's–length market prices used for transactions between unrelated units. The motivation of MNCs to manipulate transfer pricing is to maximise their global profit and minimise the total costs by avoiding or reducing taxes and tariffs in their home and host countries where their subsidiaries operate. The principal tools by which MNCs manipulate transfer pricing are underinvoicing (that is, underpricing) the exports and overinvoicing (that is, overpricing) the imports of the host country.

Many factors may influence MNCs' transfer pricing manipulation. These include tax rates and tariffs at home and in host countries, import or export restrictions, foreign exchange control, restrictions on the repatriation of profits, joint–venture partners' capability to manage and influence the pricing policy and practice, and taxation (or Customs) authorities' expertise and ability to detect and prevent transfer pricing. In general, a large international differential in taxes and tariffs would give rise to a high propensity for MNCs to use transfer prices to reduce tax payments and tariff duties in relevant countries. In addition to taxation differentials, the business environment factors such as restrictions and regulations on imports, exports and foreign exchange control, can also stimulate MNCs' incentives to manipulate transfer pricing to avoid business risks and institutional transaction costs.

For a particular host country, a set of factors may simultaneously influence MNCs' transfer pricing behaviour. Thus, the magnitude or level of transfer pricing manipulated by MNCs is determined by a group of factors. Some factors may strengthen MNCs' motivation to employ transfer prices while others could limit their capacity to practise transfer pricing. Therefore, it is essential to analyse the factors stimulating MNCs' motivation to use transfer prices and the factors limiting the scope and latitude of MNCs' transfer pricing.

MNCs' Motivation to Use Transfer Prices

As pointed out earlier, taxation, tariffs, business risks and relevant transaction costs are the major determinants of MNCs' motivation to manipulate transfer pricing. In terms of taxes and tariffs concerning FDI, China is favourably compared to many other developing countries. Under China's FIE income tax law, all FIEs, including joint ventures and foreign wholly–owned enterprises, are granted a package of special preferential tax concessions. These con-cessions include a two–year tax holiday starting at the profit–making year, and a 50 per cent tax reduction for the following three years. For FIEs invested in some industries and locations, the tax concessions are even more favourable. For example, foreign investments in low–profit industries (like agriculture and forestry) and high–technology industries are eligible for a two–year extension of the tax holiday. FDI in the special economic zones (SEZs) and economic and technology development areas (ETDAs) in the open coastal cities are eligible for a lower income tax rate after the tax holiday and a longer tax concession period. The income of FIEs in the SEZs and ETDAs is subject to a tax rate of 15 per cent compared to 33 per cent in other regions.

In addition, provinces and cities in various regions provide FDI with more generous tax concessions (for example, a longer tax holiday and tax reduction period) and other forms of preferential treatment such as lower land–using fees. Therefore, within the tax holiday and tax reduction period, MNCs do not have any particular incentive to avoid tax by using transfer prices. After the period of the tax holiday and tax reduction, FIEs are subject to the standard corporate income tax of 33 per cent. This is close to the corporate tax rates in many other countries, but is significantly higher than that in Hong Kong (only 15 per cent). Thus, the tax–induced transfer–pricing motivation would become strong for Hong Kong–based investors.

The tariffs for FIEs' exports and imports are quite preferential. According to the tariff regulation in effect, FIEs' exports are tariff free. FIEs' imports that are used as investment goods and for producing exports are also tariff free.[4] Only imports (by FIEs) used to produce goods to be sold in the domestic market are subject to some import tariffs. Therefore, tariffs applied to export–oriented FIEs in China are generous, and therefore generate no particular incentive for MNCs to manipulate transfer pricing.

Nevertheless, the business environment within China may strengthen MNCs' motivation to use transfer prices to minimise business risks, unpredictability and transaction costs. As is often claimed, developing countries usually impose more constraints on the operations of MNCs than is the case in developed countries (Plasschaert 1985). In the case of China, although the government has made great efforts to establish a legal framework for FDI and to liberalise the economy, there are still some legal and institutional factors negatively affecting the operation of FIEs.

First, the lack of well–defined laws on property rights and foreign investment protection is a major concern of foreign investors. In many cases, the property rights in enterprises are not legally clear. Although a number of laws (such as the corporation law, the bankruptcy law and the trade mark law) have been passed since the early 1980s, they are far from being fully implemented. As a result of the poor legal environment, foreign investors tend to transfer their income to low–risk countries by manipulating transfer pricing.

Second, a number of restrictive regulations, such as foreign exchange control, withholding tax on profit repatriation, and restraints on FIEs' access to the domestic markets, increase the business risks and relevant transaction costs. These restrictions motivate MNCs to use transfer prices in order to shift their income to countries with minimal restrictions. In addition, the inconvertibility of the Chinese currency is another factor inciting MNCs to keep their export income out of China. Therefore, the risk–avoiding type of transfer pricing would dominate in MNCs' transfer–pricing manipulation in the case of China.

Another important factor that deserves special attention is the ownership structure of FIEs in China. In the case of China, joint ventures including equity joint ventures and contractive joint ventures are the principal forms of FIEs. Theoretically, in Sino–foreign joint ventures both sides share profits, costs and management. In practice, however, as the interests and management goals are divergent between the two sides, each side is motivated to maximise its own interests and benefits. To reduce the profits accruing to local Chinese partners and to increase their own real profit share, MNCs have a high propensity to manipulate transfer pricing to shift profits to their parent companies or other subsidiaries located in other countries with low taxation and risks.

The Scope and Latitude of MNCs' Transfer Pricing

The above discussion indicates that MNCs' propensity and motivation to use transfer prices are quite high in China. To what extent could this propensity and motivation be realised? This is determined by many factors including the anti–transfer pricing regulation of the host–country government, the taxation and customs authorities' expertise on arm's–length market prices and their capability to detect and prevent MNCs' transfer pricing, and joint–venture partners' ability to check and prohibit MNCs' transfer–pricing practice. In general, developing countries' governments are poorly equipped, as compared with developed countries, to thwart the attempts of MNCs to manipulate transfer pricing (Plasschaert 1985). In the case of China, there is a lack of necessary regulations against transfer pricing manipulated by MNCs. The government departments, especially the taxation department and the customs authority, have recognised this problem (transfer pricing) prevailing in FIEs, but to date they do not have a special regulation against transfer pricing. This could be attributed to the difficulty in investigating MNCs' transfer–pricing practice and setting the arm's–length market prices for a large number of commodities traded by FIEs internationally.

At the firm level, the export and import business in many joint ventures are controlled by foreign investors (that is, MNCs). The Chinese partners, in general, lack professional knowledge about the channels of international trade. This excludes them from FIEs' pricing decisions for exports and imports and thus provides good conditions for MNCs to perform transfer pricing at the cost of Chinese partners' profits. In some cases, Chinese partners may participate in the decision–making process for imports and exports, but the managing power of FIEs is generally controlled by foreign partners. This is because of the particular management structure of joint ventures. As a general rule in joint ventures, foreign investors or their representatives hold the position of general manager (or chief executive) and run the enterprises at their discretion. The Chinese side takes the position of chairman (or president) of the board of directors, who are generally government officials without professional qualifications and thereby cannot manage FIEs. Therefore, the existing management structure of joint ventures leaves a large latitude for MNCs to manipulate transfer–pricing, although the existence of Chinese partners may sometimes be an impediment to transfer pricing practice and could curb to some extent MNCs' capability to underinvoice exports and overinvoice imports.

Finally, different types of FDI may vary considerably in using transfer prices, depending on the market orientations of their investment. In terms of market orientation, FDI in China can be classified into two categories: export oriented and domestic–market oriented. For the first category of FDI, the products produced by FIEs are primarily exported overseas, and the inputs can be obtained from either domestic suppliers or importing. The free–tariff regime for FIEs' exports and imported inputs used for production of exports facilitates the exports and imports of FIEs. Thus, this tariff regime is likely to induce and stimulate MNCs to overinvoice imports and to underinvoice their exports. Therefore, with the free–tariff regime, MNCs are highly inclined, and able, to manipulate transfer pricing. Consequently, a large share of FIEs' income may be transferred to MNCs' systems.

In contrast, for FDI oriented towards the Chinese domestic market, MNCs have a lower propensity and capability to use transfer prices. This is because trade between FIEs and non–affiliated enterprises in the Chinese domestic market usually use market prices. However, if FIEs use imported inputs, MNCs still have an incentive to overinvoice the imported materials from their own overseas subsidiaries. This results in a shift of some profit from FIEs in China to MNC subsidiaries in regions with lower taxes and risks. Under the current Chinese tariff regulations, FIEs' imported materials and intermediate products that are used for production of goods oriented to the domestic market, are subject to import tariff. This may curb MNCs' transfer–pricing activities.

In general, therefore, MNCs with export–oriented FDI have a higher motivation, capability and latitude to manipulate transfer pricing than MNCs whose FDI is oriented towards the Chinese domestic market. In the context of investors' origin countries, investments from Hong Kong, Taiwan and Southeast Asian countries are largely labour intensive and export oriented. By comparison, investments from the US and European countries are primarily capital/technology intensive and are oriented to the Chinese domestic market. The former is motivated by reducing the costs of production for exports by taking advantage of China's cheap and abundant labour resources, whereas the latter aims at China's huge domestic market. Therefore, under the particular circumstances of China, although transfer–pricing manipulation may exist in all types of FIEs, the frequency, scope and latitude of transfer pricing manipulated by MNCs based in Hong Kong and Taiwan may be higher or larger than that by American and European MNCs.

Some Indirect Evidence

The study of transfer pricing involves an investigation of firms' pricing policies, market orientation, accounting systems and internal financial transfers within an MNCs' system. All this information is unlikely to be released by MNCs who treat it as confidential business information. As a result, the research on MNCs' transfer pricing generally takes the form of either theoretical analysis of the conditions under which MNCs perform transfer pricing or case studies using sampled data. In the case of China, there are more than 100,000 foreign–invested enterprises operating in various industries, making a detailed investigation of these FIEs' pricing behaviour at the firm level very difficult, and certainly beyond the scope of this chapter.

As a feasible alternative, we can investigate the unit prices of China's exports to and imports from a country (or region) where most foreign investing companies are based. Trade between China and Hong Kong is a suitable case for the study of unit price ratios of the same commodities. This is because Hong Kong is the most important source of FDI in China and is also a major trade partner. The trade between China and Hong Kong is largely controlled by Hong Kong–based MNCs. FIEs are major players in China–Hong Kong bilateral trade. In the coastal provinces, trade with Hong Kong is dominated by FIEs. Therefore, the differences in the unit prices of the same commodities traded between China and Hong Kong are important indicators of transfer pricing manipulated by MNCs. By comparing the unit prices of China's exports to Hong Kong, which are reported to the Chinese Customs, with the unit prices of Hong Kong's imports reported to the Hong Kong Customs, we can measure the differences in the unit prices of the same commodities recorded by the two Customs authorities. Similarly, we can also measure the differences in the unit prices of China's imported commodities from Hong Kong, which are reported to the two Customs authorities.

To carefully study the unit prices of commodities traded between China and Hong Kong, we need to set the selection criteria for the traded commodities to be covered by this study. The criteria are: (i) the commodities have physical amounts (for example, metric ton, number, length and height) and monetary values (that is, total prices), so the unit prices can be calculated; (ii) the physical amounts of commodities reported in both the Chinese and Hong Kong's trade statistics are close to each other so that meaningful comparisons between the unit prices of the commodities can be made. The commodities that have no physical amounts or whose physical amounts are significantly divergent between the Chinese and Hong Kong statistics are excluded in this study. The data source is the *Commodity Trade Statistics* published by the United Nations in 1990 and 1994.

Using this data source and the above selection criteria, the unit prices of 90 categories of commodities exported from China to Hong Kong in 1990 and 150 categories of exports in 1994 reported by the Chinese Customs, as compared to the unit prices of the same categories of commodities reported by the Hong Kong Customs, have been calculated. The two sets of unit prices of the Chinese exports to Hong Kong (imports for Hong Kong) recorded, respectively, by the Chinese Customs and the Hong Kong Customs in 1990 and their ratios are presented in Table 6.3. Similarly, the unit prices and price ratios of 150 categories of exports from China to Hong Kong in 1994 are also calculated and presented in Table 6.3. In addition to the individual unit price ratio for each category of commodity, the weighted average unit price ratios for 90 categories of commodities in 1990 and for 150 categories of commodities in 1994 are also calculated, using the value share of each commodity category in the total value of the listed exports as the weight.

As shown in Table 6.3, the weighted average ratio of the unit price A (recorded by the Chinese Customs) to the unit price B (recorded by the Hong Kong Customs) is 0.7544 (that is, 75.44 per cent) for these 90 categories of exports in 1990, and 0.826 for the 150 categories of exports in 1994. This suggests that the prices of Chinese exports decreased by 24.56 per cent and 17.4 per cent, respectively, in the two years. This indicates that the prices of China's exports to Hong Kong are underinvoiced (underpriced) by Hong Kong traders.

Before we link this fact to MNCs' transfer–pricing manipulation, two things need to be taken into account. First, not all China's exports are provided by FIEs. For example, FIEs' exports accounted for 28.7 per cent of China's total exports in 1994 (see Table 6.1). A larger share of China's exports are from domestic firms. Thus, the unit price ratio of commodities traded between China and Hong Kong does not necessarily reflect the accurate extent to which MNCs practise transfer pricing. However, most of the trade between China and Hong Kong is controlled by Hong Kong–based trading companies. Many of them have investments and subsidiaries in China. Accordingly, for trade between China and Hong Kong, the FIEs' share should be much larger than the average share of FIEs in the total exports or imports of China. For example, in Guangdong Province where Hong Kong investment is concentrated, the exports by FIEs accounted for 44.2 per cent of the total provincial exports in 1992. The FIEs' imports accounted for 53.9 per cent of Guangdong's total imports in that year (see Table 6.1). Therefore, the unit price ratios of commodities traded between China and Hong Kong can be used as an indicator of transfer prices manipulated by MNCs based in Hong Kong.

Second, transport and insurance fees are components of the total price of exports and imports. These fees may also influence the unit prices of commodities. Since the prices of exports are calculated by the f.o.b. (free on board) price formula which does not include transportation and insurance fees, they are normally lower than the prices of the same goods as imports at the destination country. This is because the prices of imports are calculated by the c.i.f. price (cost, insurance and flight fees) formula. They are in general higher than the prices of the same goods as exports from the country of origin. The difference between the two price measurements reflects the distance from the exporting country to the importing country and insurance policies relative to trade and transportation. According to a recent estimation by Guangdong's Foreign Trade Bureau, the transport fee accounts for 3–8 per cent of the commodities' prices (depending on the distance from Hong Kong) and the insurance fee accounts for only 1 per cent. Therefore, in general the sum of transport and insurance fees are less than 10 per cent. This proportion is significantly smaller than the difference between the prices reported by the Chinese Customs and the prices reported by the Hong Kong Customs. Obviously transfer prices exist in the bilateral trade, which is dominated by Hong Kong–invested FIEs. Therefore, the prices of exports from China to Hong Kong were under–invoiced by 10–15 per cent.

In addition to exports, China's imports from Hong Kong are also subject to MNCs' transfer pricing. This can be examined by comparison of the unit prices of China's imports (from Hong Kong) reported by the Chinese Customs with the unit prices of the same commodities reported by the Hong Kong Customs. The two sets of unit prices recorded by the two Customs authorities and their ratios are presented in Table 6.4. As shown in this table, the unit prices of China's imports (from Hong Kong) reported by the Chinese Customs are generally higher than that reported by the Hong Kong Customs. Since the price of imports is calculated by c.i.f, the reported prices by the importing country's Customs should normally be higher than the prices reported (using f.o.b. price) by the exporting country's Customs by the sum of insurance and transport fees. The weighted average ratio of the unit prices reported by the two Customs Authorities for the 50 selected categories of commodities in 1990 is 1.265 (that is, 126.5 per cent). The ratio minus the transport and insurance fees as a percentage of the total price (about 10 per cent), is equal to the proportion overinvoiced by MNCs, which is 16.5 per cent. For imports in 1994, this is about 8 per cent.

This fact suggests that Hong Kong trading companies, especially MNCs investing in China, overcharged Chinese importers including FIEs by over–invoicing the imports. As imports by Chinese domestic firms are subject to relatively high import duties, they do not have any special incentive to over–invoice their imports. Therefore, the overinvoicing of imports is primarily performed by MNCs which have either direct investment in or trade relations with China. This confirms that transfer pricing manipulated by MNCs prevails in both exports and imports of China.

The effects of transfer pricing on the Chinese economy and social welfare are obviously negative. It reduces the taxation revenue for the Chinese government and lessens the profits of Chinese partners in joint ventures. As a result of transfer pricing, many FIEs report accounting losses to the taxation authority each year. For instance, 32.3 per cent of FIEs in 1992 and 31.2 per cent of FIEs in 1993 reported losses, which was even higher than that of state–owned enterprises (23.3 per cent and 28.8 per cent, respectively) (SSB 1992, 1993b). In contrast to the loss reported by FIEs, many foreign investors

Table 6.3 Unit price ratios of China's exports to Hong Kong imports, 1990 and 1994

Commodity classification	Exports of China to Hong Kong			Hong Kong imports from China			Price ratio A/B	Unit price ratio	
	Quantity	Value ($1000)	Unit price A ($1000)	Quantity	Value ($1000)	Unit price B ($1000)		Weight A %	Weighted ratio
1990									
Meat, fish, frozen	67,425	103,148	1.53	72,403	116,205	1.61	0.95	1.07	1.02
Meat, dried, salted	5,063	12,455	2.46	4,885	12,993	2.66	0.93	0.13	0.12
Meat prepd, prsvd	25,285	40,184	1.59	27,122	41,928	1.55	1.03	0.42	0.43
Milk and cream	19,361	10,681	0.55	23,001	13,317	0.58	0.95	0.11	0.11
Eggs, bird	37,492	34,329	0.92	38,999	36,028	0.92	0.99	0.36	0.35
Fish, fresh, chilled	71,583	115,880	1.62	71,966	134,345	1.87	0.87	1.20	1.04
Shellfish	55,323	215,664	3.90	47,713	190,367	3.99	0.98	2.23	2.18
Rice	43,817	16,167	0.37	53,257	20,588	0.39	0.95	0.17	0.16
Maize unmilled	60,867	7,825	0.13	13,200	1,991	0.15	0.85	0.08	0.07
Veg. etc. fish, prsvd	516,535	195,924	0.38	268,760	115,850	0.43	0.88	2.03	1.78
Fruit, fresh, dried	115,576	95,377	0.83	149,390	130,719	0.88	0.94	0.99	0.93
Fruit preserved	35,367	35,694	1.01	37,809	39,995	1.06	0.95	0.37	0.35
Sugar and honey	49,087	20,756	0.42	42,924	17,799	0.42	1.02	0.22	0.22
Sugar candy	2,719	3,548	1.31	5,186	8,073	1.56	0.84	0.04	0.03
Tea	14,417	35,455	2.46	17,310	42,159	2.44	1.01	0.37	0.37
Beverages	582,146	108,291	0.17	627,740	117,610	0.19	0.99	1.12	1.11
Alcoholic beverages	21,064	18,765	0.89	20,768	25,421	1.22	0.73	0.19	0.14
Tobacco stripped	4,248	9,386	2.21	11,503	25,298	2.20	1.01	0.10	0.10
Cigarettes	3,860	34,417	8.92	5,755	64,061	11.13	0.80	0.36	0.29
Seeds for oil	71,089	49,439	0.70	68,775	48,399	0.70	0.99	0.51	0.51
Pulp, waste paper	3,128	572	0.18	11,123	3,620	0.33	0.56	0.01	0.003
Silk	3,123	79,805	25.55	3,612	92,808	25.69	1.00	0.83	0.82

Cotton	11,281	10,552	0.94	18,022	16,556	0.92	1.02	0.11	0.11
Veg. fibre	2,726	4,799	1.76	3,887	6,743	1.74	1.02	0.05	0.05
Wool (excl.tops)	1,889	46,690	24.72	2,350	50,624	21.54	1.15	0.48	0.55
Other abrasives	1,067,000	32,345	0.03	778,026	27,085	0.04	0.87	0.33	0.29
Iron, steel scrap	52,303	4,590	0.09	62,995	11,212	0.18	0.49	0.05	0.02
Base metal ores	55,307	21,977	0.40	38,436	34,472	0.90	0.44	0.23	0.10
Animal materials	10,640	77,188	7.26	13,203	87,071	6.60	1.10	0.80	0.88
Coal, lignite, peat[a]	2,630	99,138	37.70	1,708	67,134	39.31	0.96	1.03	0.98
Petroleum products	925,912	158,914	0.17	1,077,000	225,186	0.21	0.82	1.64	1.35
Petroleum products	20,864	8,592	0.41	50,381	22,754	0.45	0.91	0.09	0.08
Fixed veg. oils,	88,249	50,702	0.58	51,972	31,816	0.61	0.94	0.52	0.49
Fixed veg. oils, other	78,854	32,368	0.41	13,819	7,385	0.53	0.77	0.34	0.26
Hydrocarbons	6,877	5,947	0.87	4,472	4,312	0.96	0.90	0.06	0.06
Alcohols, phenols	16,838	38,676	2.30	10,136	35,283	3.48	0.66	0.40	0.26
Carboxylic acids	25,993	23,459	0.90	26,441	23,293	0.88	1.02	0.24	0.25
Nitrogen	9,022	33,089	3.67	10,911	44,433	4.07	0.90	0.34	0.31
Antibiotics[b]	2,905	75,576	26.02	2,234	63,427	28.39	0.92	0.78	0.72
Essential oils	4,871	26,963	5.54	5,042	31,943	6.34	0.87	0.28	0.24
Fertilisers	5,492	810	0.15	4,928	790	0.16	0.92	0.01	0.01
Polymerisation	100,094	82,184	0.82	171,463	139,324	0.81	1.01	0.85	0.86
Cellulose derivatives	1,716	2,727	1.59	2,027	3,527	1.74	0.91	0.03	0.03
Plastic materials	1,977	9,064	4.59	1,436	6,930	4.83	0.95	0.09	0.09
Pesticides	11,810	16,963	1.44	16,248	26,822	1.65	0.87	0.18	0.15
Starch, insulin	15,978	7,220	0.45	11,295	7,210	0.64	0.71	0.08	0.05
Rubber tyres[c]	4,851	12,495	2.58	5,416	14,331	2.65	0.97	0.13	0.13
Printing, paper	19,158	15,729	0.82	16,622	15,126	0.91	0.90	0.16	0.15
Silk yarn	1,240	21,772	17.56	1,088	21,193	19.48	0.90	0.23	0.20
Synth. fibre yarn,	26,554	77,925	2.94	40,221	113,598	2.82	1.04	0.81	0.84
Discon. Syn. fibre	32,327	78,178	2.42	31,449	77,729	2.47	0.98	0.81	0.96
Regen. fibre yarn	12,822	32,670	2.55	12,369	36,742	2.97	0.86	0.34	0.29

Commodity classification	Exports of China to Hong Kong			Hong Kong imports from China			Unit price ratio		
	Quantity	Value ($1000)	Unit price A ($1000)	Quantity	Value ($1000)	Unit price B ($1000)	Price ratio A/B	Weight A %	Weighted ratio
Regen. fibre yarn	12,822	32,670	2.55	12,369	36,742	2.97	0.86	0.34	0.29
Textile fibre yarn	42,209	79,973	1.90	60,272	108,490	1.80	1.05	0.83	0.87
Other knit fab.	83,328	254,448	3.05	100,034	310,281	3.10	0.98	2.63	2.59
Sacks of textiles[c]	54,421	11,233	0.21	54,563	10,841	0.20	1.04	0.12	0.12
Blankets, etc.[c]	2,263	5,477	2.42	2,475	8,044	3.25	0.75	0.06	0.04
Carpets, knotted[d]	610	37,712	61.82	320	24,606	76.89	0.80	0.39	0.31
Lime,	59,883	2,372	0.04	43,466	1,913	0.04	0.90	0.03	0.02
Cement[a]	1,646	60,589	36.81	1,209	49,157	40.66	0.91	0.63	0.77
Glass[d]	4,349	14,109	3.24	4,771	16,555	3.47	0.94	0.15	0.14
Pig iron etc.	67,594	38,766	0.57	86,541	46,206	0.53	1.07	0.40	0.43
Iron, steel, primary	95,669	23,942	0.25	9,965	2,569	0.26	0.97	0.25	0.24
Iron, steel, shapes	413,646	117,079	0.28	387,770	118,790	0.31	0.92	1.21	1.12
Iron, steel, plate	37,590	14,348	0.38	44,040	21,984	0.50	0.77	0.15	0.11
Iron, steel hoop	3,623	1,424	0.39	8,189	6,173	0.75	0.52	0.02	0.01
Iron, steel wire	44,078	21,206	0.48	39,233	20,565	0.52	0.92	0.22	0.20
Iron, steel tubes	64,599	40,136	0.62	62,092	39,038	0.63	0.99	0.42	0.41
Copper	21,476	69,462	3.23	29,158	89,471	3.07	1.05	0.72	0.76
Aluminium	23,112	45,115	1.95	24,966	48,486	1.94	1.01	0.47	0.47
Lead	8,786	6,477	0.74	17,564	14,477	0.82	0.89	0.07	0.06
Tin	2,969	16,553	5.58	6,921	36,496	5.27	1.06	0.17	0.18
Wire products	11,928	11,055	0.93	12,889	10,988	0.85	1.09	0.11	0.12
Steel copper nails	28,297	20,372	0.72	29,877	26,516	0.89	0.81	0.21	0.17
Printing machine[e]	1,110	1,382	1.25	1,197	1,565	1.31	0.95	0.01	0.01
Metal cutting tools[e]	36,019	25,554	0.71	32,454	28,445	0.88	0.81	0.26	0.21
Centrifugal pumps[e]	32,382	1,272	0.04	11,937	1,799	0.15	0.26	0.01	0.03

	(US$ million)				(US$ million)				
Pumps for gases^c	659	2,546	3.86	1,587	9,527	6.00	0.64	0.03	0.02
Office machines^c	92,927	148,601	1.60	100,590	144,672	1.44	1.11	1.54	1.71
TV receivers^c	2,926	336,195	114.90	3,308	417,114	126.09	0.91	3.48	3.17
Radio receivers^c	174,876	1,369,774	7.83	129,584	1,307,985	10.09	0.78	14.17	10.99
Sound apparatus^c	7,362	95,165	12.93	33,742	414,151	12.27	1.05	0.98	1.04
Microphones etc.^c	246,637	58,982	0.24	441,748	116,132	0.26	0.91	0.61	0.56
Laundry equipt^e	55,146	3,816	0.07	67,547	5,295	0.08	0.88	0.04	0.04
TV picture tubes^e	172,125	8,541	0.05	382,741	18,327	0.08	0.63	0.09	0.06
Men's outwear^c	53,938	194,005	3.60	240,351	1,017,856	4.24	0.85	2.01	1.70
Women's outwear^c	233,951	923,817	3.95	310,672	1,591,257	5.12	0.77	9.55	7.37
Undergarments^c	102,470	205,195	2.00	228,703	547,032	2.39	0.84	2.12	1.78
Outerwear knit^c	1,478,000	2,293,475	1.55	332,997	1,319,252	3.96	0.39	23.72	9.29
Undergarments^c	471	2,259	4.80	497	2,503	5.04	0.95	0.02	0.02
Gas supply metres^c	151	933	6.18	170	1,180	6.94	0.89	0.01	0.01
All commodities listed above	9,669,768							100	75.44

1994	(US$ million)				(US$ million.)			Weight A %	
Bovine meat	11,433	15,201	1.33	13,272	19,506	1.47	0.91	0.10	0.09
Other meat	83,901	95,799	1.14	62,444	98,066	1.57	0.73	0.61	0.45
Meat, dry	6,077	18,339	3.02	5,953	16,822	2.83	1.07	0.12	0.13
Meat, presvd	38,607	65,337	1.69	41,513	67,457	1.63	1.04	0.42	0.44
Sausage	6,883	12,448	1.81	6,460	12,252	1.90	0.95	0.08	0.08
Poultry	3,269	8,090	2.48	3,794	9,738	2.57	0.96	0.05	0.05
Pork	21,598	33,477	1.55	26,119	37,606	1.44	1.08	0.21	0.23
Milk, cream	12,782	7,550	0.59	26,192	19,202	0.73	0.81	0.05	0.04
Eggs	30,909	22,837	0.74	30,023	25,704	0.86	0.86	0.15	0.13
Fish, frozen	12,496	31,112	2.49	6,682	13,902	2.08	1.20	0.20	0.24
Fish, dried	3,532	25,570	7.24	2,954	36,046	12.20	0.59	0.16	0.10

Commodity Classification	Exports of China to Hong Kong			Hong Kong imports from China			Unit price ratio		
	Quantity	Value ($1000)	Unit price A ($1000)	Quantity	Value ($1000)	Unit price B ($1000)	Price ratio A/B	Weight A %	Weighted ratio
Crustaceans	37,563	151,690	4.04	31,219	113,716	3.64	1.11	0.97	1.08
Fish, prepd	8,869	28,083	3.17	6,113	17,945	2.94	1.08	0.18	0.19
Rice	38,589	13,125	0.34	38,683	17,222	0.45	0.76	0.08	0.06
Maize	31,141	3,321	0.11	5,993	807	0.14	0.79	0.02	0.02
Meal, flour	8,259	1,932	0.23	8,061	2,168	0.27	0.87	0.01	0.01
Other meal	7,876	2,231	0.28	8,678	2,532	0.29	0.97	0.01	0.01
Cereal	51,669	42,050	0.81	46,519	42,281	0.91	0.90	0.27	0.24
Vegetables	492,045	174,435	0.36	304,255	160,331	0.53	0.67	1.12	0.75
Fruit, nuts	121,196	97,112	0.80	162,877	133,550	0.82	0.98	0.62	0.61
Fruit prepd	20,995	28,788	1.37	33,858	37,772	1.12	1.23	0.18	0.23
Sugar, honey	75,899	26,044	0.34	47,717	19,073	0.40	0.86	0.17	0.14
Sugar, candy	21,608	29,706	1.38	15,472	24,895	1.61	0.85	0.19	0.16
Coffee	1,097	3,733	3.40	1,078	3,675	3.41	0.10	0.02	0.02
Tea	19,213	39,520	2.06	20,871	43,781	2.10	0.98	0.25	0.25
Animal feed	212,020	40,298	0.19	189,111	34,496	0.18	1.04	0.26	0.27
Beverages[a]	698,519	184,648	0.26	683,152	188,191	0.28	0.96	1.18	1.13
Alcohol	26,740	23,168	0.87	25,395	32,509	1.28	0.68	0.15	0.10
Tobacco	4,306	9,085	2.11	4,954	12,476	2.52	0.84	0.06	0.05
Cigarettes	14,033	229,011	16.32	23,742	347,352	14.63	1.12	1.46	1.63
Oil seed	26,983	15,556	0.58	28,962	19,074	0.66	0.88	0.10	0.09
Other oil seed	26,983	15,556	0.58	28,962	19,074	0.66	0.88	0.10	0.09
Silk	5,462	95,342	17.46	5,648	104,280	18.46	0.95	0.61	0.58
Cotton	11,927	13,882	1.16	13,680	11,677	0.85	1.36	0.09	0.12
Synth. fibres	2,069	3,322	1.61	3,696	5,302	1.44	1.12	0.02	0.02
Wool	4,923	72,450	14.72	5,611	84,808	15.12	0.97	0.46	0.45

Worn clothing	4,548	2,828	0.62	5,504	2,525	0.46	1.36	0.02	0.03
Stone, sand[a]	12,608	37,836	3.00	10,929	50,154	4.59	0.65	0.24	0.16
Other mineral[a]	1,252	27,127	21.67	884	22,302	25.23	0.86	0.17	0.15
Crude animal material	7,491	51,037	6.81	10,341	67,135	6.49	1.05	0.33	0.34
Veg. material	47,111	10,202	0.22	46,531	11,365	0.24	0.89	0.07	0.06
Coal[a]	1,600	44,422	27.76	1,411	46,668	33.07	0.84	0.28	0.24
Petroleum	447,033	75,457	0.17	401,093	66,877	0.17	1.01	0.48	0.49
Fixed veg. fat	248,418	190,628	0.77	105,190	88,014	0.84	0.92	1.22	1.12
Other veg. oil	383,294	242,445	0.63	103,142	60,183	0.58	1.08	1.55	1.68
Animal fat	4,828	1,394	0.29	5,569	3,963	0.71	0.41	0.01	0.004
Carbox. acid	26,752	31,042	1.16	37,604	35,923	0.96	1.22	0.20	0.24
Organo–inorg.	7,332	65,151	8.89	9,801	76,947	7.85	1.13	0.42	0.47
Metal inorgan. acid	25,147	6,464	0.26	19,895	6,152	0.31	0.83	0.04	0.03
Metal acid	7,502	18,192	2.43	6,751	17,381	2.58	0.94	0.12	0.11
Synth. colour	19,197	74,079	3.86	17,585	69,347	3.94	0.98	0.47	0.46
Printing ink	4,371	10,962	2.51	3,195	7,718	2.42	1.04	0.07	0.07
Paints	39,336	59,507	1.51	36,252	57,443	1.59	0.96	0.38	0.36
Provitamins[a]	4,562	108,557	23.80	4,220	113,491	26.89	0.89	0.69	0.61
Prep. Oral	2,714	5,641	2.08	2,766	4,780	1.73	1.20	0.04	0.04
Soap	6,062	7,505	1.24	8,613	11,600	1.35	0.92	0.05	0.04
Detergents	30,130	17,988	0.60	26,865	14,345	0.53	1.12	0.12	0.13
Fertiliser	12,195	1,803	0.15	14,780	2,855	0.19	0.77	0.01	0.01
Polymers,eth.	7,155	4,856	0.68	11,392	8,052	0.71	0.96	0.03	0.03
Polymers,sty.	48,165	38,108	0.79	51,870	49,391	0.95	0.83	0.24	0.20
Polymers,vinyl	61,984	47,160	0.76	59,374	51,848	0.87	0.87	0.30	0.26
Polyacetal	22,660	24,080	1.06	17,617	20,773	1.18	0.90	0.15	0.14
Other plastic	11,477	11,495	1.00	18,751	22,053	1.18	0.85	0.07	0.06
Plastic tubes	14,713	14,593	0.99	13,245	15,545	1.17	0.85	0.09	0.08
Starches	13,228	4,075	0.31	11,438	3,054	0.27	1.15	0.03	0.03
Fur skins	559	25,834	46.22	999	57,425	57.48	0.80	0.17	0.13
Rubber materials	5,607	8,234	1.47	2,206	6,576	2.98	0.49	0.05	0.03

Commodity classification	Exports of China to Hong Kong			Hong Kong imports from China			Unit price ratio		
	Quantity	Value ($1000)	Unit price A ($1000)	Quantity	Value ($1000)	Unit price B (1000$)	Price ratio A/B	Weight A %	Weighted ratio
Tyres, bus	94,872	5,024	0.05	84,070	5,417	0.06	0.82	0.03	0.03
Tyres, cycles	1,983	2,143	1.08	7,692	10,871	1.41	0.77	0.01	0.01
Paper	103,504	58,441	0.57	96,550	67,503	0.70	0.81	0.37	0.30
Textile, yarn	300,322	1016,821	3.39	288,653	1103,213	3.82	0.89	6.50	5.76
Knit, crochet	148,076	525,101	3.55	160,175	576,491	3.60	0.99	3.36	3.31
Tulle, lace, etc.	14,418	106,034	7.35	14,832	87,446	5.90	1.25	0.68	0.85
Nonwoven fabr.	2,924	6,898	2.36	5,088	23,972	4.71	0.50	0.04	0.02
Coated textiles	16,700	61,565	3.69	15,089	45,754	3.03	1.22	0.39	0.48
Twine, cordage	21,063	38,097	1.81	14,749	37,043	2.51	0.72	0.24	0.18
Textile articles	62,942	13,279	0.21	31,199	9,707	0.31	0.68	0.09	0.06
Tarpaulins, sails	2,253	12,508	5.55	10,020	69,367	6.92	0.80	0.08	0.06
Household linens	401,521	215,083	0.54	638,924	353,610	0.55	0.97	1.38	1.33
Curtains	11,519	20,506	1.78	11,600	21,444	1.85	0.96	0.13	0.13
Lime, cement	748,935	74,335	0.10	601,650	52,138	0.09	1.15	0.48	0.54
Pig iron	42,892	19,766	0.46	46,082	20,638	0.45	1.03	0.13	0.13
Flat-rolled iron	68,997	26,398	0.38	99,977	36,323	0.36	1.05	0.17	0.18
Plated iron	32,782	19,093	0.58	19,604	11,825	0.60	0.97	0.12	0.12
Iron, steel, shapes	488,695	132,018	0.27	202,014	83,052	0.41	0.66	0.84	0.56
Wire of iron and steel	37,299	19,786	0.53	38,610	23,296	0.60	0.88	0.13	0.11
Tube, pipes of iron	76,874	47,897	0.62	64,643	42,615	0.66	0.95	0.31	0.29
Copper	52,898	149,298	2.82	47,360	145,350	3.07	0.92	0.96	0.88
Nickel	6,235	35,632	5.72	4,887	27,656	5.66	1.01	0.23	0.23
Aluminum	50,597	84,404	1.67	45,995	82,940	1.80	0.93	0.54	0.50
Lead	27,820	18,186	0.65	5,567	4,361	0.78	0.83	0.12	0.10
Zinc	26,857	22,797	0.85	27,865	26,289	0.94	0.90	0.15	0.13

Product									
Tin	14,221	61,940	4.36	15,772	69,659	4.42	0.99	0.40	0.39
Misc. base metal	14,450	52,838	3.66	16,708	59,896	3.59	1.02	0.34	0.35
Wire products	18,223	20,389	1.12	11,146	11,981	1.08	1.04	0.13	0.14
Nails, screws, nuts	37,557	38,969	1.04	37,277	42,786	1.15	0.90	0.25	0.23
Pistons, engines	24,453	5,508	0.23	24,487	8,133	0.33	0.68	0.04	0.02
Electric motors	694,735	197,061	0.28	968,080	478,563	0.49	0.57	1.26	0.72
Elec. generator AC	5,425	26,246	4.84	7,852	54,218	6.91	0.70	0.17	0.12
Textile machinery	12,948	4,993	0.39	23,182	16,633	0.72	0.54	0.03	0.02
Paper, pulp machine	376	1,641	4.36	528	3,225	6.11	0.72	0.01	0.01
Metal removal tools	49,370	19,912	0.40	13,776	97,676	7.09	0.06	0.13	0.01
Machinery tools	8,050	10,687	1.33	8,426	12,348	1.47	0.91	0.07	0.06
Fans, cooker hoods	16,498	156,930	9.51	47,718	453,356	9.50	1.00	1.00	1.01
Filters	1,188	12,006	10.11	1,644	17,809	10.83	0.93	0.02	0.02
Pulley tackle, winches	82,909	3,042	0.04	95,209	4,966	0.05	0.70	0.02	0.01
Derricks, cranes	69	6,809	98.68	141	15,071	106.89	0.92	0.04	0.04
Ball bearings	55,635	29,767	0.54	46,792	28,466	0.61	0.88	0.19	0.17
Taps, cocks, valves	9,397	12,456	1.33	10,435	16,323	1.56	0.85	0.08	0.07
Office machines	99,568	171,562	1.72	208,136	534,459	2.57	0.67	1.10	0.74
TV receivers	1,728	106,949	61.89	8,028	742,105	92.44	0.67	0.68	0.46
Radio receivers	58,953	445,863	7.56	206,234	2,686,099	13.03	0.58	2.85	1.66
Sound recorders	11,222	141,444	12.60	44,191	731,736	16.56	0.76	0.90	0.69
Microphones etc	675,029	219,997	0.33	679,374	283,729	0.42	0.78	1.41	1.10
Transformers	694	133,699	192.65	1,672	257,026	153.72	1.25	0.86	1.07
Laundry equipment	93,684	4,701	0.05	39,867	3,152	0.08	0.64	0.03	0.02
Refrigerators, freezers	71,912	6,718	0.09	66,925	6,798	0.10	0.92	0.04	0.04
TV picture tubes	928,101	20,126	0.02	752,028	29,499	0.04	0.55	0.13	0.07
Diodes, transistors	11,081	133,267	12.03	7,036	105,341	14.97	0.80	0.85	0.68
Passenger vehicles	82	950	11.59	3,519	70,877	20.14	0.58	0.01	0.003
Goods transport vehicles	1,307	14,174	10.85	1,796	28,158	15.68	0.69	0.09	0.06
Motor cycles	7,494	3,203	0.43	24,246	34,416	1.42	0.30	0.02	0.01

Commodity classification	Exports of China to Hong Kong			Hong Kong imports from China			Unit price ratio		
	Quantity	Value ($1000)	Unit price A ($1000)	Quantity	Value ($1000)	Unit price B ($1000)	Price ratio A/B	Weight A %	Weighted ratio
Bicycles	813	21,751	26.75	6,778	253,773	37.44	0.72	0.14	0.10
Ships, boats	472	198,447	420.44	82	47,953	584.79	0.72	1.27	0.91
Handbags	70,686	102,604	1.45	296,675	988,904	3.33	0.44	0.66	0.29
Trunks, suitcases	238,547	377,633	1.58	35,914	256,901	7.15	0.22	2.41	0.53
Men's. boys' clothing	659,411	2392,108	3.63	511,454	1861,291	3.64	1.00	15.29	15.25
Women's, girls' clothing	658,637	2331,004	3.539	488,586	2,686,596	5.50	0.64	14.90	9.59
Men's clothing, knit	279,739	226,896	0.81	518,705	491,507	0.95	0.86	1.45	1.24
Women's clothings, knit	467,585	385,153	0.82	970,826	785,565	0.81	1.02	2.46	2.51
Garments, felt textiles, fab	19,793	41,664	2.11	49,132	151,882	3.09	0.68	0.27	0.18
Pullovers etc., knit	245,637	747,497	3.04	316,180	1,828,491	5.78	0.53	4.78	2.52
T–shirts, knit	403,606	421,560	1.04	487,259	546,443	1.12	0.93	2.70	2.51
Swimwear	15,484	12,724	0.82	80,344	183,367	2.28	0.36	0.08	0.03
Other garments, not knitted	30,733	127,054	4.13	128,186	620,093	4.84	0.86	0.81	0.69
Other garments, knitted	51,523	101,551	1.97	80,344	183,367	2.28	0.86	0.65	0.56
Footwear, rubber	114,381	132,541	1.16	812,202	2,295,017	2.83	0.41	0.85	0.35
Other footwear, leather	42,415	193,114	4.55	272,277	2,388,965	8.77	0.52	1.24	0.64
Other footwear, textiles	66,105	69,259	1.05	289,524	402,953	1.39	0.75	0.44	0.33
String musical instruments	123,240	3,297	0.03	313,155	6,548	0.02	1.28	0.02	0.03
Other musical instruments	6,273	11,864	1.89	10,684	21,455	2.01	0.94	0.08	0.07

| All commodities listed above | 1,564,122 | 2,878,106 | 100.00 | 82.63 |

Notes: All units are either tonnes or numbers with the exception of
    a 1000 tonnes;
    b 1000 kilograms;
    c 1000;
    d 1000 square meters.

Sources: United Nations: Commodity Trade Statistics According to International Trade Classification, 1990, and No. 18; United Nations Statistical Office: Commodity Trade Statistics 1994, China, Rev. 3; and Hong Kong, Rev. 3.

Table 6.4 Unit price ratios of China's imports from Hong Kong, 1990 and 1994

Commodity classification	China's imports from Hong Kong			Hong Kong's exports to China			Unit price ratio		
	Quantity	Value ($1000)	Unit price A ($1000)	Quantity	Value ($1000)	Unit price B ($1000)	Price ratio A/B	Weight %	Weighted ratio
1990									
Milk and cream	1,581	1,979	1.25	1,544	1,926	1.25	1.00	0.19	0.19
Fish, fresh, frozen	636	1,020	1.60	287	269	0.94	1.71	0.10	0.17
Fish salted, smoked	32	614	19.19	33	465	14.09	1.36	0.06	0.08
Wheat meal, flour	15,413	4,552	0.30	12,874	4,234	0.33	0.90	0.43	0.39
Sugar and honey	2,367	1,385	0.59	1,726	668	0.39	1.51	0.13	0.20
Meat or fish meal	6,656	3,179	0.48	287	116	0.40	1.18	0.30	0.36
Cigarettes	3,465	42,795	12.35	7,355	78,410	10.66	1.16	4.05	4.69
Pulp, waste paper	310,796	34,382	0.11	302,212	28,058	0.09	1.19	3.25	3.88
Electric current[a]	1,925	117,020	60.79	1,797	99,375	55.30	1.10	11.06	12.16
Animal oils, fats	4,250	1,670	0.39	16,249	5,146	0.32	1.24	0.16	0.20
Fixed veg. oils, soft	43,713	24,565	0.56	6,190	3,004	0.49	1.16	2.32	2.69
Organic chemicals	136	211	1.55	9,122	13,385	1.47	1.06	0.02	0.02
Synth. Organic dyestuffs	4,469	26,505	5.93	2,279	14,024	6.15	0.96	0.51	2.42
Printing inks	1,201	5,358	4.46	1,348	5,124	3.80	1.17	0.51	0.59
Varnishes, distemper	8,373	22,388	2.67	12,472	20,851	1.67	1.60	2.12	3.39
Washing detergents	4,066	5,404	1.33	4,513	6,071	1.35	0.99	0.51	0.51
Polymerisation	264,646	280,800	1.06	527,795	487,221	0.92	1.15	26.54	30.51
Pesticides, disinfectant	2,678	6,600	2.47	2,835	5,255	1.85	1.33	0.62	0.83
Starch, insulin, gluten	11,053	17,021	1.54	14,851	19,292	1.30	1.19	1.61	1.91
Organic chemicals	766	1,643	2.15	805	1,138	1.41	1.52	0.16	0.24
Materials of rubber	1,808	3,501	1.94	807	1891	2.34	0.83	0.33	0.27

Paper, paperboard	118,166	77,560	0.66	84,169	41,244	0.49	1.34	7.33	9.82
Wool, hair yarn,	4,511	39,402	8.74	2,220	21,922	9.87	0.89	3.73	3.30
Textile fibre yarn	4,395	15,049	3.42	3,099	10,104	3.26	1.05	1.42	1.49
Woven cotton fabrics	10,103	5,661	0.56	11,093	5,529	0.50	1.12	0.54	0.60
Other knit fabrics	21,387	66,900	3.13	41,257	144,762	3.51	0.89	6.32	5.65
Man–made carpets[b]	380	5,588	14.71	38	546	14.37	1.02	0.53	0.54
Cements	103,168	5,798	0.06	84,153	3,994	0.05	1.18	0.55	0.65
Iron, steel shapes	15,381	7,884	0.51	12,538	4,530	0.36	1.42	0.75	1.06
Iron, steel univ., plate	36,794	32,353	0.88	2,136	1,197	0.56	1.57	3.06	4.80
Iron, steel hoop, strip	3,625	3,726	1.03	613	519	0.85	1.21	0.35	0.43
Iron, steel wire	7,256	5,034	0.69	12,880	7,854	0.61	1.14	0.48	0.54
Iron, steel tubes, pipes	2,027	1,703	0.84	551	389	0.71	1.19	0.16	0.19
Iron, steel tube fittings	666	1,661	2.49	876	2,060	2.35	1.06	0.16	0.17
Copper excl. cement	12,197	47,050	3.86	16,108	38,944	2.42	1.60	4.45	7.10
Aluminium	8,991	25,979	2.89	5,202	12,751	2.45	1.18	2.46	2.90
Lead	78	170	2.18	87	123	1.41	1.54	0.02	0.03
Zinc	803	1,380	1.72	1,069	911	0.85	2.02	0.13	0.26
Tin	224	1,479	6.60	347	1,700	4.90	1.35	0.14	0.19
Wire products non–electric	955	1,218	1.28	1,873	2,221	1.19	1.08	0.12	0.12
Marine piston engines[c]	282	876	3.11	153	126	0.82	3.77	0.08	0.31
Motors, generators[c]	19,305	14,504	0.75	73,705	24,339	0.33	2.28	1.37	3.12
Paper machinery	1,637	11,257	6.88	578	1,994	3.45	1.99	1.06	2.12
Other printing machine	3,088	10,308	3.34	1,697	3,880	2.29	1.46	0.97	1.42
Other machine–tools	7,395	21,156	2.86	1,084	1,548	1.43	2.00	2.00	4.01
Office machines	46,080	3,355	0.07	47,742	2,024	0.04	1.74	0.32	0.55
Digital central processors	1,486	2,728	1.84	4,410	5,523	1.25	1.47	0.26	0.38
Sound receivers, phonograph	431,763	8,641	0.02	87,028	755	0.01	2.22	0.82	1.82

Commodity Classification	China's imports from Hong Kong			Hong Kong's exports to China			Unit price ratio		
	Quantity	Value ($1000)	Unit price A ($1000)	Quantity	Value ($1000)	Unit price B ($1000)	Price ratio A/B	Weight %	Weighted ratio
Ships and boats	1,813	6,046	3.34	416	495	1.19	2.80	0.57	1.60
Undergarments[c]	446	2,082	4.67	1,006	5,002	4.97	0.94	0.20	0.19
All commodities listed above		1,057,863						100	126.46
1994									
Crustaceans, molluscs	1,168	3,415	2.92	355	657	1.85	1.58	0.17	0.27
Meal, flour of wheat	6,158	2,250	0.37	5,244	2,014	0.38	0.95	0.11	0.11
Cereal preparations	5,681	8,155	1.44	4,671	9,752	2.09	0.69	0.41	0.28
Sugar confectionery	6,676	19,807	2.97	2,903	8,706	3.00	0.99	1.00	0.99
Animal feedstuffs	28,903	11,648	0.40	6,445	1,212	0.19	2.14	0.59	1.26
Food preparations	10,122	19,768	1.95	6,832	14,795	2.17	0.90	1.00	0.90
Non-alcohol beverages	27,841	11,377	0.41	25,635	10,480	0.41	1.00	0.58	0.58
Alcohol beverages	1,658	2,099	1.27	10,363	7,350	0.71	1.79	0.11	0.19
Pulp and waste paper	316,425	32,719	0.10	295,446	24,917	0.08	1.23	1.66	2.03
Cotton	10,066	2,981	0.30	7,205	2,406	0.33	0.89	0.15	0.13
Synthetic fibres	30,256	42,053	1.39	1,440	1,711	1.19	1.17	2.13	2.49
Worn clothing, textiles	5,488	3,119	0.57	2,709	1,456	0.54	1.06	0.16	0.17
Ferrous waste, scrap	75,018	9,832	0.13	200,574	24,689	0.12	1.07	0.50	0.53
Non-ferrous waste	139,277	29,076	0.21	85,331	22,965	0.27	0.78	1.47	1.14
Electric current[a]	1,719	102,572	59.67	1,856	107,674	58.01	1.03	5.19	5.34
Animal oils and fats	17,742	4,861	0.27	16,846	5,446	0.32	0.85	0.25	0.21

Fixed veg. fat, oil soft	27,110	15,777	0.58	5,303	3,108	0.59	0.99	0.80	0.79
Animal, veg. fats	10,458	63,524	6.07	7,713	40,567	5.26	1.16	3.21	3.71
Dyeing, tanning materials	1,286	2,416	1.88	996	882	0.89	2.12	0.12	0.26
Other colouring matter	7,360	16,992	2.31	7,204	17,097	2.37	0.97	0.86	0.84
Prep. oral, dental hygiene	19,844	38,607	1.95	731	1,555	2.13	0.92	1.95	1.79
Soup	1,731	2,422	1.40	889	1,385	1.56	0.90	0.12	0.11
Polyethylene	25,604	18,466	0.72	1,546	1,221	0.79	0.91	0.93	0.85
Polymers of styrene	89,229	81,445	0.91	384,150	308,675	0.80	1.14	4.12	4.68
Polymers, vinyl	33,930	28,700	0.85	73,929	65,958	0.89	0.95	1.45	1.38
Plastic tube, pipe, hose	4,167	8,110	1.95	3,035	4,745	1.56	1.25	0.41	0.51
Other plastic	25,137	42,953	1.71	2,922	4,688	1.60	1.07	2.17	2.32
Starches, insulin	21,745	22,748	1.05	20,729	15,407	0.74	1.41	1.15	1.62
Materials of rubber	4,403	8,724	1.98	1,339	2,851	2.13	0.93	0.44	0.41
Paper and paperboard	330,121	146,590	0.44	399,725	168,590	0.42	1.05	7.42	7.81
Knit. crochet. Fabrics	126,671	278,317	2.20	117,302	248,083	2.12	1.04	14.08	14.63
Nonwoven fabrics	7,150	25,169	3.52	5,498	17,196	3.13	1.13	1.27	1.43
Lime, cement, etc.	423,584	35,054	0.08	443,335	29,673	0.07	1.24	1.77	2.19
Flat–rolled plated iron	17,764	10,904	0.61	4,641	2,616	0.56	1.09	0.55	0.60
Iron, steel shapes	115,424	42,130	0.37	72,132	22,779	0.32	1.16	2.13	2.46
Wire of iron and steel	9,355	6,638	0.71	15,259	10,247	0.67	1.06	0.34	0.36
Copper	35,948	89,175	2.48	31,564	75,784	2.40	1.03	4.51	4.66
Aluminium	29,299	43,361	1.48	23,401	31,998	1.37	1.08	2.19	2.38
Zinc	6,967	7,180	1.03	10,912	10,552	0.97	1.07	0.36	0.39
Wire products	3,871	6,300	1.63	3,224	4,002	1.24	1.31	0.32	0.42
Nails, screws	9,984	21,385	2.14	12,009	21,675	1.81	1.19	1.08	1.28
Tools[c]	2,968	14,236	4.80	7,404	11,996	1.62	2.96	0.72	2.13
Knives, forks, spoons[c]	1,206	4,363	3.62	3,613	6,634	1.84	1.97	0.22	0.44
Electric motors[c]	146,755	43,996	0.30	77,296	20,518	0.27	1.13	2.23	2.51

Commodity classification	China's imports from Hong Kong			Hong Kong's exports to China			Unit price ratio		
	Quantity	Value ($1000)	Unit price A ($1000)	Quantity	Value ($1000)	Unit price B ($1000)	Price ratio A/B	Weight %	Weighted ratio
Elec. motors, generators	597,852	7709	0.01	184,345	1,762	0.01	1.35	0.39	0.53
Other textile machinery	8,195	61315	7.48	6,792	36,618	5.39	1.39	3.10	4.31
Other printing machines	5,531	25523	4.62	2,047	8,968	4.38	1.05	1.29	1.36
Metal removal work tools	174,38	53919	3.09	12,340	27,688	2.24	1.38	2.73	3.76
Machine tools etc.	100,45	42205	4.20	6,345	21,017	3.31	1.27	2.14	2.71
Air vacuum, pump	127,447	17666	0.14	44,476	5,603	0.13	1.10	0.89	0.98
Fans, cooker hoods	400,072	6228	0.02	314,687	5,105	0.02	0.96	0.32	0.30
Machs. filter gas	83,358	38355	0.46	183,872	57,240	0.31	1.48	1.94	2.87
Ball bearings[c]	9,716	7533	0.78	4,435	2,337	0.53	1.47	0.38	0.56
Office machines[c]	4,049	12434	3.07	5,508	7,887	1.43	2.15	0.63	1.35
Automatic proc. equipt	394,389	65435	0.17	298,674	28,202	0.09	1.76	3.31	5.82
TV receivers	21,047	6676	0.32	28,401	3,804	0.13	2.37	0.34	0.80
Radios[c]	2,232	7061	3.16	2,034	6,028	2.96	1.07	0.36	0.38
Microphones etc.[c]	176,648	36327	0.21	23,147	7,329	0.32	0.65	1.84	1.19
Transformers[c]	81,827	29951	0.37	38,332	10,907	0.29	1.29	1.52	1.95
TV picture tubes	439,884	23,520	0.05	41,697	2,999	0.07	0.74	1.19	0.89
Electronic microcircuits[d]	1,017	22,478	22.10	2,067	44,431	21.50	1.03	1.14	1.17
Furniture	196,727	16,333	0.08	82,964	7,000	0.08	0.98	0.83	0.81
Trunks, suit-cases[c]	4,570	5,674	1.24	385	481	1.25	0.99	0.29	0.29

Men's, boys' clothing, knit[c]	1,583	5,552	3.51	1,706	5,105	2.99	1.17	0.28	0.33
Pullovers etc., knit[c]	28,932	43,947	1.52	34,514	50,018	1.45	1.05	2.22	2.33
Other footwear[e]	1,930	9,031	4.68	1,627	5,908	3.63	1.29	0.46	0.59
All commodities listed above	1,976,286							100.00	114.85

Notes: All units are either tonnes or numbers with the exception of

- a 1000 kwh;
- b 1000 square meters;
- c 1000;
- d 1000,000;
- e 1000 pairs.

Sources: United Nations: Commodity Trade Statistics According to International Trade Classification. 1990, Vol.40, No.10 (pp.1–80) and No.18 (pp.95–158); United Nations Statistical Office: Commodity Trade Statistics 1994, China, Rev. 3; and Hong Kong, Rev. 3.

actually expanded their investment in these 'loss-making' enterprises. This suggests that the loss of some FIEs is artificially created by MNCs using transfer prices.

The existence of transfer pricing is also evidenced by the fact that the pre–tax profit rate in FIEs is lower than that in state–owned enterprises on average. As is well known, Chinese state–owned enterprises are characterised by low efficiency and low profitability, and many of them are run on fiscal subsidies from the government. Therefore, it is incredible that the pre–tax profit rate in FIEs is even lower than that in state–owned enterprises. For instance, the pre–tax profit rate (weighted average) for FIEs in the industry sector was 5.27 per cent in 1992 and 9.05 per cent in 1993, compared to 11.38 per cent and 11.11 per cent for state–owned enterprises, respectively (SSB 1992, 1993b).

The above indirect evidence reveals that MNCs actually manipulate transfer pricing at the cost of Chinese government and local partners in FIEs, resulting in taxation and profit losses. For foreign investing companies, the manipulation of transfer pricing is motivated by maximisation of their global profit and minimisation of their business risks. In terms of the economics of multinational corporations, transfer pricing is an MNC's pricing behaviour in response to market imperfection caused by government interventions including tax, tariff and other risks. Transfer–pricing activities tend to improve the overall efficiency of allocation of resources in the world (Chudson 1985). In terms of income distribution, however, transfer pricing is harmful to host countries, especially for developing countries that are poorly equipped in legal systems and professional expertise. These are the two aspects of the impact of transfer pricing.

CONCLUSION AND POLICY IMPLICATIONS

This chapter has discussed the impact of FDI on the foreign trade of the host country in the context of China. It is found that in general, FDI is trade–creating in the case of China, therefore confirming the Kojima hypothesis, which argues that foreign investment in the host country's comparatively advantaged industries tends to promote trade. As the empirical study shows, FDI has played an important role in Chinese export expansion, and therefore sparked a strong stimulus to export–led economic growth over the past 18 years.

However, the trade deficits of FIEs partly offset the trade surplus created by the Chinese domestic sectors, and thus to some extent discounted the positive impact of the FIEs' export boom. Among the factors contributing to the persistent trade deficit of FIEs, the importation of capital goods is expected to affect the Chinese capital formation and economic growth positively. However, transfer pricing manipulated by MNCs for FIEs' exports and imports would have a negative impact on the Chinese economy, especially reducing the government taxation revenue and local partner's operating profits. This study finds that under the current Chinese legal framework and economic environment, MNCs have a higher propensity to use transfer prices for FIEs' trade. The indirect evidence presented in this chapter confirms the existence of transfer pricing in FIEs' foreign trade.

Some policy implications can be drawn from the findings of this study. First, FDI, especially export–oriented FDI, should be continuously encouraged. In terms of industrial composition, the comparatively advantaged industries (which are largely labour–intensive manufacturing industries) are expected to be the major industries for MNCs' investment. Second, to reduce the trade deficit of FIEs, some policies should be formulated and further implemented, such as input localisation, and removal of tariff–free import of intermediate inputs for FIEs, which can be produced domestically. Third, the government should formulate anti–transfer pricing laws or regulations and implement them with concrete and effective measures. To do so, government departments such as Customs and the Ministry of Foreign Trade and Economic Corporations (MOFTEC) should regularly monitor the market prices of major commodities traded between China and her major trading partners and formulate some necessary accounting criteria governing or measuring the prices of traded commodities reported by traders including FIEs.

NOTES

1. Calculated by using the 1981 exchange rate (US$1 = 1.7051 renminbi, the Chinese currency).
2. Calculated from *Statistical Yearbook of China 1996.*
3. *Economic Daily* (*Jingji Robao*), 17 May 1995, p.2, which cited from SSB data.
4. The Chinese government recently modified the tariff policy on FIEs' imports. The standard tariff will be applied to the imports of FIEs including capital goods and other products, since 1997, under the new rule.

REFERENCES

Arndt, H.W., 1974. 'Professor Kojima on the macroeconomics of foreign direct investment', *Hitotsubashi Journal of Economics* **14**, 26–35.

Buckley, P.J., 1983. 'Macroeconomic versus international business approach to direct foreign investment: a comment on Professor Kojima's interpretation', *Hitotsu–bashi Journal of Economics*, **24**, 95–100.

Casson, M.C. and Pearce, R.D., 1988. *Economic development and international trade*, Macmillan, Basingstoke and London.

Chudson, W.A., 1985. 'The regulation of transfer prices by developing countries: second–best policies?', in A.M. Rugman and L. Eden (eds), *Multinationals and Transfer Pricing*, Croom Helm, London and Sydney.

Corden, W.M., 1974. 'The theory of international trade', in J.H. Dunning (ed.), *Economics analysis and the multinational enterprise*, Allen & Unwin, London.

Dunning, J.H., 1985. 'The eclectic paradigm of international production: an update and a reply to its critics', Mimeo, University of Reading.

Geroski, P.A., 1979. 'Review of direct foreign investment by Kiyoshi Kojima', *Economic Journal*, **89**, 162–4.

Gray, H.P., 1993. 'The role of transnational corporations in international trade', in H.P. Gray (ed.), *Transnational corporations and international trade and payments*, Routledge, London and New York.

Helleiner, G.K., 1973. 'Manufactured exports from less developed countries and multinational firms', *Economic Journal*, **9**, 361–74.

Hone, A., 1974. 'Multinational corporations and multinational buying groups: their impact on the growth of Asia's exports of manufactures: myths and realities', *World Development*, **2**, 145–9.

Johnson, H.G., 1973. 'Trade, investment and labour, and changing international division of production', in H. Hughes (ed.), *Prospects for partnership, industrialisation and trade policies in the 1970s*, World Bank Publication, Washington, DC.

Kojima, K., 1973. 'A macroeconomic approach to foreign direct investment', *Hitotsubashi Journal of Economics*, **14(1)**, 1–21.

Kojima, K., 1975. 'International trade and foreign investment: substitutes or complements', *Hitotsubashi Journal of Economics*, **16(1)**, 1-12.

Kojima, K., 1982. 'Macroeconomic versus international business approach to direct foreign investment', *Hitotsubashi Journal of Economics*, **23(1)**, 1–19.

Lecraw, D.J., 1985. 'Some evidence on transfer pricing by multinational corporations', in A. M. Rugman and L. Eden (eds), *Multinationals and transfer pricing*, Croom Helm, London and Sydney.

Lee, C.H., 1984. 'On Japanese macroeconomic theories of direct foreign investment', *Economic Development and Cultural Change*, **32**, 713–23.

Mason, R.H., 1980. 'A comment on Professor Kojima's "Japanese style versus American type of technology transfer"', *Hitotsubashi Journal of Economics*, **20**, 42–52.

Ministry of Foreign Trade and Economic Corporations (MOFTEC) of China, 1995, *Almanac of China's foreign economic relations and trade, 1984–1994*, China Statistical Publishing House, Beijing.

Mundell, R.A., 1957. 'International trade and factor mobility', *American Economic Review*, **47(3)**, 321–35.

Ohlin, B., 1933. *Interregional and international trade*, Harvard University Press, Cambridge, Massachusetts.

Plasschaert, S.R.F., 1985. 'Transfer pricing problems in developing countries', in A. M. Rugman and L. Eden (eds), *Multinationals and transfer pricing*, Croom Helm, London and Sydney.

Purvis, D.D., 1972. 'Technology, trade and factor mobility', *Economic Journal*, September, 991–9.

Rana, P.B., 1985. 'Exports and economic growth in the Asian region', *Asian Development Bank Economic Staff Paper*, 75.

State Statistical Bureau (SSB), 1992. *Statistical Yearbook of Chinese Industry*, China Statistical Publishing House, Beijing.

State Statistical Bureau (SSB),1993a. *China Foreign Economic Statistics 1979–1992*, China Statistical Publishing House, Beijing.

State Statistical Bureau (SSB), 1993b. *Statistical Yearbook of Chinese Industry*, China Statistical Publishing House, Beijing.

State Statistical Bureau (SSB),1995. *China Foreign Economic Statistics 1994*, China Statistical Publishing House, Beijing.

State Statistical Bureau (SSB), 1996. *Statistical Yearbook of China 1996*, China Statistical Publishing House, Beijing.

United Nations, 1992. *World Investment Report 1992*, New York.

7.   Causality Between FDI and Economic Growth

Jordan Shan, Gary Tian and Fiona Sun

INTRODUCTION

The linkage between FDI and economic growth has been the subject of considerable research for many decades. However, the link between FDI and economic growth which has been subjected to empirical scrutiny remains the subject of debate. There is renewed interest in this area of research in recent years largely due to the globalization of the world economy and due to the recognition that multinational corporations play an increasingly important role in trade, capital accumulation and economic growth in developing countries. Three developments have added an additional twist to the literature on the FDI–led growth study, particularly in the area of empirical studies. First, previous econometric studies based on the assumption that there is one–way causality from FDI to GDP growth have been noted and criticised in more recent studies (see, for example, Kholdy 1995). In other words, not only can FDI 'Granger–cause' GDP growth (with either positive or negative effects), but GDP growth can also affect the inflow of FDI.[1] Failure to consider either direction of such a causality can lead to an inefficient estimation of the impacts of FDI on economic growth and hence is subject to the problem of simultaneity bias. Second, the so–called 'new growth theory' has resulted in some reappraisal of the determinants of growth in modelling the role played by FDI in the growth process. Third, new developments in econometric theory, such as time–series concepts of cointegration and causality testing, have further expanded the debate on the FDI–growth relationship.

Since the early 1990s, China has become one of the most important FDI recipient developing countries in the world. During 1980–95, the annual growth rate of actual FDI was 40 per cent, and accompanying this persistent strong FDI inflow, China has achieved a remarkable economic growth rate (9.5 per cent per annum).[2] Therefore, did FDI lead economic growth in China or was it the other way around? The hypothesis can be further divided into three competing, although not mutually exclusive, hypotheses: (i) the FDI–

led growth hypothesis; (ii) the growth–driven FDI hypothesis; and (iii) the two–way causality hypothesis, which is a combination of (i) and (ii).

This chapter contributes to the debate on the FDI–led growth hypothesis by constructing a six–variable vector autoregression (VAR) model for the Chinese economy on the basis of quarterly time–series data in a production function context. Four distinct features in this chapter stand out as follows: first, the FDI–led growth study on China, which uses Granger no–causality testing procedure, is the first attempt in the literature; second, we have gone beyond the traditional two–variable relationship by building a six–variable VAR model in the production function context to avoid the possible specification bias; third, we follow Riezman, Whiteman and Summers (1996) to test the hypothesis, while controlling import growth to avoid producing a spurious causality result; and finally, the methodology by Toda and Yamamoto (1995) is expected to improve the standard *F*–statistics in the causality test process.

The rest of the chapter is organised as follows. First, we provide a review of some of the empirical literature and then describe the model and data employed in the chapter. This is followed by analyses of the empirical results. The final section concludes the chapter.

A LITERATURE REVIEW

Empirical studies on the FDI–growth nexus can be categorised into two broad groups: (i) the studies which focus on the role of multinational firms and on the determinants of FDI; and (ii) the studies which, very recently, applied casualty tests based on time–series data to examine the nature of causal relationship between FDI and output growth. Some noteworthy studies in the first group are Scaperlanda and Mauer (1969), Dunning (1970) and Vernon (1971). More recently, Rugman (1994), Root and Ahmed (1978), Graham and Krugman (1989), O'Sullivan and Geyikdagi (1994), Lin (1995), Cable and Persaud (1987), Tsai (1994) and Chao and Yu (1994), among others, have examined the factors that influence the inflows and outflows of foreign direct investment.

In the second group of studies on the FDI–growth nexus, some scholars have applied time–series data analysis and directed their FDI–led growth studies towards the use of the Granger no–causality testing procedure. These include, for instance, Karikari (1992), Saltz (1992), de Mello (1996), Kasibhatla and Sawhney (1996), Kholdy (1995), Pfaffermayr (1994) and United Nations (1993). However, one of the problems with these studies is their arbitrary choice of the lag length used for causality test[3] (see, for example, Kasibhatla and Sawhney 1996). Furthermore, these studies have applied *F*–test statistics for the causality test (see, for example, United Nations 1993). It is now well established in the econometric literature that the

F–test statistic is not valid if times series are integrated (for example, if they are $I(1)$ variables) as argued by Zapata and Rambaldi (1997) and Gujarati (1995)).

Some empirical studies have examined the FDI–led growth hypothesis in the case of the Chinese economy. Recent attempts include Chen, Chang and Zhang (1995), Zhang (1995), Chen (1996), Pomfret (1991), Kueh (1992), Plummer and Montes (1995), Sun (1996), Wei (1996), Lee (1994) and Wang and Swain (1995). However, these studies suffer from two major problems. First, none of these studies have tested for the direction of causality between GDP growth and FDI inflow; they have implicitly assumed a one–way causality running from FDI to GDP growth and estimated the impacts of FDI based on such a causality which cannot yield reliable conclusions. Second, most of these studies have used cross–section data, the validity of which is also subject to debate.

The main arguments against the use of cross–section data and in favour of the use of times–series data have been: cross–country studies implicitly impose or assume a common economic structure and similar production technology across different countries which is most likely not true; and further, the economic growth of a country is influenced not only by FDI and other factor inputs, but also by a host of domestic policies such as monetary, fiscal and external policies. Finally, the significance of the conclusions drawn from cross–section data is claimed not to be sufficient in finding a long–run causal relationship (for example, Enders 1995, Marin 1992). Some studies have attempted to overcome the problems with cross–section data analysis and the simultaneity bias by using a simultaneous equations model (for example, Gupta and Islam 1983, Lee and Rana 1986, Snyder 1990). How-ever, these studies, as pointed out by White (1992a, 1992b), suffer from the problems of both inadequate theoretical foundations and poor econometric methodology.

As far as the model specification is concerned, most of these studies have used a simple two–variable relationship. It should be pointed out that the approach of using a simple two–variable framework in the causality test without considering the effects of other variables (such as export, import and investment growth) is subject to a possible specification bias. It is established in the econometric literature that causality tests are sensitive to model selection and functional form (Gujarati 1995). Riezman, Whiteman and Summers (1996) have pointed out an important finding that omitting the import variable in the VAR estimation process can result in both 'type I' and 'type II' errors, that is, spurious rejection of one causality as well as spurious detection of it.

Another problem that has often been ignored and/or has not been dealt with adequately in the literature, yet far more important, is the endogenous nature of a production function as argued by Greenaway and Sapsford (1994). Therefore, studies which do not consider the endogenous nature of the growth process are subject to a simultaneity bias. The use of a VAR model has proved to generate more reliable estimates in an endogenous context (Gujarati 1995).

Although the choice of the optimal lag length in the causality test has been noted in some studies, very few studies have considered the problem of the sensitivity of the causality test results under different lag structures. It is vital to obtain consistent causality results for at least some consecutive lag structures along with the optimal choice of the lag, using some conventional criterion such as Akaike Information Criteria (AIC) and/or the Schwartz Criterion (SC).

Theoretically, the causality between FDI and GDP growth could run in either direction: FDI could promote further GDP growth as postulated, among others, by Todaro (1982), Chenery and Strout (1966), Dunning (1970), the World Bank (1993) and Krueger (1987). Recently some economists, in the line with the 'new growth theory', argue that through the capital accumulation in the recipient economy, FDI is expected to generate non–convex growth by encouraging the incorporation of new inputs and foreign technologies in the production function of the recipient economy. Further, through knowledge transfers, FDI is expected to augment the existing stock of knowledge in the recipient economy through labour training and skill acquisition, on the one hand, and through the introduction of alternative management practices and organisational arrangements, on the other (de Mello and Sinclair 1995). As a result, foreign investors may increase the productivity of the recipient economy and FDI can be deemed to be a catalyst for domestic investment and technological progress.

However, the causality could also run the opposite way: rapid GDP growth could induce the inflow of FDI (for example, Dowling and Hiemenz 1982, Lee and Rana 1986). This is because rapid GDP growth will usually create a high level of capital requirement (and a resource gap) in the host country, and hence the host country will demand more FDI by offering concessional terms for FDI to attract overseas investors. Further, rapid economic growth in the host country (for example, in China) will build up the confidence of overseas investors investing in the host country. More importantly, rapid economic growth, accompanied by an increased higher per capita income, will create huge opportunities for FDI to invest in industrial sectors, consumer durable goods production and infrastructure in the host country.

It should be pointed out that the direction of the causality between FDI and GDP growth depends on many economic as well as political and cultural factors, such as the level of economic development, the productivity of FDI and the policies shaping FDI inflow. Ultimately, we shall have to 'let data speak'.[4] China's case fits neatly into this context. Since the adoption of the open–door policy, China has achieved high rates of economic growth. Some sectors, such as the infrastructure, became a serious bottleneck to further economic development, which has become available for the introduction of foreign capital. During the 1990s, China's rapid economic growth was increasingly dependent on the huge FDI inflow, while its rapid economic growth also attracted more capital from overseas.

THE MODEL AND DATA

The Model

Based upon the review in the previous section, the FDI–led growth hypothesis is tested according to a six–variable VAR model, which is built upon the following augmented production function:

$$Y_t = f(Inv_t, Lab_t, Imp_t, FDI_t, En_t) \tag{7.1}$$

where Y is industrial output; Inv_t, Lab_t, Imp_t, FDI_t and En_t, respectively, are capital, labour, imports, FDI inflows to China and the consumption of energy, respectively.

The Granger Causality Procedures

Testing for Granger no–causality in multiple time series has been the subject of considerable research in recent econometric literature. It has been argued that the traditional F–test in a regression context for determining whether some parameters of the model are jointly zero, for example, in the form of a causality test (in a stable VAR model), is not valid when the variables are integrated and the test statistic does not have a standard distribution (see, for example, Gujarati 1995). Therefore, several alternative procedures have been developed which attempt to improve the size and power of the Granger no–causality test (see, for example, Toda and Phillips 1993, and Mosconi and Giannini 1992). Unfortunately, these tests are considerably cumbersome and 'the simplicity and ease of application have been largely lost' (Rambaldi and Doran 1996, p.1).

   In this chapter, we apply the Granger no–causality methodology, developed by Toda and Yamamoto (1995), to test the hypothesis that 'industrial growth in China is Granger–caused by FDI growth', versus the alternative hypothesis that 'industrial growth has driven the inflow of FDI in China'.

   The advantage of using Toda and Yamamoto's (1995) method of testing for Granger causality lies in its simplicity and the ability to overcome many shortcomings of alternative econometric procedures. Some studies have applied the cointegration technique by Johansen and Juselius (1990). However, this method involves transforming the suggested relationship into an Error Correction Model (ECM) and identifying the parameters associated with the causality. If the case involves more than two cointegration vectors, this is not practically simple. Further, there is growing concern among applied researchers that the cointegration likelihood ratio (LR) tests of Johansen (1988) and Johansen and Juselius (1990) have often not provided the degree of empirical support that might reasonably have been expected for a long–run relationship. Furthermore, using a Monte Carlo experiment, Bewley and Yang (1996) argue that the power of LR tests is high only when the correlation between the shocks that generate the stationary and non–stationary components of typical macroeconomic series is sufficiently large and also that the power of LR tests deteriorates rapidly with over–specification of the lag length. This concern has also been supported by the simulation studies of Ho and Sorensen (1996).

The procedure developed by Toda and Yamamoto (1995) utilises a modified WALD test for restrictions on the parameters of a VAR(k), or MWALD procedure (where k is the lag length in the system). This test has an asymptotic χ^2 distribution when a VAR($k + d_{max}$) is estimated (where d_{max} is the maximal order of integration suspected to occur in the system). A Monte Carlo experiment which included the above three alternative test procedures, presented in Zapata and Rambaldi (1997), provides evidence that the MWALD test has a comparable performance in size and power to the LR and WALD tests if (i) the correct number of lags for estimating $k + d_{max}$ is identified and (ii) no important variables are omitted, provided a sample of 50 or more observations is available.

Rambaldi and Doran (1996) have demonstrated that the MWALD method for testing Granger no–causality can be computationally simple by using a seemingly unrelated regression (SUR) which can be routinely computed by several of the available econometric packages, such as Shazam. We have therefore built the following six–variable VAR system in a SUR form:

$$
\begin{bmatrix} Ind_t \\ En_t \\ Lab_t \\ Imp_t \\ Inv_t \\ FDI_t \end{bmatrix}
=
A_0 + A_1
\begin{bmatrix} Ind_{t-n} \\ En_{t-n} \\ Lab \\ Imp_{t-n} \\ Inv_{t-n} \\ FDI_{t-n} \end{bmatrix}
+
\begin{bmatrix} \varepsilon_{Ind} \\ \varepsilon_{En} \\ \varepsilon_{Lab} \\ \varepsilon_{Imp} \\ \varepsilon_{Inv} \\ \varepsilon_{FDI} \end{bmatrix}
\tag{7.2}
$$

The advantage of this procedure, as argued by Zapata and Rambaldi (1997), is that it does not require the knowledge of cointegration properties of the system. It has a normal standard limiting chi–square distribution and the usual lag selection procedure to the system can be applied, even if there is no cointegration and/or the stability and rank conditions are not satisfied, 'so long as the order of integration of the process does not exceed the true lag length of the model' (Toda and Yamamoto 1995, p.225). In addition, Toda and Yamamoto (1995) have shown how VARs can be estimated using data in levels and 'testing general restrictions even if the process may be integrated or cointegrated of an arbitrary order'.

It should be added that, by using a SUR–type VAR model, we can compromise between the theory–driven and the data–driven approaches, since we have included the relevant set of variables in our VAR system following the recent literature of 'new growth theory', and at the same time, the simultaneity bias can be overcome by the VAR model. Gujarati (1995) points out that the VAR model is a truly simultaneous system in that all variables are regarded as endogenous considering the feedback effects in the system, and that it can be estimated by ordinary least square (OLS) without resorting to any system methods such as two–stage least squares (2SLS).

To examine the first causality (from FDI to growth), we should test whether FDI_{t-n}, appears in the first equation (the *Ind* equation), that is, H_0: $\alpha_1^{(1)} = \alpha^{(2)} = \alpha^{(3)} = ... = \alpha^{(n)} = 0$; where $\alpha_1^{(i)}$ are the coefficients of FDI for $1, ..., n^{th}$ lags in the first equation of the system (7.2).

The causality from FDI to growth can be established by rejecting the null hypothesis, $\alpha_1 = \alpha_2, ..., ..., = \alpha_n = 0$ (that is, 'FDI does not Granger–cause industrial growth') which requires finding the significance of the MWALD statistic for the group of the lagged independent variables identified above. Similar restrictions and the testing procedure can be applied to examine the second causality (that is, industrial growth to FDI). This involves testing the following linear restrictions in the system (7.2): H_0: $\alpha_6^{(1)} = \alpha^{(2)} = \alpha^{(3)} = ...$ $= \alpha^{(n)} = 0$; where $\alpha_6^{(i)}$ are the coefficients of Ind for $1, ..., n^{th}$ lags in the 6th equation of the system (7.2), that is, the FDI growth equation.

Thus we shall test whether Ind_{t-n}, appear in the *FDI* equation. The existence of the causality from industrial growth to FDI can be established by rejecting the hypothesis of 'industrial growth does not Granger–cause FDI growth' which requires finding the significance of the MWALD statistic for the group of the lagged independent variables identified above.

Data

The VAR model is estimated using quarterly and seasonally–adjusted data, in logarithms and real terms (in 1990/1991 prices) over the period 1985:2–1996:2.[5] The size of the VAR model requires quarterly rather than annual series to generate enough degrees of freedom for estimation. Therefore, we first collected monthly data for imports (*Imp*), industrial output (*Ind*), energy consumption (*En*), labour force (*Lab*), foreign direct investment (*FDI*) and capital expenditure (*Inv*). They were then converted into quarterly data and inflation–adjusted using the consumer price index except FDI data which is in current price in US dollars. Monthly data, seasonally adjusted flow variables, on exports, industrial output, labour force, total investment and energy consumption, were collected for the period 1985:2–1996:2 from various issues of *China Monthly Statistics* (CMS) of China Statistical Bureau (China Statistical Information and Consultancy Service Centre), and was cross–referenced with the annual data from the IMF's *International Financial Statistics*.[6] They were then transformed into quarterly data. The details of each series are as follows: Total Industrial Output Value (Ind): Table 2.1 series in various issues of CMS; Exports (Exp) and Imports (Imp): Table 7.1 series in CMS; Labour Force (Lab): Table 14.1 series in CMS; Total Investment (Inv): it was obtained by adding 'Total Capital Construction Investment' and 'Total Technical Updating and Transformation Investment'. They are from Tables 4.1 and 4.2 series in CMS; Energy Consumption (En): Table 3.5 series measured in Standard Coal Equivalents (SCEs) from CMS. The quarterly data on FDI is from *China Economic Information Centre*, State Statistical Bureau, Beijing.

EMPIRICAL RESULTS

Prior to testing for a causality relationship between the time series, it is necessary to establish that they are integrated of the same order. To this end, an Augmented Dickey–Fuller test (ADF) was carried out on the time series in undifferenced levels and differenced forms. The results of the ADF tests suggest that each series is a $I(1)$ variable at the 95 per cent level of confidence.[7] After the ADF test, we proceeded to the Granger no–causality test. Results derived from these methods are presented in Table 7.1.

The results reported in Table 7.1 suggest that, in the case of China, both the null hypothesis of 'Grange no–causality from FDI to growth' and the null hypothesis of 'Granger no–causality from growth to FDI' can be rejected strongly at the 99 per cent significance level. These indicate that there is a two–way causality running between industrial growth and FDI in China. Therefore, both FDI–led growth and growth–driven FDI hypotheses are supported by the empirical evidence from China.

Even though we have used AIC and SC to aid in the choice of lag length,[8] we have estimated the model using several different lag structures to ensure that results are not sensitive to the choice of the lag length. As Pindyck and Rubinfeld (1991, p.217) point out, 'it is best to run the test for a few different lag structures and make sure that the results are not sensitive to the choice of *m* (lag length)'. Bahmani–Oskooee and Alse (1993) have also warned about

Table 7.1   Results of Granger causality test: China

H_0:	FDI does not cause GDP		Ind does not cause FDI	
Optimal lag (VAR order)	6 (7)		6(7)	
P–values	0.0040		0.0009	
R^2	0.9895		0.9895	
	Test statistic		*Test statistic*	
Lag structure (VAR order)	P–value	MWALD statistic	P–value	MWALD statistic
3(4)	0.5504	2.5689	0.5541	2.5978
4(5)	0.5710	2.0067	0.5748	1.9884
5(6)	0.1058	7.4073	0.0360	10.2773
6(7)	0.0040	10.0005	0.0009	85.1379
7(8)	0.0030	16.9845	0.0060	14.2302
8(9)	0.0008	84.2364	0.0007	84.5609

Notes: *Ind* = real industrial;   *FDI* = foreign direct investment flows in real terms; Optimal lag length is determined by AIC and SC. The results for other equations are not reported for simplicity. Numbers in parenthesis represent VAR order. VAR order = $k + d_{max}$, where: k is the lag length used in the system; d_{max} is the maximum order of integration in the system, in our system is $I(1)$.

the danger of an arbitrary choice of lag length, and one must 'select a strategy for choosing the optimum number of lags on each other when there is more than one independent variable' in a VAR model (Bahmani–Oskooee and Alse 1993, p.540).

Table 7.1 indicates that the results are consistent with each other for different lag lengths, so we can conclude that our results are robust or sturdy, in a similar sense of Leamer's Extreme Bound Analysis (EBA), avoiding a fragile statistical inference.[9]

The fact that both FDI–led growth and growth–driven FDI hypotheses are supported by our analysis of Chinese data indicates that the FDI–led growth hypothesis, in the sense of a unidirectional causal ordering from FDI inflows to output growth, is not valid for China. The results merely demonstrate that both economic growth and FDI inflow reinforce each other in the course of economic development.

The observations on China's recent economic development process fit into the above argument. The empirical evidence for the causality running from economic growth to FDI in the case of China indicates that the rapid economic growth has accelerated the inflow of FDI into China. Along with the fast economic growth during 1988–96, there have been swift structural changes within the Chinese economy, which attracted investment from multinational corporations (MNCs) in the areas of capital– and skill–intensive manufacturing and service sectors.   Further, rapid economic growth, along with the rising per capita income in China, has created huge domestic markets and business opportunities for overseas investment and hence has strengthened business confidence for investing in China. At the same time, closer economic ties, through economic complementarities, between China and Hong Kong, Taiwan, Korea and Japan, have resulted in a favourable investment environment in China and hence have made it increasingly attractive to foreign investment.

The econometric evidence in our chapter for the FDI–led growth hypothesis is also consistent with China's recent economic record. This can be partly explained by the dynamic benefits brought about by FDI as it induces and creates the production from other industries which can be measured by the 'backward linkage index'. Sun (1996), for instance, has shown that the inflow of FDI in China has contributed to the expansion of the industrial networks in China by the so–called 'spillover effect'.[10] The large multinational investment projects in China, especially from the OECD countries and the US, have contributed significantly in the transfer of technology; managerial training; linkage effects; renovating the state–owned enterprise sector; easing the development bottleneck; and establishing high–tech industries in China. It has been argued that under import protection, dynamic gain of learning, by introducing these MNCs, might offset the losses of static allocative efficiencies (Chao and Yu 1994).

CONCLUDING REMARKS

This chapter has used the methodology of the Granger no–causality test developed by Toda and Yamamoto (1995) to examine the causality link between FDI growth and real industrial growth in China, in the context of the FDI–led growth hypothesis.

The test was based upon quarterly time–series data, in a six–variable VAR model, for the period 1988 to 1996. After surveying the literature on the topic, a VAR model built upon an augmented production function was applied to overcome the dual problems of simultaneity bias and weak theoretical foundations underpinning the models of previous studies. In particular, we have allowed for import growth and investment growth to be included in the VAR model. The rigorous econometric method of causality testing, developed by Toda and Yamamoto (1995), has improved the power of the test as compared to the traditional *F*–test statistic. Further, we have tested the sensitivity of the causality tests using different lag structures, along with the choice of the optimal lag structure.

Our results indicate a two–way causality running between industrial growth and FDI growth in China. The results reported here do not lend support, in the sense of a unidirectional causal ordering, to the FDI–led growth hypothesis. In other words, the inflow of FDI and rapid industrial growth in China have reinforced each other. On the one hand, the exceptional economic performance in China during the 1990s was propelled by a strong FDI inflow,   helping China's access to overseas markets, improving technology and supplementing domestic saving and investment. On the other hand, China has benefited from a very rapid growth of domestic demand and hence a high level of domestic investment, which enabled the country to achieve rapid economic growth rates and industrial restructuring. Therefore, as an outcome of this rapid growth in China, the emergence of huge domestic markets and increased per capita income, along with the emergence of a large middle class in urban and rural areas, have attracted foreign investments into China in order to capture China's huge domestic market and to take advantage of China's natural and labour resources.

The implication of our research concerning the two–way causality between growth and FDI inflow is that a host country such as China should adopt a policy of promoting FDI inflows (for example, by offering concessional terms) to promote economic growth. At the same time, the country should adopt a policy of mobilising domestic resources and promoting further GDP growth (for example, by a continued commitment to an economic reform policy) to attract new inflows of FDI. In other words, the efforts of promoting further economic growth using a set of well–designed domestic policies is no less important than relying on FDI inflows.

NOTES

1. Granger (1981, 1988a and 1988b) has introduced the concept of causality in the framework of bivariate VAR, defining *Y* is said to be Granger–caused by *X* if the information in past and present *X* helps to improve the forecasts of the *Y* variable.
2. Calculations based upon State Statistical Bureau, *China Statistical Yearbook*, 1994 (pp.32 and 527 for growth rate of FDI, and pp.42 and 597 for the nation's economic growth rate).
3. Pindyck and Rubinfeld (1991, p.217) point out, when doing causality tests, that 'it is best to run the test for a few different lag structures and make sure that the results are not sensitive to the choice of m (lag length)'.
4. There is a debate in the literature of econometrics on choosing the theory–driven or the data–driven approach as the appropriate methodology (see Leamer 1985 and Cooley and Le Roy 1985). Marin (1992, p.690) argues that both techniques seem not to be adequate for

testing theories, since "the former assumes that the model is true and makes the data consistent with it; while in the latter many models ... let the data "speak" themselves'.

5. A plot of time series prior to the estimation of the model indicated some time trend in the data, hence the data was de–seasonalised using the method of Pindyck and Rubinfeld (1991).
6. The data was de–seasonalised using the method of Pindyck and Rubinfeld (1991).
7. The results are not reported in this chapter. The ADF regression equation is: $\Delta Y_t = \alpha_0 + \alpha_1 Y_{t-1} + \alpha_2 t + \sum \gamma_j \Delta Y_{t-j} + \varepsilon_t$ where ε_t for $t = 1, ..., N$ is assumed to be Gaussian white noise. This equation is with constant and trend denoted by α_0 and α_2. The lag length was determined using AIC and SC.
8. Both AIC and SC minimised at the lag length = 6 (that is, VAR is 7).
9. Leamer (1978, 1983) has discussed the importance of the model selection and model search in his EBA analysis in which, he distinguishes between *free* and *doubtful* variables. He suggested the construction of a range or a bound for the estimates from a set of different combinations of free and doubtful variables. The smaller the bound, the more robust the estimates or *fragile* the inference will be.
10. In essence, it refers to inter–sectoral relations or potential inter–sectoral impacts within an economy, induced by input demand from a given industry in which FDI locates. Sun (1996) has calculated this index for FDI in China and concluded that first, FDI activities are concentrated in the industries with high backward linkage effects; second, such backward linkage effects were realised by FDI to a considerable extent and further, FDI in China 'induces and stimulates exports from the local firms through the backward linkage effects'(Sun 1996, p.23).

REFERENCES

Bahmani–Oskooee, M. and Alse, J., 1993. 'Export growth and economic growth: an application of cointegration and error correction modelling', *Journal of Developing Areas,* **27**, 535–42.
Bewley, R. and Yang, M., 1996. 'On the size and power of system tests for cointegration', in M. McAleer, P. Miller, and K. Leong (eds), *Proceedings of Econometric Society Australasian meeting 1996*, **3**, 1–20, Perth, Australia.
Cable, Vincent and Persaud, Bishnodat, 1987. 'New trends and policy problems in foreign investment: the experience of commonwealth countries', in V. Cable and B. Persaud (eds), *Developing with foreign investment*, Croom Helm, London, 45–67.
Chao, Chi–chur and Yu, E.S.H., 1994. 'Foreign capital inflows and welfare in an economy with imperfect competition', *Journal of Development Economics,* **45**, 141–54.
Chen, C., Chang, L. and Zhang, Y., 1995. 'The role of foreign direct investment in China's post–1978 economic development', *World Development*, **23(24)**, 691–703.
Chen, C.H., 1996. 'Regional determinants of foreign direct investment in mainland China', *Journal of Economic Studies*, **23**, 18–30.
Chenery, Hollis and Strout, W., 1966. 'Foreign assistance and economic development', *American Economic Review*, **66**, 679–733.
Cooley, T. and Le Roy, S., 1985. 'A theoretical macroeconometrics' *Journal of Monetary Economics*, **16**, 283–308.
de Mello, L.R., 1996. 'Foreign direct investment–led growth: evidence from time series and panel data', mimeo, Department of Economics, University of Kent at Canterbury.

de Mello, L.R. and Sinclair, M. Thea., 1995. 'Foreign direct investment, joint ventures, and endogenous growth', Mimeo, Department of Economics, University of Kent, UK.

Dowling, J.M. and Hiemenz, U., 1982. 'Aid, savings and growth in the Asian region', *The Developing Economies*, **21**, 3–13.

Dunning, J.H., 1970. *Studies in direct investment*, George Allen & Unwin, London.

Enders, W., 1995. *Applied econometric time series*, John Wiley & Sons, New York.

Granger, C.W.J., 1981. 'Some properties of time series data and their use in econometric model specification', *Journal of Econometrics*, **16**, 121–30.

Granger, C.W.J., 1988a. 'Some recent developments in the concept of causality', *Journal of Econometrics*, **39**, 199–211.

Granger, C.W.J., 1988b. 'Causality, cointegration, and control', *Journal of Econometric Dynamics and Control*, **12**, 551–9.

Graham, E.M. and Krugman, P.R., 1989. *Foreign direct investment in the United States*, Institute for International Economics, Washington, DC.

Greenaway, D., and Sapsford, D., 1994. 'What does liberalisation do for exports and growth?', *Weltwirtschaftliches Archives*, **130**, 152–74.

Gujarati, D., 1995. *Basic econometrics*, 3rd edition. McGraw–Hill, New York.

Gupta, K.N. and Islam, M., 1983. *Foreign capital, savings and growth: an international cross section study*, Reidel Publishing Company, Boston.

Ho, M.S. and Sorensen, B.E., 1996. 'Finding cointegration rank in high dimensional systems using the Johansen test – an illustration using data based on Monte Carlo simulations', *Review of Economics and Statistics,* **78**, 726–32.

Johansen, S., 1988. 'Statistical analysis of cointegration vectors', *Journal of Economic Dynamics and Control*, **112**, 231–54.

Johansen, S. and Juselius, K., 1990. 'Maximum likelihood estimation and inference on cointegration – with applications to the demand for money', *Oxford Bulletin of Economics and Statistics*, **52**, 169–210.

Karikari, J.A., 1992. 'Causality between direct foreign investment and economic output in Ghana', *Journal of Economic Development*, **17**, 7–17.

Kasibhatla, K and Sawhney, B., 1996. 'Foreign direct investment and economic growth in the U.S.: evidence from co–integration and Granger causality tests', *Rivista Internazionale di Scienze Economiche e Comerciali*, **43(2)**, 411–20.

Kholdy, S., 1995. 'Causality between foreign investment and spillover efficiency', *Applied Economics*, **27**, 74–749.

Krueger, A.O., 1987. 'Debt, capital flows and LDC Growth', *American Economic Review*, **13**, 159–64.

Kueh, Y.Y., 1992. 'Foreign investment and economic change in China', *China Quarterly*, **132**, 637–89.

Leamer, E., 1978. *Specification searches: ad hoc inference with nonexperimental data*, John Wiley & Sons, New York.

Leamer, E., 1983. 'Reporting the fragility of regression estimates', *Review of Economics and Statistics*, **65**, 306–17.

Leamer, E., 1985. 'Vector autoregressives for causal inference?', *Carnegie Rochester Conference Series on Public Policy*, **22**, 255–304.

Lee, J., 1994. 'Regional differences in the impact of the open–door policy on income growth in China', *Journal of Economic Development*, **19(1)**, 215–33.

Lee, J. and Rana, P., 1986. 'The effect of foreign capital inflows on developing countries of Asia', *Asian Development Bank Economic Staff Paper*, 4.

Lin, A, 1995. 'Trade effects of foreign direct investment: evidence for Taiwan with four ASEAN countries', *Weltwirtschaftliches Archiv*, **131(4)**, 737–47.

Marin, D., 1992. 'Is the export–led hypothesis valid for industrialised countries?', *Review of Economics and Statistics*, **74**, 678–87.

Mosconi, R. and Giannini, C., 1992. 'No–causality in cointegrated systems: representation, estimation and testing', *Oxford Bulletin of Economics and Statistics*, **54**, 399–417.

O'Sullivan, P. and Geyikdagi, Y., 1994. 'Japanese direct investment in the United States', *Rivista Internazionale di Scienze Economiche e Commerciali*, **9(41)**, 761–73.

Pfaffermayr, M., 1994. 'Foreign direct investment and exports: a time series approach', *Applied Economics*, **26**, 337–51.

Pindyck, R.S. and Rubinfeld, D.L., 1991. *Econometric models and economic forecasts*, McGraw–Hill, New York.

Plummer, M. and M.F. Montes, 1995. 'Direct foreign investment in China: an introduction', in Sumner J. La Croix, M. Plummer and K. Lee (eds), *Emerging patterns of East Asian investment in China, from Korea, Taiwan and Hong Kong*, M.E. Sharpe, Armonk, New York.

Pomfret, Richard, 1991. *Investing in China: ten years of the open door policy*, Iowa State University Press, Ames, Iowa.

Rambaldi, A.N. and Doran, H.E., 1996. 'Testing for Granger non–causality in cointegrated systems made easy', *Working Papers in Econometrics and Applied Statistics*, No.88, Department of Econometrics, University of New England.

Riezman, R., Whiteman, C.H. and Summers, P.M., 1996. 'The engine of growth or its handmaiden? A time–series assessment of export–led growth', *Empirical Economics*, **21**, 77–110.

Root, A. and Ahmed, A., 1978. 'The influence of policy instruments on manufacturing direct foreign investment in developing countries', *Journal of International Business Studies*, **9**, 81–93.

Rugman, A., 1994. *Foreign investment and NAFTA*, University of South Carolina Press, Columbia.

Saltz, I.S., 1992. 'The negative correlation between foreign direct investment and economic growth in the third world: theory and evidence', *Rivista Internationale di Scienze Economiche e Commerciali*, **7(39)**, 617–33.

Scaperlanda, A.E. and Mauer, L.J., 1969. 'The determinants of U.S. direct investment in the E.E.C', *American Economic Review*, **59**, 558–68.

Snyder, D., 1990. 'Foreign aid and domestic savings: A spurious correlation', *Economic Development and Culture Change*, **45**, 175–81.

Sun, H., 1996. 'Direct foreign investment and linkage effects: the experience of China', *Asian Economies*, **25**, 1–28.

Toda, H.Y. and Phillips, P.C.B., 1993. 'Vector autoregressions and causality', *Econometrica*, **61**, 1367–93.

Toda, H. Y. and Yamamoto, T., 1995. 'Statistical inference in vector autoregressions with possibly integrated processes', *Journal of Econometrics*, **66**, 225–50.

Todaro, M., 1982. *Economics for a developing world*, 2nd edition, Longman, London.

Tsai, P.L., 1994. 'Determinants of foreign direct investment and its impact on economic growth', *Journal of Economic Development*, **19(1)**, 137–63.

United Nations, 1993. *Foreign investment and trade linkages in developing countries*, New York.

Vernon, R., 1971. *Sovereignty at bay: the multinational spread of O.S. enterprises*, Basic Books, New York.

Wang, Z.Q. and Swain, N., 1995. 'The determinants of foreign direct investments in transforming economics: empirical evidence from Hungry and China', *Weltwirtschaftliches Archiv*, **131**, 358–82.

Wei, S., 1996. 'Foreign direct investment in China: sources and consequences', in T. Ho and A. Krueger (eds.), *Financial deregulation and integration in East Asia*, University of Chicago Press, Chicago, 77–105.

White, H., 1992a. 'The macroeconomic impacts of development aid: critical survey', *Journal of Development Studies*, **28(2)**, 163–240.

White, H., 1992b. 'What do we know about aid's macroeconomic impacts? An overview of the aid effectiveness debate', *Journal of International Development*, **4(2)**, 121–37.

World Bank, 1993. *East Asia miracle: economic growth and public policy*, Oxford University Press, London.

Zapata, H.O. and Rambaldi, A.N., 1997. 'Monte Carlo evidence on cointegration and causation', *Oxford Bulletin of Economics and Statistics*, **59**, 285–98.

Zhang, Z., 1995. 'International trade and foreign investment: further evidence from China', *Asian Economic Journal*, **23**, 23–56.

PART III

Foreign Direct Investment and Regional
Economies

(China)

R1 ♯

F21 815

8. Changing Patterns of FDI in Shanghai

P33

Gary Tian

INTRODUCTION

There are two main types of foreign–invested enterprises (FIEs) in China: the cost–reduction–oriented type and the market–oriented type. Typically, the first type characterises investment in small–scale, labour–intensive industries. They import the equipment and key raw materials, process them in China using Chinese workers, and export to the overseas market. The second type of investment targets China's domestic market. Most of them are large or medium–sized enterprises holding specific technological advantages (Kim 1995, pp.208–9). The small export FIEs are considered to be better suited to capitalizing on major aspects of China's comparative advantage, that is abundant labour, which is the success of FDI flowing into China (Pomfret 1991). These projects are easy to set up, avoid expensive and lengthy negotiations, involve quick returns, and can be readily terminated (Shapiro et al. 1991, p. 29). In addition to its proximity and cultural similarity to Hong Kong, the success in attracting foreign direct investment (FDI) in South China depends largely on its inflow of the capital from Hong Kong and other newly industrialising economy (NIE) investors, the majority of which own small export FIEs. Another similar issue is one concerning the nationality of FDI in China. In particular, it is argued that, compared with US investors and other Western investors, Japanese direct investments have concentrated on labour–intensive, export–oriented, low–technology projects and have remained quite small compared with Japan's large share of China's total trade. In this chapter we shall look at these issues in the case of Shanghai.

In recent years FDI in Shanghai has grown very quickly, following the implementation there of the Pudong policy.[1] In 1994, Shanghai once more became the second largest place for attracting FDI (Guangdong is the largest). One of the primary reasons for this change is that multinational corporations (MNCs) have increasingly concentrated their investment in

Shanghai's capital or skill–intensive manufacturing and service sectors.[2] In comparison with the other coastal provinces where most FDIs are located in labour–intensive sectors to exploit Chinese cheaper labour, is FDI in Shanghai driven more by a motive of accessing the domestic Chinese market by transferring advanced technology and/or the global division of labour? What is the cause of the success of MNCs in the city? Is it Shanghai's dynamic comparative advantage (brought about by the more comprehensive nature of industrial structure, the larger number of research institutes and universities and the larger size of its skilled labour pool), or its more biased policy which favours these MNCs' activities over activities in other coastal regions? Does the success of MNCs' market–oriented activities in Shanghai suggest that the 'firm–specific asset' (FSA)[3] theory is more useful in explaining the pattern of FDI in Shanghai than in most other regions in China where FDI is small scale, and the largest investors are from the NIEs.[4] Then what is the economic cost and benefit for these MNCs' activities in China?

The organisation of this chapter is as follows. Recent trends and major characteristics of FDI in Shanghai are examined first. The major features and contributions of FDI in manufacturing to Shanghai's technology improvement, expansion of exports and changes in commodity composition are then investigated. This is followed by an evaluation of the performance of capital–intensive and labour–intensive FIEs in Shanghai and discussions about policy implications.

SECTORAL DISTRIBUTION

Policy Shift

Shanghai emerged as a major centre for attracting FDI after 1984 when the announcement of the 14 open coastal cities policy presaged the spread of special economic zone (SEZ) conditions to Shanghai and other areas.[5] China's investment environment was also improved by the introduction of more relevant laws and regulations.[6] FDI boomed in the city in 1984 and was further driven by the overheated domestic economy in 1985 (see Table 8.1).

During the investment boom period 1984–88, the pattern of sectoral distribution of FDI started to shift its focus from manufacturing to the service sector in Shanghai. The service sectors in which foreigners were allowed to invest at that time included only some real estate (mainly hotels), tourism facilities, commerce and the catering industry. Hotels were es–

Table 8.1   Shanghai: contracted and actual FDI, 1980–94

	Number of projects	Contracted FDI			Actual FDI		Realiza– tion ratio (%)
		Value (US$m)	Size	Annual growth rate (%)	Value (US$m)	Annual growth rate (%)	
1980–83	17	113.7	6.7	n.a.	17	n.a.	15.0
1984	41	389.1	9.5	427	28.3	66	7.3
1985	94	710.8	7.6	83	62.4	120	8.8
1986	62	297.4	4.8	–58	97.5	56	32.8
1987	76	246.6	3.2	–17	212	117	86.0
1988	219	333.3	1.5	35	364	72	109.3
1989	199	360.0	1.8	8	422	16	117.2
1990	201	375.0	1.9	4	177	–58	47.2
1991	365	450.0	1.2	20	175	–1	38.9
1992	2,014	3,357.0	1.7	646	1,259	619	37.5
1993	3,650	7,016.0	1.9	109	2,318	293	33.1
1994	3,803	10,025.8	2.6	42.9	2,623	13	26.2

Sources: 1980 from *Shanghai Shi Duiwai Jingji Tongji Nianjian* (*Foreign Economic Statistical Yearbook of Shanghai*) (EC 1949–88, pp.153–4). 1989 figures from EC (1985, 1992, 1993, 1994). 1994 figures from *Xinwenbao*, 6 February 1995.

pecially encouraged by the Chinese officials because they found that accommodation facilities had to be improved to attract foreign business people to China before a further inflow of FDI could be expected. Foreign partners preferred investing in these service sectors, and particularly in hotels, because as long as the projections proved sound, receipts would be in foreign currency, and consequently profit repatriation was not hampered by the yuan's inconvertibility.

The share of foreign–based projects in hotels in Shanghai's total contract FDI rose sharply from 51.1 per cent in 1984 to 92.7 per cent in 1985. This figure still remained as high as 79.9 per cent in 1986 and then fell to 42.4 per cent in 1987, 35.8 per cent in 1988 and 43.5 per cent in 1989. The lag of the rate of inflow into manufacturing projects was improved by the different equity ratio of foreign funds/Chinese funds as between manufacturing projects and hotel projects. In manufacturing projects, by mid–1987, the equity ratio of foreign funds/Chinese funds was 1.23:1, while in hotel projects the ratio was 5.66:1.

The upward trend reversed itself sharply in 1986. The sharp decline in 1986 can be attributed to a number of factors. First, Chinese domestic austerity policies had been introduced to curb the 'overheated' economy after the second half of 1985. As a result, the authorities began screening new investments more tightly. Access to imports by domestic enterprises and FIEs was also tightened. Second, there were serious problems associated with investment in Shanghai after the euphoria of 1984 and the first half of 1985. These problems included high costs, price gouging, low levels of productive labour, exchange controls, limited domestic market access and excessive government bureaucracy. The most dramatic confrontation of 1985 had been over joint ventures (especially in the case of technologically advanced enterprises (TAEs)) where there were foreign exchange problems.[7] As a result, on an approval basis, the FDI in Shanghai fell from US$712 million in 1985 to US$297 million in 1986, a 58 per cent reduction. Even during the boom time, as early as 1984–85, the city experienced a very low realisation ratio (between contractual commitments and investment realised): 7.3 per cent in 1984 and 8.8 per cent in 1985, which was even lower than the 15 per cent realised in the initial period 1980–83 (when large–scale manufacturing projects, which would usually take a longer negotiation period, were mainly implemented).

In response to the decline in FDI, the State Council issued the 22 Articles, which allowed foreign exchange swap centres to be set up in Shanghai and Shenzhen in 1987, adding another alternative to foreign exchange constrained joint ventures, especially to those in the manufacturing sector.[8] Investment opportunities for foreigners were further broadened by allowing their products to be *partially* sold in the domestic market in order to attract TAEs (so called 'swapping market for technology strategy').

Beyond the 22 Articles, Shanghai offered additional incentives for foreign investors by issuing its local 16 article provisions supplementing the national legislation. These local provisions extended the national tax exemptions by up to a further three years, reduced land–use charges, guaranteed priority delivery of urban services for the same price paid by state enterprises, and promised another set of preferential treatments for enterprises operating in Shanghai's three economic technical development zones (ETDZs): Minhang, Hongqiao and Caohejing. China's top economic and technological planners have promoted the creation of high–technology zones (the Caojejing microelectronics zone in the case of Shanghai) in the belief that a technologically advanced economy depends on spatial concentration.[9] The changes in the national FDI policy and local attitudes also accounted for the reduction of the drawbacks referred to earlier, especially in removing most of the bureaucratic obstacles which made small export–oriented investments appear to be not worth the effort (Pomfret 1991). These export–oriented projects are typical of the SEZs and the Pearl

River Delta region in the earlier years.[10] The major purpose of these policy shifts was to increase the competitiveness of manufactured goods, to expand exports and to implement import substitution by attracting foreign capital and technology.

By contrast, the government has become more selective in its approval of service activities since then. The move away from service projects was strengthened in late 1988, when the national austerity programme was extended to cover some joint ventures, while the slowdown of hotel occupancy presented another problem.[11] Further changes in China's official attitude to FDI which have taken place relate to the removal of a fixed duration for joint ventures and acceptance of wholly foreign–owned enterprises (WFEs). In addition, towards the end of the 1980s, the rising domestic labour costs and the real appreciation of currencies in the newly industrialising Asian economies, such as Taiwan and Korea, played a significant role in attracting FDI flows into China and Shanghai as well.[12] All of these changes resulted in both a very fast growth rate of FDI on an actual basis and an increase in the proportion of FDI flowing to manufacturing projects after 1986 (Table 8.2). Also, Shanghai experienced a sharply increasing trend in the realization ratio from a very small base during 1980–85 to 32.8 per cent in 1986 and further to 86 per cent in 1987. This figure rose again, to 109 per cent in 1988 and 117 per cent in 1989 when the environment was further improved. Disrupted by the Tiananmen Square Event and the later implementation of the economic austerity policy, on an actual basis, the FDI in Shanghai fell from US$422 million in 1989 to US$177 in 1990, representing a 58 per cent reduction in that year.[13]

The Central government's decision to develop the Pudong new area and promulgation of an amended law on Sino–foreign joint ventures in April 1990 markedly improved the investment environment in Shanghai.[14] In 1992, Shanghai, together with Beijing, Tianjin, Guangzhou, Dalian, Qiandao and the SEZs, was granted rights to open more tertiary industries to foreign investors. In the service sector these included finance, insurance, land rent, retail, wholesale sectors, telecommunications and so on. These industries were initially monopolized by the state–owned enterprises because they were regarded as the arterial industries which have important impacts on the whole economy of China. This was partly due to economic consideration because these industries, especially wholesale and retailing, are highly profitable in China.

In addition to the opening of the service sector, FDI in the six priority industrial sectors has been particularly encouraged since the 1990s when Shanghai began shifting to high–tech and capital–intensive industries by selecting six industries as its pillar industries of the eighth Five–year Plan (1991–96). These six industries included iron and steel, automobiles, tele–

Table 8.2 Shanghai: contracted FDI by sector, 1980–94

	1980–83	1984	1985	1986	1987	1988	1989	1990	1991	1992	1993	1994
Agriculture												
Contracted	0	0.5	0.2	0.0	0.0	4.1	1.6	0	10.2	1.6	5.4	12.9
Growth (100%)	n.a.	n.a.	-0.6	-1.0	n.a.	n.a.	-1.0	-1.0	n.a.	-0.8	2.4	1.4
Number	0	1	2	0	0	3	3	0	4	6	21	19
Size	n.a.	0.5	0.1	n.a.	n.a.	1.4	0.0	n.a.	2.6	0.3	0.3	0.7
% of total value	0	0	0	0	0	1	1	0	2	1	0	0
Construction												
Contracted	0	9.2	3.4	0.0	0.9	0.1	0.1	0.3	0.2	27	104.2	105.6
Growth (100%)	n.a.	n.a.	-0.6	-1.0	n.a.	-1.0	85.0	-1.0	-0.3	134	2.9	0
Number	0	6	9	0	4	1	1	1	2	77	162	197
Size	n.a.	1.5	0.4	n.a.	22.5	0.1	8.6	0.3	0.1	2.9	0.6	0.5
% of total value	0	2	0	0	0	0	0	0	0	1	1.5	1

Manufacturing											
Contracted	99.4	175.5	32.5	52.3	115.6	199.3	181.2	359.6	338.3	1781.3	2387.1	3671.8
Growth (100%)	n.a.	1.4	-0.8	0.6	1.2	0.7	0.2	0.5	-0.1	4.3	0.3	0.5
Number	10	15	41	40	52	196	174	188	331	1,600	2,427	2503
Size	9.9	11.7	0.8	1.3	2.2	1.0	1.4	1.9	1.0	1.1	1.0	1.5
% of total value	79	45	5	18	47	60	50	96	75	53	34	36.6

Tertiary industry											
Contracted	14.5	203.9	674.8	245.2	130.1	129.8	176.9	14.8	101.4	1,547	4,520	6,236
Growth (100%)	n.a.	n.a.	2.3	-0.6	-0.5	0.0	0.9	-0.9	5.9	14.3	1.9	0.4
Number	7	19	42	22	20	19	21	12	28	320	1,040	1,101
Size	2.1	10.7	16.1	11.1	6.5	6.8	8.4	1.2	3.6	4.8	4.3	5.7
% of total value	11	52	95	80	45	39	49	4	23	46	64	62

Note: Agriculture refers to primary industry in China, while secondary industry includes building and manufacturing sectors.

Sources: Data are from Shanghai Statistical Bureau (various issues) and EC (various issues).

communications and household electrical appliances. These six pillar industries manufactured 120 billion yuan–worth of products, earned 144 billion yuan from sales and generated 25 billion yuan in profits and taxes in 1994, or 36 per cent, 45 per cent and 55 per cent of Shanghai's total products, sales and profits and taxes, respectively. This change in sectoral distribution indicates the dramatic policy shift from a focus on industrial production during 1986–91 to a focus on both industrial production and a more open service sector.

Outcome

The purpose of this new move was to utilize foreign capital specifically to improve Shanghai's infrastructure and tertiary sector. This was necessitated by fast industrial growth in the early 1990s which caused infrastructure to become a serious bottleneck to further economic development. In addition, Shanghai, as the most important city, is still lagging behind in the development of its service sector, even compared with other Asian countries, with a 33.2 per cent relative share in the city's GDP in 1992. (This figure is, of course, much larger than the 18.6 per cent in 1978 when the reform started.) The focus on infrastructure and the tertiary sector followed the consensus by Chinese governments that development of the service industries is the key to building the city into an economic, financial and trade centre in China. Shanghai's mushrooming service industry has in turn become a new boom area for overseas investment since 1992.

In recent years, foreign investment in service industries has surpassed that in the secondary industries. Moreover, the overseas investment has expanded to about 30 sectors of the service industries, including banking, real estate, advertising, culture, recreation, information consultation, catering, design, decoration, education and health care.[15] The sectoral distribution of FDI within the service sector, therefore, has been changed since then. On an approval basis, although the share of FDI in real estate in total FDI in the service sector rose again from 20 per cent in 1990 to 76 per cent in 1993 (Table 8.3), the rapid increase was attributed as much to an increase in the investment in land lease as to office and hotel projects. This pattern can be compared with the situation during the period up to 1990 when 98 per cent of FDI in real estate in Shanghai was allocated to hotel projects. The most significant phenomenon is a jump of FDI in finance and insurance from a very low base in 1990 to US$519.6 million in 1993, representing a share of 11.5 per cent of total FDI in the service sector in the city in 1993 (Table 8.3). Thirty foreign financial institutions had set up branches in Shanghai by the end of October 1994, some 20 of them ranking among the 50 largest in the world. These banks have promoted the

Table 8.3 *Shanghai: contracted FDI in service industry, 1980–93 (US$ million)*

	1980–89	1990	1991	1992	1993
Transport, communi–cation and posts	16.0 (1%)	0.4 (2.7%)	9.9 (9.8%)	36.4 (2.4%)	42.7 (1%)
Commercial and catering	11.8 (1%)	10.0 (67.6%)	3.0 (3%)	104.1 (6.7%)	432.0 (9.6%)
Real estate, public utilities**	1,564.0 (96%)	2.9 (20%)	63.3 (62%)	1,298.2 (84%)	3,411.2 (76%)
Hygiene, sports	n.a.	n.a.	5.1 (5%)	15.9 (1%)	31.7 (1%)
Education, culture	n.a.	n.a.	0 (0%)	2.5 (0%)	4.4 (0%)
Science, technology	n.a.	n.a.	0.1 (0%)	1.7 (0%)	4.1 (0%)
Finance, insurance and others	34.6* (2%)	1.5* (1.5%)	20.1 (20%)	88.8 (6%)	519.6 (12%)
Total	1,626.4	14.8	101.4	1,547.6	4,519.5

Notes
* Denotes these figures actually include FDI in hygiene, sports, education, culture, science and technology only. FDIs in finance and insurance were allowed to be invested only after 1991.
** Public utility in service sector includes gas, electricity, sewage and so on.

Sources: EC (1990, p.109), EC (1985, p.84), EG (1992, p.170), EG (1993, p.116), EG (1994, p.222).

introduction of overseas investment in China. The loans from banks for basic infrastructure development in the city is estimated to have topped US$250 million in 1994, compared with US$100 million to US$150 million in the previous two years. Also, some branch banks from Japan introduced companies from their country to invest in Shanghai in a bid to develop their own clients.[16]

The commercial and catering sectors are other areas in which FIEs grew very fast during recent years in Shanghai. Among commercial and catering sectors, the retail and wholesale sector in the city became a boom area for foreign investors after late 1992. Yaohan International, a Japanese retailer with headquarters in Hong Kong, was the first retailer to win State Council approval for a huge complex in Pudong with the Shanghai Number One Department Store, China's largest store (in terms of sales volume) to date. The store, to be jointly operated by the two partners, was scheduled to open at the end of 1995. In the legal agreements constituting this project, the Japanese party was granted the right to import goods from overseas by China's Central government. Imported products can constitute up to 30 per cent of the goods sold in the new department store. Other State Council–approved projects include a joint venture between the China Resources Group of Hong Kong and the Shanghai Hualian Shopping Centre, China's number four store.

The objective of the policy of the liberalization of the retail sector is to improve the lives of the Chinese people through efficient and profitable investment and to meet the needs for imported products which resulted from a dramatic rise in the purchasing power of its residents in big cities following the reform. This is particularly true for Shanghai because until recently it was more difficult to access imported luxury goods than in other cities, especially those in southern China.[17] The narrowing of these disparities in prices and access to imported consumer goods for Shanghai by liberalizing the retail sectors in major cities to FDI will allow resources to be distributed more efficiently within China.

As a result of faster growth of FDI in service sectors after 1991, on an actual basis, FDI in services accounted for 45 per cent of total FDI, which is close to that of FDI in manufacturing which accounted for 54 per cent of total FDI up to the end of 1993. The use of overseas investment has improved the city's whole industrial structure. The gross national product of the service industries accounted for 40 per cent of the total in 1994 compared with 33 per cent in 1992.

Along with the change in sectoral distribution of FDI in the city, the years after 1992 also saw a second boom of FDI inflows into Shanghai. On an approval basis, FDI jumped more than 15 times between 1991 and 1993, that is, from US$450 million to US$7,016 million. In 1994, FDI in Shanghai still *grew* fast (by 43 per cent) in comparison to an overall *decline* of FDI in the country as a whole (by 26 per cent, *The Age*, 8 April 1995). However, in common with the country as a whole, FDI in Shanghai has also experienced a declining trend in the realisation ratio (actual value/approval value) since the early 1990s.[18] By comparison, the realisation ratios of both Hong Kong and Taiwan are lower than that of any Western investor. The realisation ratios for Hong Kong and Taiwan are 29 per cent and 14 per cent, respectively. These figures are much smaller than those for the US (56 per cent), Japan (47 per cent) or Germany (100 per cent). The city municipality has revoked the business licences of over 140 FIEs since late 1994, as their capital funds failed to arrive long after registration.[19] A new system to strengthen the supervision of the arrival of foreign capital for enterprises

was established by the Municipal Foreign Investment Management Committee and the Municipal Industrial and Commercial Administration in
order to crack down on enterprises involved in illegal or illicit business
activities.

Furthermore, there still remained a low rate of inflow of FDI into the
priority areas in Shanghai (such as infrastructure construction, transport,
communication/postal, education/culture and science/technology) up to the
date of this publication. In addition, worsening pollution and ecological
damage have become major obstacles to Shanghai's further economic
growth and the plan for it to become a multi–functional international city.
The upgrade of the above facilities has been largely dependent on borrowing
external loans, permitted since the reform. This high risk sphere of
economic activity needs relatively large amounts of investment, and with a
lower rate of return in the short term it faces some difficulty in covering its
foreign exchange expenses. By contrast, FDI is largely concentrated on
hotels, land leasing and offices where, to some extent, the investment has
been driven by speculation, especially during 1993.

Therefore, in early 1995, government policy concerning FDI was
formulated to work in two ways. On the one hand FDI in real estate has been
brought under control on a national level. Building affordable housing
rather than the construction of luxury buildings will be encouraged by a new
policy, in order to prevent the consumer service facilities from growing too
fast.[20] Although the city municipality temporarily stopped approving further
luxury building projects, the service industry in general in the city is still a
big magnet for overseas investment.[21] There will still be a huge demand for
luxury buildings, because the office space (0.5 million square metres) in
Shanghai is still much smaller than that in Tokyo (60m), New York (50m),
Hong Kong (6.9m) and Singapore (6m). On the other hand, the Central
government introduced more preferential policies for FDI in the basic
infrastructure projects in April 1995. These policies include offering low–
interest loans to foreign investors in the basic infrastructure project areas
such as agriculture, transportation and energy; first 5 years of tax
exemption; and 50 per cent reduction in taxation for the next 5 years (5/5)
(compared to 2/3 for other ventures) for those with at least 15 years of
operation in port construction.[22] In addition to these tax concessions, and
even more important, is further market liberalisation, which is necessary to
convince foreign investors that they can earn returns on massive infrastructure investments.

FDI IN THE MANUFACTURING SECTOR

Major Features of Shanghai's Manufacturing FIEs

Now let us have a close look at FDI in manufacturing in Shanghai by examining its scale and distribution of sectors, because the distribution of FDI in manufacturing provides a first approximation of where FDI's technology contribution takes place and its contribution to exports.

The average scale of FDI in Shanghai's manufacturing sector fell substantially from as high as US$10 million per project during 1980–83 to only US$1 million in 1988 (Table 8.2) and rose then to US$1.5 million in 1994.[23] Therefore, the gap in the scale of FDI between that in Shanghai and that in the country as a whole diminished after the mid–1980s.[24] The declining average FDI scale per project after the mid–1980s reflected the increased relative importance of small and medium–sized ventures in the manufacturing sector. This result also suggests the changes in local government's attitudes after the mid–1980s towards those small and medium–scaled enterprises which are usually export oriented.

However, because there is a bipolar distribution in the scale of FDI in Shanghai and its extent is greater than that in the country as whole, Shanghai's large–scale manufacturing FDI projects occupied a very important role in China. This has been particularly true since 1990 when more and more large MNC investments have been flowing into Shanghai. There are 281 projects funded by 142 world famous MNCs in Shanghai, such as AT&T, Dupont, Hitachi, Mitsubishi, Hochu, Siemens, Bell, Pilkington, Volkswagen and Philips (up to the end of October 1994). These MNC projects amounted to US$4,800 million which accounted for more than 20 per cent of total FDI in the city on a contractual basis.[25] The average scale of these projects contracted in 1994 is about US$20 million as compared with US$14 million in 1993 (SSSA 1994, p.70) and US$11 million on average during the period up to 1992 (SSSA 1993, p.115).

In Shanghai, FDI projects larger than US$100 million accounted for 81 per cent of national FDI in the same project size during the period up to the end of November 1994. The figures for FDI projects larger than US$50 million and US$20 million in the city were 56 per cent and 37 per cent, respectively, of the national total FDI in same–sized projects. The second important region is Beijing, which is followed by Guangdong, Liaoning, Zhejiang, Shandong and Fujiang (Table 8.4). It is clear that Shanghai has attracted more MNC activity, which is usually more technologically sophisticated, than elsewhere in China.

Within the manufacturing sector, the top four sectors include medical and pharmaceutical products, machinery, chemical products and electronic

*Table 8.4   Registered capital of top manufacturing FIEs by November
               1994*

	>US$100 million	>US$50 million	>US$20 million
Shanghai	563 (81.2)	662 (56)	839 (37)
Beijing	130 (18.8)	248 (21)	309 (14)
Guangdong	0 (0)	60 (5)	181 (8)
Liaoning	0 (0)	52 (4)	163 (7)
Zhejiang	0 (0)	0 (0)	128 (6)
Shandong	0 (0)	108 (9)	108 (5)
Fujian	0 (0)	0 (0)	91 (4)
Others	0 (0)	50 (4)	377 (15)
China total	693 (100)	1,180 (100)	2,196 (100)

Note: The figures in the brackets are percentage shares of total national FDI at the same size projects.

Sources: *Asian Wall Street Journal*, 22 November 1994, *Doing Business with China*, published by Kogan Page Ltd., London, 1994.

equipment products. All these industries are either human capital–intensive or physical capital–intensive industries. If all the industries are grouped by factor intensity, FDI in industries which are human capital–intensive ranked first, with US$1,068 million up to the end of 1993, or 62 per cent of total actual FDI in the city. FDI in labour–intensive industries ranked second with US$1,172 million, or 42 per cent of total actual FDI followed by FDI in physical capital–intensive industries. Table 8.5 also tells us that the average size of physical capital–intensive industries is the highest, followed by that of human capital–intensive and labour–intensive industries, in accordance with traditional wisdom. Therefore, it can be said that more FDI in Shanghai has taken place in capital–intensive industries (especially human capital–intensive industries) than in labour–intensive industries. This pattern of the sectoral distribution of FDI is quite different from that of the country in general and southern Chinese provinces in particular, where most FDI is located in labour–intensive, export–oriented sectors in order to exploit cheap Chinese labour.

Sources of FDI in Shanghai

Since 1987, Hong Kong has been the largest investor in Shanghai (Table 8.6).[26] On an actual basis, during the period up to the end of 1993, Hong Kong still ranked first but with a relatively lower percentage share of the total value (40 per cent) followed by the US (per cent), Japan (11 per cent), Germany (5 per cent), Switzerland (3 per cent) and then Taiwan and Singapore (2 per cent each).

Table 8.5   Sectoral distribution of FDI in Shanghai's manufacture by 1993*

	No. of cases	Approval (US$m)	Scale	Actual (US$m)	Share (actual)
Manufacturing total	5,081	5,648.5	1.11	2,776	100.0
Labour intensive					
Textile manufacture	270	330.5	1.22	262.3	9.4
Clothing	790	394.4	0.50	242.6	8.7
Leather and fur manufacture	192	94.6	0.49	47.3	1.7
Cultural, education and sports materials	194	152.4	0.79	94.4	3.4
Arts and crafts	149	80.6	0.54	44.5	1.6
Rubber and plastic manufacture	407	546.3	1.34	265.1	9.5
Building materials and other non–metal goods	145	218.1	1.50	95.7	3.5
Metal products	384	463.5	1.21	120.2	4.3
Total	2,531	2,280.4	0.95	1,172.1	42.2
Human capital intensive					
Medical and pharmaceutical industry	90	111.3	1.24	71.7	25.9
Machinery	313	487.7	1.56	373.7	13.5
Transportation equipment	94	254	2.70	163.1	5.9
Electric equipment	255	212.8	0.83	312.3	11.2
Electronic and telecommunication equipment	553	654.3	1.18	123.3	4.4
Instruments, meters and other equipment	102	81.7	0.80	24.2	0.9
Total	1,407	1,801.8	1.39	1,068.3	61.8
Physical capital intensive					
Chemical industry	282	556.3	1.97	366.8	13.2
Chemical fibres	49	105.4	2.15	16.8	0.6
Total	331	661.7	2.06	383.6	13.8

Note: * The sectoral distribution and industries are classified by factor intensity in accordance with Zhang (1991, p. 131).

Sources: Calculated from EG (1994, pp. 216–8).

Table 8.6   Shanghai: contracted and utilised FDI by major sources and
              size, 1985–94

	1985	1986	1987	1988–91	1992	1993	1994
Hong Kong							
Contracted	206.2	19.8	122.3	447.8	1,765.1	4,337.8	6,424
% of total	29	7	50	29.5	53	61.8	64.1
Number	52	17	34	488	1,036	1718	1,596
Size	4.0	1.2	3.6	0.9	1.7	2.5	4.0
Actual	n.a.	n.a.	27.9	351.7	338.3	9248	n.a.
United States							
Contracted	283.8	158.22	55.95	238.7	303.0	598.6	521
% of total	40	53	23	15.7	9	8.5	5.2
Number	14	10	10	115	241	467	453
Size	20.3	15.8	5.6	2.1	1.3	1.3	1.2
Actual	n.a.	n.a.	41.8	175.7	85.8	613.6	n.a.
Japan							
Contracted	148	7.95	5.7	310.2	281.2	370.2	688
% of total	21	3	2	20.4	8.4	5.3	6.9
Number	15	10	13	134	163	298	476
Size	9.9	0.8	0.4	2.3	1.7	1.2	1.4
Actual	n.a.	n.a.	28.2	322	55.6	175.7	n.a.
Germany							
Contracted	0.7	1.8	2.7	33.02	13.7	57.9	n.a.
% of total	0	1	1	2.2	0.4	0.8	n.a.
Number	1	2	1	7	6	2.5	n.a.
Size	0.7	0.9	2.7	4.7	2.3	2.3	n.a.
Actual	n.a.	n.a.	n.a.	23.5	109.6	50.7	n.a.
Taiwan							
Contracted	0	0	0	143.2	250.6	530.0	463.3
% of total	0	0	0	9.4	7.5	7.6	4.6%
Number	0	0	0	102	302	604	574
Size	n.a.	n.a.	n.a.	1.4	0.8	1.0	0.8
Actual	0	0	0	12	18.0	94.8	n.a.

	1985	1986	1987	1988–91	1992	1993	1994
Singapore							
Contracted	n.a.	36.6	12.81	30.06	115.9	175.5	n.a.
% of total	0	12	5	2.0	3.5	2.5	n.a.
Number	0	6	4	24	38	108	n.a.
Size	n.a.	6.1	3.2	1.3	3	1.6	n.a.
Actual	n.a.	n.a.	1.5	47.5	7.7	53.9	n.a.

Notes: 1994 figures are estimated from the data to the end of November 1994 (from *Shanghai External Economic Monthly Statistics,* November 1994 published by Shanghai Statistics Bureau). The figures for Germany refer to West Germany before 1990. The figure of cumulative capital for West Germany both contracted and utilized (1980–92) refers to the combination of cumulative figures for West Germany between 1980 and 1989 and Germany between 1990 and 1992.

Sources: Shanghai Statistical Bureau (various issues), 1992 figures from EC (1993, pp.55–62), 1993 figures from EG (1994, p.220).

Based on approximate figures, the average scale of FDI projects in manufacturing by Germany (US$4.7 million per case), Japan (US$2.3 million) and the US (US$2.1 million) were all larger than those of Hong Kong (US$0.9 million), Taiwan (US$1.4 million) and Singapore (US$1.3 million) during the period between 1988 and 1991.[27] Because the rise in the scale of Hong Kong's projects was caused mainly by its heavy investment in the Shanghai's service sectors with large–scale items during 1992–94, the distribution of scale within the manufacturing sector by Hong Kong after 1991 could remain the same as the period before 1991.

Let us have a further look at the type of FIEs by nationality. By the end of 1992 the US, Western European and Japanese ventures dominated the 112 TAEs in the city: the US accounted for 39 per cent of total TAE cases; Western European countries for 21 per cent and Japan for 13 per cent. Hong Kong alone had significant commitments in the export enterprises (EEs) category. Its 661 EEs accounted for half of the total EE projects in the city (Table 8.7). The percentage share of Western investors in TAE investment on a capital basis will be larger than that based on number if it is available because the average scale of Western investors is larger than that of Hong Kong and other Asian countries. The statistics also show that 90 per cent of the investment in Shanghai by MNCs came from the US, Japan and Europe in Shanghai.[28] In other words, many Organisation for Economic and Co–operative (OECD) companies which invest in Shanghai are MNCs.

It is clear that Western European and American, and to a lesser extent Japanese, investors emphasized larger projects in manufacturing, while most

Table 8.7   Distribution of FDI projects in TAEs and EEs in Shanghai, 1980–92

Source	TAEs		EEs	
	No. of projects	Per cent of total	No. of projects	Per cent of total
Hong Kong	19	17.0	661	49.8
Japan	15	13.4	171	12.9
United States	44	39.3	134	10.1
Western European countries	23	20.5	33	2.5
Other countries	11	9.8	329	24.8
Total TAEs/EEs	112	100	1328	100

Note: TAEs stands for technologically advanced enterprises and EEs stands for export enterprises.

Source: SSSA (1993, p.114).

investment from Hong Kong and other Asian countries tended to be in small or medium–sized manufacturing projects which were export oriented using low–level technology which had already succeeded in their sourcing countries and regions, or otherwise it was concentrated in real estate and service industries in Shanghai.

It used to be a heated issue that the US and Western European firms were more aggressive towards the Shanghai market in contrast to Japanese conservatism. The former invested in more large–scale projects than the latter, especially during the period before 1988.[29] It may be true that unlike Western investors who feel they must manufacture in China in order to gain access to the domestic market, the Japanese have been able to avoid investing because they have been so successful in exporting to China. The success of Japanese exporting was due to, among other things, Japan's linguistic, cultural and geographic proximity to China, and an abundance of credit and concessionary financing, which was typically tied to the purchase of Japanese products (Westendorff 1989). This argument is based mainly on the assumption that if China had not depended on such large Japanese hardware imports (by high tariffs and so on), Japanese firms would have increased their manufacturing investment in China. The case of the Association of Southeast Asian Nations (ASEAN) countries is a good example. Even before the mid–1980s, most Japanese manufacturers relocating to ASEAN countries were final producers assembling for the local market because of high import tariffs imposed by these host countries.

From the latter half of 1986, as the Japanese yen continued to appreciate and wage rates were allowed to rise, Japan no longer possessed a comparative advantage in the manufacture of many items which had generated her export revenue before. Besides the need to circumvent ever stricter laws in Japan against pollution of the environment, many Japanese firms were obliged to relocate in order to remain competitive in the face of competitors and imitators from the West and from the NIEs (Phongpaichit 1990, pp.61–3). Since then, Japanese investment with large–scale projects in China has increased. Up to the end of April 1995, more than half of the 190 leading overseas consortia represented in the city were from Japan. Nine out of the 33 overseas–funded banks and insurance companies are Japanese.[30] However, it is still clear that the Japanese are more interested in investing in China's service sector such as Hong Kong than in the manufacturing sector. Therefore, the high percentage share for Japanese exports in China's domestic market and fear of Chinese competitiveness will still be the factors influencing Japanese investors to have a cautious attitude towards investment in China.

In addition to the difference in terms of scale, technological intensity and type, the management style is also different between Western investors and Hong Kong and other NIEs, as well as Japan. Hong Kong and other NIE investors adopted a family–based management style which is quite different from that of Western countries. It is true that this kind of management is very allocation efficient for small–scale enterprises, which may be the reason for the success of their FDI in South China. However, for large–scale enterprises in Shanghai it is often inappropriate to introduce this sort of management style. The statistics actually show that the percentage share of WFEs is very high in Hong Kong (15.6 per cent), Japan (29.4 per cent) and Taiwan (22.9 per cent) compared with that in the US (9 per cent) (SSSA 1994, p.79). Investors from Western countries have very few cases of WFEs. This pattern is related to the higher ratio of export–oriented–type enterprises in the former countries because they are dependent on imported materials and exports market, while Western investors who focus on the domestic market have to rely on the purchasing from, and sale on, the domestic market and therefore cooperating with Chinese partners becomes a very important factor for their success. However, in the case of Shanghai, where large–scale state–owned enterprises (SOEs) still have a higher percentage share of its total economic output, it is important to introduce more equity FIEs in order to reform the SOEs.

Furthermore, Shanghai has also benefited more from learning marketing skills, organizational skills and management techniques and the ability to gain access to the world markets through MNCs, but small–scale FIEs normally cannot undertake substantial training or research and development. Moreover, it appears that little of the most modern technology is likely to be transferred by small–scale enterprises. In this case, local 'market forces' alone will not achieve the objective of modern technology use.

Although the type of investment project (labour–intensive or capital–intensive) of each nation's FDI in Shanghai is similar to that in China as a whole, the pattern of distribution of some nations' FDI differs. For instance, although Hong Kong partners were the largest group in Shanghai with 32 per cent of total FDI up to the end of 1992, this figure is much smaller than that of the nation as a whole (62 per cent).[31] By contrast, up to the end of 1992, the share of the US and Japan of total FDI in Shanghai was more than that in the country as a whole (Table 8.8). A more compatible Hong Kong FDI figure, the Hong Kong–based FDI figure (which adds the PRC–controlled FDI to Hong Kong's FDI in the city), also indicates that Hong Kong–based FDI accounted for 46 per cent of total FDI in the city, which is still smaller than that in the country as a whole.[32] Furthermore, the total FDI from Hong Kong, Macau, Taiwan, Singapore, Thailand and the Philippines (with large ethnic Chinese communities) accounted for 70 per cent of total national actual FDI, in comparison with the same figure for Shanghai of 52 per cent during the same period.[33] A similar pattern can be observed on an approval basis between the two. Therefore, the FDI from the US, other

Table 8.8   Comparison of the share of major sources in total FDI in China and Shanghai by 1992

	Hong Kong (%)	United States (%)	Japan (%)	Major Asian countries with large ethnic Chinese communities (%)**
Actual value				
Shanghai	31.5(46.3*)	13.8	16.2	52.2*
China	62.0	9.3	11.3	70.1
Contract value				
Shanghai	39.9(48.0*)	16.0	12.3	60.5*
China	69.6	7.4	5.6	80.9

Notes
* Estimated by adding contracted PRC–controlled FDI to Hong Kong's FDI in Shanghai.
** The countries include Hong Kong (which includes PRC–controlled FDI in Hong Kong, in Shanghai's case), Macau, Taiwan, Singapore, Thailand and Philippines.

Sources: Shanghai's figures from EG (1993, pp.114–5), China's figures from Shi and Zhou (1995).

Western countries and Japan played a much more important role in Shanghai's FDI inflow than in that of the country as a whole during the reform era.

Exports from Manufacturing FIEs

This is a topic that must be touched on in an assessment of investment–export links. Export expansion using overseas management techniques and technology has increasingly been the 'line' for Shanghai. The contributions made by exports from FIEs to Shanghai's export growth and commodity structure changes during that time will now be examined.

Direct exports by FIEs rose sharply from US$99 million in 1988 to US$1,815 million in 1994, representing a rise in its share of Shanghai's total exports from 2 per cent in 1988 to 20 per cent in 1994 (Table 8.9). The rapid growth after 1988 partly reflects the time lag between setting up a joint venture and the venture becoming an exporter, but, more importantly, it reflects the increased willingness to accept Shanghai as a suitable platform for small–scale export–oriented FDI, a trend which was accelerated by the 1986 Provisions. By streamlining approval procedures and then essentially leaving the joint ventures alone to sink or swim, the municipal authorities have boosted exports by attracting foreign funds and technology and, most importantly, export–marketing expertise.

Among the regions in Shanghai, the ratio of exports per dollar invested in Minghang is much higher than that in Caohejing and in Pudong New Area (PNA), although the exports from FIEs in the PNA rose dramatically to US$252 million in 1994 which is about equal to that in Minghang (Table 8.10). If the statistics are available, the figures from the Jinqiao export processing zone (EPZ) in PNA rather than the whole PNA area would be more compatible with those of the other two ETDZs because the majority of exports by FIEs in PNA are from the Jinqiao EPZ. The much higher ratio of exports per dollar invested should be attributed to the conditions in the Minhang ETDZ attracting labour–intensive export–oriented FIEs, which were similar to conditions in the SEZs. By the end of 1993, some 232 FIEs had been approved in these two ETDZs, of which 112 enterprises were in the Minhang Zone which contains only foreign–invested ventures.

It also reflects the different time phase they experienced: Minhang started in 1984, Caohejing in 1988 and PNA in 1991. The ratio of exports per dollar invested in Minhang grew relatively steadily after 10 years of development, while the figure for Caohejing grew faster and the figure for PNA, especially for Jingqiao EPZ, can be expected to show a big rise in the near future. The rise of exports of FIEs in PNA in general and Jingqiao in particular reflects the benefits gained from the PNA policy since 1990.

Table 8.9 Exports and imports by Shanghai's FIEs, 1985–92 (US$ million)

	1985	1986	1987	1988	1989	1990	1991	1992	1993	1994
Exports										
FIE enterprise exports	21	42	59	99	186	297	497	1,040	1,610	1,815
	(0)	(7)	(28)	(39)	(189)	(299)	(645*)	(1,070*)		
Share of Shanghai's total exports (%)	0.6	1.2	1.4	2.2	3.7	5.6	8.7	15.9	21.8	20.0
Annual growth rate of FIE exports (%)	n.a.	100	40	68	88	60	67	109	55	12
Imports										
FIEs' imports	45	159	250	215	326	257	492	829		
							(1,348*)	(2,247*)		
Share of Shanghai's local imports (%)	2.5	9.8	14	12.3	116	12.2	21.4	25.9		
FIE imports as per cent of exports	1,125	3,815	424	151	175	86	209	213		

Notes: Export figures of FIEs from SSSA (various issues), while the figures in bracket are from EC (various issues). * denotes that the figures during 1991–92 are Customs figures (all the other figures are Ministry of Economic Relations and Trade (MOFERT) figures). The difference between Customs and MOFERT figures in 1991 (larger by 28 per cent) for FIE exports is because there is larger proportion of processing and assembly trade in FIE exports than in total exports.

Sources: The figures of FIE exports: 1989–90 figures from SSSA (1991, p.403), SSSA (1992, p.358), 1985 and 199–94 figures from SSSA (1994, pp.316–7) (1994 figures are predicted). Exports by FIEs in bracket: 1985–87 and 1989–90 from EC (1985–90, p.17) (the figure for 1988 in that yearbook is too small, I take the figures in EC (1990, p.26); 1991 and 1992 from EC (1993, p.18). Imports by FIEs: 1985–90 from EC (1985, p.28), 1991 and 1992 from EC (1993, p.25). Customs figures (1991–92 exports and imports figures) from XWB, 2 March 1993. 1994 figure is estimated from CBI, 21 April 1995.

Table 8.10   Exports from Minhang and Caohejing ETDZs, 1989–94

	1989	1990	1991	1992	1993	1994
Utilized FDI in						
Shanghai	422	177	175	1,259	2,318	n.a.
Minhang	29	38	54	61	61	n.a.
	(7%)	(21%)	(31%)	(5%)	(3%)	
Caohejing	21	7	12	23	44	n.a.
	(5%)	(4%)	(7%)	(2%)	(2%)	
PNA	n.a.	n.a.	29	177	784	n.a.
			(16%)	(14%)	(34%)	
Exports from the FIEs in	189	299	503	1,070	1,610	1,815
Minhang	102	104	166	212	232	n.a.
	(54%)	(35%)	(33%)	(20%)	(14%)	
Caohejing	1	7	14	36	59	n.a.
	(1%)	(2%)	(3%)	(3%)	(4%)	
PNA	n.a.	n.a.	n.a.	n.a.	191	252
					(12%)	(14%)
Exports/Actual FDI in	0.45	1.69	2.87	0.85	0.69	n.a.
Minhang	3.52	2.74	3.07	3.48	3.80	n.a.
Caohejing	0.05	1.00	1.17	1.57	1.34	n.a.
PNA	n.a.	n.a.	n.a.	n.a.	0.24	n.a.

Sources: 1989 figures from EC (1985–90, pp.132–4), 1990–91 figures from EC (1992, pp.154–7) 1992 figures from EC (1993, pp.88–9). PNA figures: 1992 export figure from Zhao (1994, p.134); 1994 export figure from *CBJ*, 14 April 1995; actual FDI figures from EG (1993, p.235 and 1994, p.297).

The importance of the exports from Minhang declined after 1990. Minhang's share in total exports by FIEs in Shanghai fell from 35 per cent in 1990 to 14 per cent in 1993, while the share of Caohejing and PNA in total exports by FIEs increased to 4 and 12 per cent, respectively, in 1993. As a result of the decline of the export share by the FIEs in all three zones, the exports by FIEs outside these zones increased their share in total exports by FIEs in the city from 63 per cent in 1990 (assuming there were no exports from FIEs in PNA at that time) to 70 per cent in 1993. This implies that the preferential PNA policy towards the FIEs in the zones has spread over all the areas in Shanghai since the early 1990s.

The Caohejing project was viewed as the city's most important effort to create an advantageous electronics industrial base which results from

Shanghai's comparative advantage in skill– and knowledge–intensive ind–ustries (Simon 1988, p.137). The low level of ratio of exports per dollar invested is mainly because the FIEs in Caohejing were largely capital–intensive enterprises, in comparison with that in Minhang where mostly labour–intensive export–oriented enterprises are located. Overall, the ratio of exports per dollar actually invested experienced a rise from 0.45 in 1989 to 2.87 in 1991 and then declined to 0.69 in 1993. This trend of exports from FIEs in the city is strongly linked to the change in the average scale of each FDI project. The FIE export share of Shanghai's exports of 16.8 per cent in 1992 is still much lower than that of Guangdong which has 43 per cent (He 1994) and even lower than the national average of 20 per cent in the same year.

However, the narrowing of the disparities in the ratio of exports per dollar between the Caohejing and Minhang zone is partly due to the fact that some former import–oriented FIEs have increasingly exported their capital–intensive products to the world markets. This change happened not only in the zone but also outside the zone as well. Shanghai Yaohuo–Pilkington Glass, for example, became the largest FIE exporter, exporting US$26 million of products in 1991.[34] This result suggests that Shanghai's potential comparative advantage in skilled labour–intensive industries tended to be realised. This has contributed to a rise of non–traditional sophisticated products in its total exports, though at a slow pace.

In order to understand the contribution of FIEs to Shanghai's export composition, let us compare their export composition with those of the city's total exports. Table 8.11 reveals that electronic and machinery exports from FIEs accounted for 25.2 per cent in 1993, while electronic and machinery exports accounted for only 18.3 per cent of Shanghai's total exports in the same year. Such a result tentatively suggests that exports from FIEs are much more capital intensive or skilled labour intensive than those of Shanghai's total.

This conclusion does not seem to hold true for the exports from FIEs within the labour–intensive sector of textile and clothing. Textile and clothing exports together accounted for about the same percentage share of both total exports from FIEs in the city and the city's total exports during 1991–92. However, the ratio between clothing and textiles exported by Shanghai's FIE enterprise (86/14) was higher than that of total exports taking Shanghai as a whole (63/37). Taking the fact that low value–added products, such as cotton–made products, cotton yarn and piece goods, still accounted for a high percentage share of Shanghai's total textile exports, the higher proportion of clothing exports would in fact suggest that FIEs exploited Shanghai's relatively higher–skilled labour in the clothing industries. In many years of garment production, Shanghai has built up a

Table 8.11   *Comparison of product mix of total exports and exports by*
FIEs in Shanghai, 1991 and 1992 (US$ million)

	Shanghai's total exports	Exports by FIEs
1991		
Total exports	5,912(100%)	645(100%)
Textile products (SITC 65)	903(15.3%)	n.a.
Clothing (SITC 84)	1,533(25.9%)	213(23.0%)
Electronic and machinery goods*	1,098(18.6%)	171(26.5%)
1992		
Total exports	6,297(100%)	1,055(100%)
Textile products (SITC 65)	n.a.	60(5.6%)
Clothing (SITC 84)	n.a.	384(36.4%)
Electronic and machinery goods*	1,442(22.9%)	306(29.0%)
1993		
Electronic and machinery goods*	1,351(18.3%)	405.9 (25.2%)

Notes: * The electronic and machinery products include machinery and transportation equipment
(SITC 7), manufactured metal products (SITC 69), professional, scientific and control equipment
(SITC 87) and photo equipment, optics and watches and clocks (SITC 88) (State Statistical Bureau
1989, p.146). The figure in brackets is percentage share of total exports.

Sources: *XWB*, 28 February 1993 and 2 March 1993. 1993 figures are calculated from *XWB*, 6
February 1995.

huge and continuing supply of skilled labour in this domestic trade. Despite
the abundance of labour in other regions, it is more difficult for such regions
to train a labour force adequately in a short period of time. This suggests
that the value–added is higher in the exports from FIEs, even in the clothing
and textile sectors.

Furthermore, the higher percentage share of electronic and machinery
exports from FIEs depends on its higher export–processing activities more
than do the total exports from Shanghai as a whole. The re–exports from
processed imports by FIEs accounted for 63 per cent of FIE total exports in
1991, which is more than that of 47 per cent for the city as a whole in 1990.
Similarly, processing and assembly accounted for 14 per cent of total exports
by FIEs, which is much larger than that of 5 per cent for Shanghai's total
exports.[35] This would suggest that the higher percentage share of non–

traditional export products, especially electronic and machinery products by FIEs, can be attributed to their higher processing activities (which involved more labour content) than that of the city's total exports as a whole. The implication then is that exports are not actually so capital intensive as suggested by the export composition itself. Nevertheless, the commodity composition of FIEs exports is more sophisticated than that of the profile of Shanghai's total exports.

Another issue is that the *net* exports of FIEs were negative until 1989 because of their high level of import demands. Imports by FIEs surpassed exports again between 1990 and 1992 and this situation is expected to continue if Customs figures are applied. This may represent inter–temporal problems, as the dramatic growth in the number of such ventures in 1992–94 means that at any moment their international trade is dominated by the new joint ventures' and WFEs' purchases of foreign equipment. Therefore, if the MOFERT figures are adopted (that is, imports of producer capital goods were excluded), exports were larger than imports during 1991–92.

In addition to the FIEs' contribution to exports, the goal of technology transfer has been successfully met by introducing capital–intensive FIEs in the manufacturing sectors and service sectors. The majority of these FIEs involve advanced technology and are related to industrial production such as motor vehicles, telecommunications, machinery and electronics, computers, fine chemicals, biotechnology and pharmaceuticals (forced growing infant industries called 'six pillar industries'). This policy has been implemented vigorously since the early 1990s in Shanghai and other cities. Other investment projects are related to finance, trade, information services and real estate. Since the early 1990s, these six manufacturing sectors have expanded very rapidly.

A number of large–scale capital–intensive projects have played a very important role in the fast growth of these rising six pillar industries in the city since early 1990s. For example, the Shanghai Volkswagen Automobile Company has built a total of 425,000 Santana cars, occupying half of the domestic car market. The Shanghai Bell Telephone Equipment Manufacturing Company has provided automatic telephone switchboards with a total of 13.6 million lines to 1,200 telephone offices in 29 province–level areas since its establishment in 1984. With the ultimate goal of producing the products from these industries designed and manufactured domestically, the central government is trying to implement a local content ratio.

Overall, a major recent survey revealed that the average rate of return on investment (ROI) of the US ventures situated in the major urban centres of Shanghai (16.2 per cent), Guangzhou (13.3 per cent) and Beijing (13.2 per cent), or in Shenzhen (13.6 per cent), is higher than that of other SEZs (11.4 per cent), coastal cities (10.9 per cent) and inland cities (10.1 per cent).[36]

Not all the special economic zones selected by the Chinese government have proved ideal in performance. Among more than 7,000 FIEs which have gone into operation in the city, 80 per cent of them are profitable, a ratio of 17 percentage points higher than the national average, ranking first in the country. The industrial output expanded steadily to 86 billion yuan in 1994, accounting for 20.5 per cent of the city's gross industrial output. They delivered more than 4.8 billion yuan to the state in taxes and profits at the same time, an increase of 30 per cent over the previous year.[37]

CONCLUSION: ASSESSMENT OF CAPITAL–INTENSIVE FIES IN SHANGHAI

The success of the large–scale capital–intensive FDI in Shanghai from OECD countries can be attributed to the following factors.

On the demand side it can be attributed to, first, Shanghai's advantage in its comprehensive industrial base, relatively advanced technology, superior infrastructure and the availability of a large pool of skilled labour. Shanghai's particular attractiveness to OECD investors also derives from its role as a consular, business centre and as China's emerging major financial centre with a relatively large international community. The local investment incentives plus the creation of three ETDZs and PNA contributed to an environment more congenial to non–Chinese business people than anywhere else in the PRC (Pomfret 1991). These advantages provide OECD investment (especially their technology–intensive FDI) with a favourable environment. This is also the cause of the rapid rise in MNC investment in service sectors, especially those capital–intensive ones, after 1992 when these sectors were allowed to be opened to the FDI. Shanghai's huge domestic market as well as its emergence as entrepôt centre for its hinterland has attracted largely the market–oriented FIEs. However, it should be pointed out that Shanghai's role as an entrepôt is largely restricted by China's regional protectionism which prevents it from taking full advantage of integration with its hinterland in the Shanghai economic zone (Tian 1994). Therefore its comparative advantage in the service sector has not until now been adequately utilised.

Second, the improvement in the city's infrastructure and service sector in turn generated increasing returns to scale and economies of agglomeration to all the sectors in the economy by lowering long–run average costs of production. Economies of scale, combined with low transport costs with external markets suggest that there is a tendency for clusters of manufacturing activities as well as service sectors in the city.[38] Along with the inflow of foreign capital, the city's comparative advantage is moving further towards being a more capital–intensive one. Therefore, among the other things, the success of investing in those sectors in the city has been largely dependent on the FIEs' effective exploitation of the dynamic comparative advantage in Shanghai. Since financial and trade sectors are more capital or skilled intensive than manufacturing sectors, skilled labour supply and the state of infrastructure become key determinants as to whether growth will accelerate or not.

Third, it may reflect the fact that Shanghai has relatively strong trade relations with non–Asian countries. Countries that have large–scale trade activity with China (or a particular province) tend to be more familiar with the economic system, market environment and business practices, knowledge that is undoubtedly useful in assisting them in setting up investment operations (Grub and Lin 1991, p.83). Guangdong and Hong Kong are the best examples. Both Guangdong's trade and foreign investment became more concentrated in Hong Kong. Japanese FDI in Shanghai, as well as in China as a whole, is an exception to this observation. Compared with its higher percentage share in Shanghai's total exports and local imports, Japanese direct investment is a relatively small proportion of Shanghai's FDI.

Finally, even without the advantage in location and dialects that southern provinces have, Shanghai absorbed a dramatically increasing amount of investment from Hong Kong which mainly focused on Shanghai's service sectors, especially in the real estate and retail sectors, banking and land development, after 1992. On an approval basis, Hong Kong's FDI rose from US$128 million in 1991 to US$6,424 million in 1994, representing a sharp rise in percentage share of total FDI in the city, from 28 per cent in 1991 to 64 per cent in 1994. The average scale of FDI projects by Hong Kong investors also jumped to US$2.5 million in 1992 and US$4 million in 1994. The reason for the sharp rise in Hong Kong's investment in the retail sector, for example, is due to its ability to adapt better to balancing foreign exchange (forex) and negotiating China's antiquated bureaucracy and distribution systems than their Western counterparts.[39] This result also suggests that the city's comparative advantage in its sophisticated industrial structure, skilled labour and existing and improving infrastructure facilities has increased its competitiveness and attracted more of Hong Kong's capital since 1992 when policy was equalized between Shanghai and Guangdong, where Chinese compatriots have apparent cultural or proximity advantages.

On the supply side, the competitive advantage in technology and management by OECD investors, especially MNCs, together with their eagerness to exploit new business opportunities and the advantages of using the industrial base in Shanghai, led to a surge in their investment activities in the form of large–scale capital–intensive projects. These MNCs have enormous resources, such as FSA and long–term plans to invest in China.

The success of MNCs in Shanghai suggests that the FSA theory is more useful in explaining the pattern of FDI in Shanghai than most other regions in China where FDI is small scale, and the largest investors are from the NIEs.

It is clear now that due to its comparative advantage in capital–intensive industries and its role as the centre of commerce and finance, Shanghai has attracted more large–scale market–oriented technological projects from Western countries. The remaining question is whether this pattern fits Shanghai's economic development.

It is true that the labour immobility (which caused Shanghai's comparative advantage to further move towards the more capital–intensive industries) should encourage the inflow of foreign capital to Shanghai's hinterland in line with the conventional wisdom that capital chases labour.[40] However, this does not happen in Shanghai. In addition to the preferential policy, it should be Shanghai's comparative advantage in skilled labour and its improving urban infrastructure and comprehensive manufacturing sectors (which generate increasing return and economies of agglomeration) that attracts the foreign capital into the city. In recent years when Shanghai's compulsory remittance of its local revenue to the centre had been relaxed, a large amount of net capital flowed from inland provinces to the city compared with the situation before 1990 when Shanghai transferred large amounts of capital to the inland provinces. This result further supports my argument about reasons for inflow of MNC capital into China. On the economic efficiency ground, the free movement of capital between regions should be encouraged in order to exploit the increasing returns to scale. However, it is impossible to fully release the mobility of labour into big cities in China because of its huge social cost (the already congested environment).

It can also be argued that the success of MNCs in Shanghai is a result of the deliberate national and/or provincial policies which are in favour of these large–scale capital–intensive projects. The economic efficiency issue should then be raised in assessing the MNCs' activities in Shanghai. The national policies include ones such as the heavy import–substitute policy under which the distorted price system is in favour of capital–intensive production. Like most developing countries, China is anxious to acquire the latest, state–of–the–art technologies. These companies therefore have a strong bargaining power with China and have secured various incentives from the Chinese authorities. In addition, in persuading the authorities to allow them to establish their dominance in the Chinese market, these companies have also used strong bilateral political influence. For instance, US companies argued for the US government to 'go easy' on China by supporting legislation to renew China's status as a most favoured nation.[41] In addition to the protection from high import tariffs, the Chinese authorities can ensure that any domestic–market–oriented venture makes an accounting profit by controlling prices, material allocation and demand, but the joint venture may be socially undesirable in so far as the output could be imported at a lower domestic resource cost.

China, like many other developing countries, is seeking to attract export–oriented investment in a context where there is a high level of protection, which raises domestic costs. This makes it difficult to export and to attract FDI into export activities (Cable and Persaud 1987, p.12). Then it has exaggerated existing problems facing FIEs in Shanghai, such as energy shortages, transportation bottlenecks and poor quality and insecure supply of inputs – including raw materials. Inputs were purchased at costs above world market levels from indigenous firms operating under protection. These problems contributed to a central difficulty facing many export–oriented joint ventures, that of meeting international quality standards. For example, copper tube was priced as high as 16 thousand yuan per tonne when selling to FIEs in Shanghai in 1988, while copper tube imported (and of higher quality) was priced at only 11 thousand yuan per tonne. Moreover, the domestic suppliers usually sold the raw material to FDI partners at a price higher than that to a non–FDI firm. One estimate (Gu and Xu 1989, p.19) shows that 80 per cent of manufacturing FIEs in Shanghai had problems with raw material supply, because when an enterprise became a FIE enterprise, the material supplied at the 'planned' price was automatically cancelled. Therefore, the contribution of foreign investment to exports have been somewhat limited, presumably due to built–in bias in favour of large–scale capital–intensive projects and policy conflicts (Ariff and Lim 1987, pp.117–8).

Local policies are important because since decentralization local authorities, especially those in the coastal region, have been granted more autonomy which has enabled them to grant more incentives to the investment involved in capital–incentive projects in order to fulfil their local industrial policy. Besides, the open–door policy itself is coastal region biased. However, as seen from the previous discussion, the capital–intensive biased FDI policy in the city has been largely changed into policy which is export–oriented friendly. So we can assume that there is not much difference between Shanghai and the rest of the country in terms of incentive measures offered to MNCs. In other words, what Shanghai can offer MNCs all the other provinces can follow (tax concession and so on).

However, one of the significant arguments against tariffs and quotas to protect such industries as automobiles and steel from foreign competition is that protection removes the incentive to be efficient and competitive. It is clear that China should reduce its very strong overall import protection to a moderate one in order to achieve the goals of both economic efficiency (by introducing fair competition) and protection of its infant industries.[42] But the point is how to implement this process. It is not necessary to act in favour of all export–oriented FIEs or against all import–substitute ones. After several years of operating in the domestic market, some import–substitute capital–intensive FIEs then turned to exporting their products to overseas markets. Therefore, the point is how to determine the potential comparative advantage when enterprises are likely to be mainly temporary import–substitute FIEs like this. Under the distorted price system, comparison of profits between different sectors would be meaningless. However, the comparison of profit within one sector would approximately reflect the economic profit and cost. Actually, Shanghai has performed much better in terms of profit in the manufacturing sectors, especially in the capital–intensive ones, than the other cities. The automobile is one example. Where comprehensive liberalisation is not feasible, the 'second–best' solution is to close down those companies running at a loss and leave in operation only those producers who are economically efficient enough to break even or make a profit.

In a country like China, where the market mechanism is not fully functional and the legal framework tends to be weak, strong government interference in selecting the survivals in capital–intensive industries is not always a bad thing, in order to avoid duplication and lowering of economies of scale. Even in the well–functioned market economy, if very large economies of scale are possible in the case of natural monopolies, it makes no sense to have many small firms producing the same thing at much higher costs. Governments need to regulate monopolies to which they have granted exclusive licences. China's National Automotive Industry Corporation is anxious to see consolidation in the auto parts industry and has no intention of preserving small local producers that cannot achieve economies of scale and a national market position. Although some local government agencies and their original equipment manufacturer customers may seek to protect such producers, the consolidation process is already under way and can be expected to continue for a decade or more. Many failing auto parts plants are being converted into auto service centres, since the auto repair business is both small scale and local.[43]

While to some extent a government presence is valid, in other areas China needs further economic reform to remove the obstacles to the introduction of further foreign capital. An example is the auto parts industry. For the immediate future, the most important problem facing this industry remains the existence of captive supplier–original equipment manufacturer re-lationships, remnants of China's state–planned economy. In addition, the insulation of the Chinese economy and society from international influences for forty years meant that Chinese workers and managers were usually unaware that quality was even a difficulty and, even when they understood the problem, they were unsure what to aim for.

In addition, within the joint ventures, the Chinese partners generally tried to keep a grip on finance, labour management, and other keys to management. They tried to maintain joint ventures which followed the wage systems, welfare and benefit systems, and promotion systems of the existing state–owned enterprise systems which it is in their interest to preserve. The firing of employees was strongly opposed by the Chinese side. The policy of separating technology and management and the hope that technology can be absorbed while maintaining existing employment and compensation systems impedes the transfer of technology. It was China's existing economic and management system that made foreign firms less confident in deciding to place their manufacturing investment in China than in East Asian and ASEAN countries. Excessive interference also appears through almost the whole process, from the start of negotiations to the operation of the venture. This gives the government authorities too much power in effecting the venture and inevitably results in much corruption, distortion and unfairness (Shi and Zhou 1995).

The other major area which impedes the inflow of FIEs, especially MNCs, is the foreign trade sector where national trading companies still feel a predominant right to engage in foreign dealings. Before investing in the host country, a big MNC often markets products or provides services in the country and occupies the target market share. To do this, an FIE would import some products from its home company and then sell them in the Chinese market. The national trading companies, however, who have benefited a lot from the existing system, impose pressure on the relevant government department (Shi and Zhou 1995).

Therefore China needs to further its economic reform and the improvement of its legal framework in its state–owned enterprises before she can maximize her benefit from introducing the technology of both hardware and software from FDI firms.

In short, although labour–intensive industry is one area in which China presently does have a comparative advantage, the long–established urban centre of Shanghai offers other advantages which have not, until now, been adequately utilised. In moving away from the static comparative advantages approach to a more dynamic one, I argue that the increasing returns to scale, or economies of agglomeration, as well as the comparative advantage in skill and knowledge–intensive industries, combined with the existing Chinese policy were important factors in determining the rapid inflow of large–scale MNC projects. Therefore Guangdong's successful experience with small export–oriented enterprises may not suit Shanghai. This, however, is not to say the small export–oriented enterprises are not important in Shanghai's growth because they still exploit Shanghai's static comparative advantage.

These projects contributed a lot in obtaining technology and managerial training from foreigners, especially from the US and European countries.

188   *Foreign Direct Investment and Regional Economies*

Therefore, one of the major roles of FDI in Shanghai is to renovate the SOE sector, which is the largest in China, with foreign capital. They are also very important in easing the development bottleneck and establishing the industries with dynamic comparative advantage even though the short–term costs might be higher. However, the shift of these import–oriented projects to export–oriented ones may be more difficult than the encouragement of 'fresh' export–oriented investors since it requires strategies (Bennett and Sharpe 1979). Therefore, it is important to improve the economic efficiency of these capital–intensive FDI projects by reducing the import protection to push these firms to be enable to compete in the world markets. Upgrading the skilled labour sectors by attracting more FDI and expanding the exports from these sectors is equally important as in the case of activities built on unskilled labour.

NOTES

1. In mid–April 1990, the Chinese government announced a plan to open and develop Pudong, a decision through which Pudong New Area was granted similar special privileges that the special economic zones (SEZs) had, in order to resume Shanghai's financial, trade and economic centres in the West Pacific region in the future.
2. It is argued that supporting industries of international trade (shipping, air transport, communications, finance, insurance and business services) are more capital or skill intensive than manufacturing (Sung 1991, p.32).
3. The concept of FSA was first introduced by Coase (1937). Dunning developed this theory in his 'eclectic approach'(Dunning 1970). Examples of FSAs include technical knowledge, managerial expertise, distribution networks, product complementarities, credit advantages, brand recognition, and internalised economies of scale. These advantages permit the firm to overcome disadvantages inherent in entering new or unfamiliar markets where it would have to compete with existing domestic firms and adjust to a different regulatory and business framework (Plummer and Montes 1995, p.7).
4. It is argued that a major share of FDI in China is small scale, and the largest investors in China are from the NIEs. The FSA that most small foreign investors in China appear to possess is knowledge of retail and wholesale markets in advanced countries for specific products. Therefore China's recent FDI experience suggests that FSA theory is incomplete in its application to intra–Asian FDI flows (Plummer and Montes 1995, p.9).
5. Despite initial enthusiasm within and outside China following the dramatic policy change in 1978 permitting FDI, actual FDI was very limited before 1984 outside of SEZs. This was mainly because the overall environment in China for attracting foreign investment was still poor during 1979–83.
6. These include detailed joint–venture regulations ('Detailed Rules for the Implementation of Sino–Foreign Joint Venture Law of PRC') in late 1983 and clearer patents legislation ('Patent Law of PRC') in mid–1984; both were designed to encourage foreign investment to grow. By the end of 1984, investment protection treaties had been signed with a number of Western countries and others were being negotiated.
7. Various regulations introduced by the State Council forced the FIEs to export their products to repatriate their earnings (Shi and Zhou 1995).
8. The decline of FDI inflow led the Chinese authorities to reassess their attitudes towards FDI and to issue 'the 22 Articles' (Provisions for the Encouragement of Foreign Investment) by the State Council in October 1986. The 22 Articles have allowed joint ventures with surplus

foreign exchange to swap this at negotiated rates for renminbi from joint ventures with foreign exchange deficits.

9. See *Chinese Business Review (CBR)*, March–April 1990, p.50.
10. The local emergence of a positive Shanghai attitude towards foreign investors among policy makers was an equally important change. Such an attitude was apparent first in Guangdong and Fujian Provinces. The Shanghai authorities signalled that they would work actively to create a good climate for foreign–invested ventures, including using their power to determine prices and availability of inputs under the plan to ensure a reasonable return for joint ventures.
11. During the period 1985–87, Shanghai was hard put to accommodate the large number of tourists and foreign businessmen rushing to take advantage of the new open–door policy, although the hotel occupancy rate fell from 94 per cent in 1985 to 84 per cent in 1987. However, after 1988 there were too many new hotels and not enough visitors. The growth rate of room availability in new hotels became higher than that of the increase in the population of tourists from overseas. Shanghai hotels' occupancy fell drastically from 85 per cent in 1986 to 67 per cent in 1988. With the collapse of foreign tourism immediately after 4 June 1989, the occupancy rate fell further to 53 per cent. The occupancy rate recovered somewhat to 57 per cent in 1990 and 58 per cent in 1991.
12. Taiwanese FDI received another boost in July 1988 when China promulgated Regulations on Encouraging the Investment of Taiwanese. In July 1988, Beijing announced that Taiwanese investors could put money into any project on the mainland, as compared with foreigners who were limited to industries targeted for development. It also promised to speed their investment application process, and guaranteed that there would be no nationalisation of Taiwanese–owned assets and that secrecy would be maintained (*Financial Times*, 7 July 1988, as cited in Fukasaku et al. 1994, p.91).
13. This policy largely affected the FIEs which were newly created because China lacked matching funds. Companies that already had been established in the coastal region, however, continued to do business. Some well–publicised Western corporations maintained or even expanded their commitments.
14. With the main points being: (i) no nationalization of joint ventures; (ii) permission for the appointment of foreign nationals as board chairman; (iii) abolition of restrictions on the duration of most joint ventures.
15. See *Chinese Business Journal (CBJ)*, 21 April 1995.
16. See *CBJ*, 17 November 1994.
17. During the early 1980s, the purchase of imported consumer products without a MOFERT's exit (province) permit from Guangdong was allowed by other local provincial governments but under a limited range and quantity of products being involved. In addition there were a lot of individual salesmen who sold imported products illegally, mostly cigarettes, in their small shops or simply on the street. It was estimated that there were over 100 thousand people who sold imported cigarettes in Shanghai alone. After the late 1980s, local governments (especially those within the coastal regions) loosened their control over the purchasing of imported consumer products or light industrial raw materials from Guangdong bought without permit in order to meet the requirement of strong demand for imported products. Shanghai's wholesalers and retailers, however, had to purchase the products which were imported by Guangdong through middlemen in other provinces, because they were not permitted to purchase directly from Guangdong by the local government. This more controlled procedure resulted in a rise in price of these imported products in Shanghai and unsatisfied demand for imported products which grew rapidly.
18. The main reason behind this is perhaps the new proneness to boasting and exaggeration. It is reported that many lower–level officials try their best to find 'foreign devil', no matter if they are 'genuine or false', 'credible or noncredible', and sign joint–venture contracts with them in order to fulfil a quota of utilisation of FDI which was received from their superiors. How the project will be implemented is not their concern (Shi and Zhou 1995).
19. See *CBJ*, 27 April 1995.
20. See *CBJ*, April 1995.
21. See *Xinwenbao (XWB)*, 8 February 1995.
22. See *Independence Daily*, 10 April 1995.

23. In this period, annual totals for contracted FDI were dominated by the presence or absence of these large projects, mostly equity joint ventures. In 1980, the enterprise Schindler Elevators Co accounted for US$3 million investment, more than 90 per cent of total contracted FDI in that year. In 1981, Shanghai United Wooltex accounted for US$2.4 million, about 90 per cent of the total. In 1982 and 1983, both numbers and value of FDI projects increased substantially, but the value increase was mainly due to two and then three projects, respectively. There were Foxboro, Squibb and Shanghai Joint–Operation Building, involving a total of US$22 million in 1982 and Yaohuo Pilkington and the firm Shanghai Bell, involving a total of US$70 million in 1983.

24. China's figures, however, are skewed by the amount of investment in contractual oil ventures, without which average FDI per project would be smaller. A survey by Nai–Ruenn Chen ('Foreign investment in China: current trends', in *China Business Review*, May–June 1988, p.57, and *Intertrade*, February 1988, pp.27–9) shows that the average size of contracted FDI in China amounted to US$0.82 million during 1979–87. If contractual oil ventures is not included, the average size would be only US$0.61 million (source: Shapiro et al. 1991, pp.28–9).

25. See *Independence Daily*, 16 November 1994.

26. Before 1986, the US investment in Shanghai was larger than that of Hong Kong and Japan together. The US share of total contracted FDI in Shanghai was 40 per cent and 53 per cent in 1985 and 1986. The share of American investment, however, fell from 53 per cent in 1986 to 17 per cent in 1988 and was only 12 per cent in 1989 (which is largely because of the Tiananmen Incident), increasing to 24 per cent in 1990. As a result, after 1986 the US position was surpassed by Hong Kong. During the last 6–year period, between 1989 and 1994, the position of the US investment was surpassed by Japan. Taiwanese investment grew rapidly after 1990 in Shanghai. In 1990 Taiwanese FDI projects approved in Shanghai amounted to US$102 million, representing 27 per cent of total FDI approved which is larger than that of Japan in that year. Taiwan's share of contracted value of Shanghai's total FDI became smaller than that of Japan in 1991 and 1992, but increased to 8 per cent in 1994, again surpassing that of Japan.

27. There are no separate figures available for average scale of FDI in the manufacturing sector by country (what we have are the figures for aggregate average scale by country). However, since manufacturing FDI dominated FDI in the city during 1988–91, we can assume that the aggregate scale figures by country largely reflect those in the manufacturing sector during the same period.

28. The average scale of Hong Kong's FDI projects is actually larger than that of the US and Japan up to the end of 1994, but the FDI from the US and Japan vary widely between a few very large–scale projects and many small–scale projects.

29. The average scale of FDI projects by the American investors amounted to US$20.3 million, US$15.8 million and US$5.6 million in 1985, 1986 and 1987, respectively. The average scale of Japanese FDI projects amounted to US$9.9 million in 1985, but became very small in 1986 and 1987 at US$0.8 million and US$0.4 million (Table 8.6).

30. See *CBJ*, 6 May 1995.

31. Hong Kong's FDI involvement in the PRC can be overestimated mainly because some Hong Kong companies act as representatives of foreign countries. However, there will not be any serious problems when we compare Hong Kong's share in Shanghai and in China because we can assume that the proportion of these Hong Kong companies that actually represent other foreign investors in total Hong Kong investment will be approximately the same as in China as a whole.

32. The reason for doing this is because the figures for Hong Kong investment in the country as a whole include the PRC–controlled FDI, while there are separate figures for the FDI from PRC–controlled firms in Shanghai (which can be found from a newly published *Yearbook of Shanghai Foreign Economic Relations and Trade Statistics (EG)* recent issues). These PRC–controlled FDI enterprises were located mostly in Hong Kong and used as joint–venture partners to facilitate raising funds in Hong Kong or to obtain joint–venture tax and trading privileges. Therefore, it will be more accurate to analyse Sino–foreign FDI by nationality of partner by applying Shanghai's data.

33. Having advantages due to shared dialect and culture and close location, these FDIs are located in southern Chinese provinces much more than elsewhere.
34. It is, however, unclear whether these joint ventures sold their products at a loss on the world market, because they must export to earn the necessary foreign exchange which is required by Chinese officials, as argued by Yang (1990, p.40).
35. See *XWB*, 3 March 1991 and 2 March 1992.
36. See *CBR*, November–December 1992, pp. 54–6.
37. See *CBJ*, November 1994 and 28 April 1995.
38. Hoover (1937) discussed the economies of agglomerations in the context of the US. Myrdal (1957) discussed the 'circular causation' of development and Hirschman (1958) discussed backward linkages in the context of developing economies. See also Krugman (1991a, 1991b, 1991c).
39. See *CBR*, January–February 1994, p.26.
40. Before the reform, population mobility was restricted for people moving from rural to urban areas under the house registration and identity system. Although the relative easier access to daily necessities made it possible for farmers to settle down in cities, the government still control large–scale inflow of population to cities for fear of social instability.
41. See *Business Week*, 13 June 1994.
42. A social cost–benefit analysis would require case–by–case evaluation, however, and that is beyond the scope of this chapter.
43. See *CBR*, March–April 1994, pp.24–30.

REFERENCES

Ariff, M. and Lim, C.P., 1987. 'Foreign investment in Malaysia', in V. Cable and B. Persaud (eds), *Developing with foreign investment*, Croom Helm, London.

Bennett, D. and Sharpe, K.E., 1979. 'Transnational Corporations and the political economy of export promotion: the case of the Mexican automobile industry', *International Organization*, **33(2)**, 177–201.

Cable, V. and Persaud, B., 1987. 'New trends and policy problems in foreign investment: the experience of commonwealth countries', in V. Cable and B. Persaud (eds), *Developing with foreign investment*, Croom Helm, London.

CBJ (*Chinese Business Journal*), various issues. Electronic daily journal on Chinese business in the US.

CBR (*Chinese Business Review*), various issues. Bimonthly journal on Chinese business, published in the US.

Coase, R.H., 1937. 'The nature of the firm', *Economica*, **4**, 386–405.

Dunning, J.H., 1970. *Studies in direct investment*, George Allen & Unwin, London.

EB (Editorial Board), various issues. *Yearbook of Shanghai foreign economic relations statistics*, compiled by Shanghai Statistical Bureau, Science and Technology Publishing House, Shanghai.

EC (Editorial Committee), various issues. *Foreign economic statistical yearbook of Shanghai*, compiled by Shanghai Statistical Bureau, Science and Technology Publishing House, Shanghai.

EG (Editorial Group, Shanghai's Foreign Economic Relations and Trade), various issues. *Yearbook of Shanghai foreign economic relations and trade statistics*, Shanghai Kexue Jisu Chubanshe, Shanghai.

Fukasaku, K., Wall, D. and Wu, M., 1994. *China's long march to an open economy*, OECD, Paris.

Grub, P.D. and Lin, J.II., 1991. *Foreign direct investment in China*, Quorum Books, New York.

Gu, G.X. and Xu, X.M., 1989. 'A survey on sanzi enterprises in Shanghai', *Fudan Xuebao (Social Science Edition)*, **4**, 14–20.

He, G.S., 1994. 'A comparative study of exports of Guangdong and Shanghai', *Shanghai Investment*, **6**, 4–6.

Hirschman, A.O., 1958. *The strategy of economic development*, Yale University Press, New Haven, Conn.

Hoover, E., 1937. *Location theory and the shoe and leather industry*, Harvard University Press, Cambridge, Mass.

Independence Daily, a Chinese daily newspaper published in Australia.

Intertrade, monthly journal on China's foreign trade, published MOFERT.

Kim, S.J., 1995. 'Korean direct investment in China: perspectives of Korean investors', in Sumner J. La Croix, M. Plummer and K. Lee (eds), *Emerging patterns of East Asian investment in China, from Korea, Taiwan and Hong Kong*, M.E. Sharpe, Armonk, New York.

Krugman, P., 1991a. 'Increasing returns and economic geography', *Journal of Political Economy*, **99(3)**, 483–99.

Krugman, P., 1991b. *Geography and trade*, Cambridge, MIT Press, Mass. and London.

Krugman, P., 1991c. 'History and industrial location: the case of the manufacturing belt', *American Economic Review*, papers and proceedings, May, 80–83.

Myrdal, G., 1957. *Economic theory and underdeveloped regions*, Duckworth, London.

Phongpaichit, P., 1990. *The new wave of Japanese investment in ASEAN: determinants and prospects*, ASEAN Economic Research Unit, Institute of Southeast Asian Studies, Singapore.

Plummer, M. and Montes, M.F., 1995. 'Direct foreign investment in China: an introduction', in Sumner J. La Croix, M. Plummer and K. Lee (eds), *Emerging patterns of East Asian investment in China, from Korea, Taiwan and Hong Kong*, M.E. Sharpe, Armonk, New York.

Pomfret, R., 1991. *Investing in China: ten years of the open door policy*, Iowa State University Press, Ames, Iowa.

Shanghai Statistical Bureau, various issues. *The statistical yearbook of Shanghai*, Statistical Publishing House of China, Beijing.

Shapiro, J.E., Behrman, J.N., Fischer, W.A. and Powell, S.G., 1991. *Direct investment and joint ventures in China: a handbook for corporate negotiators*, Quorum Books, New York.

Shi, H.L. and Zhou, L.P., 1995. 'A study of foreign direct investment in China', Paper presented at China's Economy Towards 2000: Opportunities and Challenges at La Trobe University.

Simon, F., 1988. *Technological innovation in China: the case of the Shanghai semiconductor industry*, Ballinger Pub. Co., Cambridge, Mass.

SSSA (Shanghai Social Science Academy), various issues. *The economic yearbook of Shanghai*, Shanghai Sanlian Shudian, Shanghai.

State Statistical Bureau, 1989. *Interpretation of major national economic statistical terms*, Zhonguo Tongji Chubanshe, Beijing.

Sung, Y.W., 1991. *The China–Hong Kong connection, the key to China's open–door policy*, Cambridge University Press, Cambridge.

The Age, an Australian daily newspaper.

Tian, G., 1994. 'The emergence of Shanghai's role as entrepot centre since the mid–1980s', *Journal of Contemporary China*, Fall, 3–27.

Westendorff, D., 1989. *Foreign direct investment and technology transfer: the case of Shanghai, PRC 1978–88,* Working papers planning, Cornell University, Ithaca, New York.

XWB, Xinwenbao (Daily News), published in Shanghai.

Yang, G., 1990. 'The pattern of foreign direct investment in China', PhD thesis, National Centre for Development Studies, Australian National University, Canberra, unpublished.

Zhang, X.H., 1991. 'The classification of China's industries by factor intensity and the corresponding trade pattern', in *China: trade and reform*, Chinese Students' Society for Economic Studies (Australia) (ed.), Australian National University, Canberra,

Zhao, Q.Z., 1994. *New century and new Pudong*, Fudan University Press, Shanghai.

9. FDI and Industrial Restructuring in Xiamen

Qi Luo

INTRODUCTION

The recent resumption of direct shipping links between mainland China (Xiamen and Fuzhou) and Taiwan (Kaohsiung), for the first time since 1949, has once again brought the world's attention to the Taiwan Straits and the two cities along the Fujian coast. Within China, this new development came at the time when Xiamen and Fuzhou, like most of China's special economic zones (SEZs) and coastal open cities (COCs), were increasingly losing their policy advantages to inland regions due to the adjustment of the 'Special Policy', which was originally designed to give the SEZs and COCs greater autonomy in developing their export–oriented economies. Thus, Xiamen and Fuzhou will certainly be using this unique opportunity to give themselves an edge over other Chinese cities and regions in the fierce competition for a greater inflow of foreign investment. Some local officials even hope that this latest development will eventually lead their economies to a 'second take–off'.

In the case of Xiamen, which has been one of the hot spots for Taiwanese investment in the mainland since 1988, the local government had been anticipating the opening of the direct link with Taiwan for years and hence has taken a series of measures to restructure the local industry in order to make it more open and competitive. A salient feature of Xiamen's industrial restructuring is the authorities' strategy of using FDI to facilitate the transformation of local, long–established enterprises. Experience in many developing countries shows that FDI tends to be very effective in creating employment opportunities and increasing export earnings for the host economy but less so in transferring technology and management expertise, to say nothing of facilitating local industrial restructuring.

So, can Xiamen fulfil its goal of using FDI to promote local industrial restructuring? This chapter seeks to assess the performance of the strategy. After providing an overview of the economic development in Xiamen since 1980, the chapter will discuss the city's policy towards industrial restructuring, examine the achievements it has made, and analyse the problems it has encountered in the process of utilising FDI. The study will conclude with an assessment of the role of FDI in Xiamen.

OVERVIEW OF THE XIAMEN ECONOMY

The Xiamen Municipality (*Xiamen shi*) consists of the Xiamen Island, the Gulangyu Islet, the coastal part of the northern bank of the Jiulongjiang River on the mainland and Tong'an County, with a total area of 1,516 square kilometres and a population of 1.2 million (at the end of 1995). The 2.2–kilometre Gaoji Causeway built in 1955 connects the Island with the mainland.

When China launched the reform and open–door policy in the late 1970s, Xiamen was already a medium/small–sized industrial city within the country's old, command economic structure. It possessed an outmoded but all–embracing industrial system, encompassing 33 of the 40 major industrial sectors identified in China (EG 1989, p.124). By the early 1980s, six of them, food–processing, chemicals and pharmaceuticals, machinery, textiles, paper and stationery, and building materials, had emerged as key sectors. With some 500 enterprises and a 110,000–strong workforce, Xiamen's industry generated about 60 per cent of the city's GDP and 12.5 per cent of Fujian's total gross value of industrial output (GVIO) in 1985 (EC 1986, pp.113, 131, Fujian Statistical Bureau 1985, p.486).

In July 1980, the State Council approved the proposal presented by the Fujian Provincial government to open up an area of 2.5 square kilometres in the Huli District, northwest of the Xiamen Island, as the Xiamen SEZ.[1] In March 1984, after Deng Xiaoping made a high–profile visit to Xiamen, the Central government decided to expand the Xiamen SEZ into the whole Xiamen Island, including the Gulangyu Islet. It covers a total area of 131 square kilometres and, at the end of 1994, had a population of 426,196, representing 8.6 and 35.7 per cent of the Xiamen Municipality's totals, respectively (EC 1995, pp.239, 244–5).

After 16 years of development as an SEZ, Xiamen has achieved a spectacular growth. As can be seen from Table 9.1, its GDP in 1995 was 13 times bigger than that of 1980 while its exports expanded by an astonishing 23.8 times, with the average annual growth rates hitting 19.3 and 23.9 per cent, respectively. These two rates compare favourably with the 10.2 and 14.6 per cent for the country as a whole over the same period, and with the 12.9 and 16.9 per cent for Xiamen's own record over the pre–SEZ period of 1950–79.[2] Compared with Shenzhen, China's most–developed SEZ, Xiamen had a lower growth in GDP because the bulk of its economy consisted of old industrial enterprises, but it enjoyed a higher growth in exports due to the

Table 9.1   Growth of Xiamen's GDP and exports, 1980–95

Year	GDP (RMBm. at 1980 price)	Change over preceding year (%)	Exports (US$m)	Change over preceding year (%)
1980	647.6	n.a.	140.3	n.a.
1981	707.1	9.2	141.1	0.7
1982	822.3	16.3	132.0	−6.4
1983	860.4	4.6	128.3	−3.0
1984	1,061.4	23.4	145.9	14.1
1985	1,374.5	29.5	165.3	13.0
1986	1,495.4	8.8	163.7	−0.6
1987	1,823.9	22.0	261.1	59.2
1988	2,343.9	28.5	576.1	120.7
1989	2,764.3	17.9	646.8	12.3
1990	3,144.1	13.7	781.5	20.7
1991	3,732.0	18.7	1,150.6	47.4
1992	4,456.0	19.4	1,765.7	53.4
1993	5,668.1	27.2	2,355.3	33.4
1994	7,323.1	29.2	3,390.9	44.0
1995	9,132.0	24.7	3,481.8	2.7
Average annual growth rate (%)		19.3		23.9

Sources: Xiamen Statistical Bureau (1991, pp.9, 15), EC (1991, pp.227, 236; 1992, pp.246, 255; 1993, pp.219, 229; 1994, pp.246, 254; 1995, pp.289, 299), and *China Economic Review*, July 1996, p.32.

massive influx of foreign–invested export–oriented companies since the early 1980s. For example, between 1990 and 1995 the average annual growth rates for Xiamen's GDP and exports were 23.8 and 34.8 per cent, respectively, in contrast with Shenzhen's 30.4 and 32.4 per cent.[3]

At the same time, Xiamen's economic structure has also been upgraded significantly, with agriculture's share in GDP dropping from 21.6 per cent in 1980 to 6.9 per cent in 1994 and manufacturing's from 57.8 to 48.7 per cent, while the services sector's share has risen from 20.6 to 44.4 per cent (EC 1991, p.247 and 1995, p.283).

As a result, Xiamen's profile in the country has also been raised. Its GDP per capita in 1994 (15,662 yuan) rose to 13th place among 188 major Chinese cities, despite the fact that the size of its economy ranked beyond 40th in the country (EC 1993, p.4 and 1995, p.499). In 1995, its export volume (US$3.48 billion) was the fourth–largest among all the Chinese cities, behind Shenzhen, Shanghai and Guangzhou (Lu 1996, p.26). Before the opening of the SEZ, Xiamen's seaport was very small and could not accommodate large vessels of over 8,000 tons. Today, its seaport, with a handling capacity of 13.1 million tons a year (in 1995), is classified as a Class–I large port (*daxing yilei gangkou*) in the country, ranking 6th in terms of volume of containers handled and 11th in terms of foreign trade goods handled. Linked with over 60 ports in more than 40 countries and regions, the seaport now has 65 berths, of which 11 are capable of serving large ships of over 10,000 tons (EC 1995, pp.56–7 and 1996, p.132). Xiamen's international airport, on the other hand, is currently used by 26 airlines providing flights to 53 domestic and overseas destinations. All these indicate that the establishment of the SEZ and especially the implementation of the 'Special Policy' has created greater economic prosperity in Xiamen, making it one of the strong economic growth centres in southern China.

THE POLICY OF INDUSTRIAL RESTRUCTURING

Unlike the Shenzhen SEZ, which was built on the basis of a little fishing village, the Xiamen SEZ was converted wholesale from the old city. The enlargement of the SEZ in 1984, therefore, has not only increased its territory from 2.5 to 131 square kilometres but, more significantly, embedded the 588 existing enterprises situated in the old city area, in addition to the 180 already established in the Huli District since 1981. As a result, it became clear that the performance of the mainstay of the SEZ's economy, that is, the 588 long–established enterprises, was crucial to the success of the SEZ. This meant that the restructuring of these enterprises should become the priority of Xiamen's industrial reform and development.

Accordingly, soon after the expansion, the Xiamen authorities started to readjust the SEZ's industrial restructuring policy. The new policy included the following ambitious goals:

> To rationalise the industrial structure and upgrade technology in the enterprises through introducing foreign direct investment. As an economic zone, Xiamen should make maximum use of FDI to import as much as possible advanced foreign technology and management expertise into local industrial enterprises. ... From the strategic point of view, the electronics industry should be chosen as the leading industry because it not only represents modern advanced technology but

also has a great bearing on technological transformation of other industries. (EG 1989, p.139).

Clearly, the Xiamen authorities tried to use FDI to promote the restructuring of local, long–established enterprises. By 1994, this strategy became more apparent – the government promulgated a tentative provision to encourage foreign businesses to invest in local industrial enterprises, especially state–owned enterprises (SOEs), and form joint ventures with them. These joint ventures are given additional preferential terms on top of the package of 'Special Policy' applied to all the SEZs. For example, they can enjoy three more years of tax exemption, have priority in getting water, power, transport and communication facilities installed, are to be charged at the rate of domestic users for the use of local utilities, and will, if their products are classified as 'hi–tech products', be allocated more preferential loans and larger quotas for the domestic sale of their products.[4]

Experience in many developing countries indicates that industrial restructuring generally involves structural adjustment to the changing world economic environment, which may require not only substantial investment in new lines of production but also a thorough renovation of existing industries. However, how to use FDI to facilitate the restructuring of local, long–established enterprises, especially SOEs, still remains largely untried. So, can Xiamen fulfil this unprecedented and ambitious goal?

EFFECTS OF FDI ON THE LOCAL ECONOMY

The inflow of FDI into Xiamen started as soon as it was designated as an SEZ in 1980. By the end of 1995, as shown in Table 9.2, Xiamen had concluded 3,450 contracts covering the major forms of FDI – equity joint ventures (EJVs), contractual management enterprises (CMEs), and wholly foreign–owned enterprises (WFEs). These contracts committed foreign investors to make investments in cash (usually foreign currencies), equipment, machinery and technology totalling US$10.3 billion. Of this amount, US$4.7 billion had already been delivered, resulting in over 2,000 FIEs in operation.

From a provincial perspective, although taking only 18.5 per cent of 2,729 contracts signed by Fujian with foreign investors in 1995, Xiamen successfully attracted 23.2 per cent of the total foreign commitment (US$8.9 billion) and 32.7 per cent of the actual invested amount (US$4 billion) in the province within that year. Thus, the average capitalisation of the FDI pro–jects in Xiamen (US$4.08 million per project) was 24.9 per cent higher than Fujian's level (US$3.26 million) and 65.3 per cent higher than the national

Table 9.2   Growth of FDI in Xiamen, 1983–95

Year	No. of contracts signed	Change over previous year	FDI pledged (US$m)	Change over previous year (%)	FDI realised (US$m)	Change over previous year (%)
1983	24	n.a.	37.2	n.a.	–7.8	n.a.
1984	86	258.3	149.7	302.9	40.4	421.8
1985	105	22.1	242	61.7	73.3	81.2
1986	34	–67.6	27.6	–88.6	33.9	–53.7
1987	50	47.1	56.7	105.6	17.5	–48.3
1988	180	260.0	155.6	174.5	48.0	173.6
1989	201	11.7	514.5	230.6	129.8	170.6
1990	262	30.4	485.6	–5.6	72.7	–44.0
1991	213	–18.7	519.8	7.0	132.6	82.3
1992	443	108.0	1,697.0	192.7	563.0	324.7
1993	655	47.9	2,404.0	41.7	1,037.0	84.2
1994	692	5.7	1,864.9	–22.4	1,241.0	19.7
1995	505	–27.0	2,062.4	10.6	1,321.6	6.5
Total	3,449	28.9*	10,261.7	39.8*	4,721.3	53.5*

Note: * Average annual growth rate between 1983 and 1995.

Sources: EC (1986, p.92; 1990, p.327; 1991, p.50; 1992, p.40; 1993, pp.37–8; 1994, p.55; 1995, p.66; and 1996, p.472).

level (US$2.47 million).[5]

In terms of the source of FDI, most of the investors came from the Asia–Pacific region, with Hong Kong (and Macau) and Taiwan taking the lead. In 1995, for example, Hong Kong investment accounted for 53.5 per cent of the total FDI in the SEZ, Taiwan 16.7 per cent, the US 5.7 per cent, Great Britain 5.4 per cent, Japan 3.9 per cent, Singapore 2.6 per cent and Malaysia 2.4 per cent (EC 1996, p.473).

As a result of this infusion of foreign capital and, above all, the dynamism associated with it, two important structural changes have taken place in Xiamen's industry. Firstly, as illustrated in Table 9.3, in terms of sectoral structure, the electronics sector, which was non–existent in 1981, has

Table 9.3 Composition of Xiamen's industry by major sector, 1981 and 1994

Industries	1981		1994	
	GVIO (RMBm at 1980 prices)	Share (%)	GVIO (RMBm at 1990 prices)	Share (%)
Electronics	n.a.	n.a.	468.1	20.8
Machinery	19.8	18.2	446.6	19.8
Food processing	26.5	25.5	245.2	10.9
Textiles	12.9	12.4	240.7	10.7
Chemicals and pharmaceuticals	19.8	19.1	158.9	7.0
Paper and stationery	4.5	4.3	129.7	5.8
Building materials	3.7	3.6	n.a.	n.a.
Sub–total	86.2	83.1	1,689.2	75.0
Others	17.5	16.9	566.3	25.1
Total	103.7	100.0	2,255.4	100.0

Sources: EC (1995, pp.334–5; 1986, p.72).

emerged as the largest industrial sector in Xiamen. By 1994, it accounted for nearly 21 per cent of the SEZ's GVIO, whereas the food–processing sector, which was the largest until the mid–1980s, has been relegated to third place, with its share plunging from 25.5 per cent in 1981 to 10.9 per cent in 1994. The other two major sectors, machinery and textiles, experienced only a small change, with the former's share increasing from 18.2 to 19.8 per cent while the latter's dropped from 12.4 to 10.7 per cent. The share for the chemical and pharmaceutical sector, on the other hand, shrank sharply because the category of 'rubber' was no longer included in this sector. Thus, it appears that Xiamen's overall industrial structure has been improved markedly.

Second, in terms of ownership structure, the FIE sector has replaced the SOE sector to become the largest manufacturing force in the Xiamen economy. As illustrated in Table 9.4, the FIE sector's share in the SEZ's GVIO rose from nothing in 1981 to an astonishing 70.45 per cent in 1994 while that for the SOE sector dived from 78.6 to a mere 17.5 per cent.

Table 9.4 Composition of Xiamen and national GVIO by ownership, 1981 and 1994 (%)

	Xiamen		China	
Sectors	1994	1981	1994	1981
SOE sector	17.5	78.6	34.1	77.5
Collective–owned enterprise sector	6.7	21.3	21.8	21.7
FIE sector	70.5	0.0	8.6	0.0
Private individuals	0.2	0.1	11.5	0.8
Others	5.1	0.0	24.0	0.0
Total	100.0	100.0	100.0	100.0

Sources: EC (1995, pp.67, 322; 1986, p.71), State Statistical Bureau (1981, p.268; 1995, pp.375, 380–81).

Compared with the country as a whole, the ownership structural change in Xiamen was much more radical, transforming the industry from one dominated by inefficient SOEs to one dominated by dynamic FIEs.

Can we therefore reach the conclusion, based on the above two changes, that Xiamen has largely completed its goal of using FDI to facilitate the local industrial restructuring, as claimed by the authorities? A further analysis of the electronics industry and the FIE sector as a whole, however, suggests that such a claim may be premature.

PROBLEMS IN UTILISING FDI

The strategy of using FDI to restructure local industry, especially to develop electronics as the leading sector, may be very appealing to developing countries, particularly those with a heavy presence of obsolete industry in their economies, but it will inevitably conflict with the objectives of foreign investors. In the case of Xiamen, most of the investors want to make use of the local cheap but relatively skilful workforce to produce labour–intensive products for export, while a few intend to use Xiamen as their stepping–stone to enter China's vast domestic market. Clearly, these objectives bear little congruence with Xiamen's goal for utilising FDI. As a result, Xiamen has encountered the following four major problems in the process of using FDI to restructure the local enterprises.

Table 9.5   Composition of the electronics industry in Xiamen by major product group, 1987

	1987		1990		1994	
	GVIO (RMBm at 1980 prices)	%	GVIO (RMBm at 1980 prices)	%	GVIO (RMB mil. at 1990 prices)	%
Consumer goods	543.9	63.1	1,423.5	68.4	2,014.8	43.0
Simple tele–communicatio n equipment	256.4	29.8	246.4	11.8	839.7	17.9
Components and parts	57.7	6.7	303.7	14.6	1,238.8	26.5
Computers	0.22	0.1	36.5	1.8	54.1	1.2
Others	3.1	0.3	70.5	3.4	533.5	11.4
Total	861.32	100.0	2,080.6	100.0	4,680.9	100.0

Sources: Xiamen Statistical Bureau (1988, p.39; 1991, p.43; 1995, p.192).

The first has been the lack of linkage between the electronics sector and other industrial sectors. Table 9.5, showing the change in the composition of the electronics sector's GVIO by major product group from 1987 to 1994, tells us that consumer goods, composed mainly of coloured TV sets, radio cassettes, video recorders, and camcorders, still took the lion's share in 1994 (43 per cent), while simple telecommunication equipment, largely made up of telephones and walkie talkies, accounted for nearly 18 per cent. Computer manufacturing, on the other hand, played only a minor role in the sector, contributing a mere 1.2 per cent in 1994. This left components and parts and other unspecified products to take the rest of the share (nearly 38 per cent).

Experience in other export processing zones (EPZs) suggests that the electronics industry tends to have a low propensity to use local inputs (see Basile and Germidis 1984, pp.48–9). This was not exceptional in Xiamen, where most of the electronics products were made of imported components and parts and, once assembled or processed, re–exported to their overseas markets. In 1994, for example, the electronics sector imported about 93 per cent of its input and exported nearly 83 per cent of its output (Chen 1995, p.46). In other words, the producers, most of which were FIEs, were in fact engaged in enclave–type export–processing activities. Obviously, an industry like this can hardly play the role of so–called 'leading industry', that is, to stimulate the technological transformation of other industries through linkage effects, as originally envisaged by the Xiamen authorities.

The second problem has been the lack of linkage between the FIEs and the local enterprises. This was due largely to the domination of WFEs in the FIE sector. Table 9.6 shows that the share of WFEs in the total number of the FIEs in Xiamen rose steadily from 5.7 per cent in the period of 1981–85 to a peak of 78.6 per cent in 1990. By 1994, it still hovered around 60 per cent. To some extent, this large swing from EJVs to WFEs, rare in the history of FDI within developing countries, was caused by the large–scale influx of Taiwanese capital, which accounted for 40–50 per cent of the total FDI in Xiamen in during the late 1980s and early 1990s (EC 1990, p.329; 1991, p.51; 1992, p.315).

Compared with other foreign investors in Xiamen, the Taiwanese preferred wholly–owned ventures to other forms of investment and, in many cases, emphasised their independence by supplying their own raw materials and export markets.[6] For example, in 1990 more than three–quarters of all the raw materials, components and parts needed by the Taiwanese firms in Xiamen were imported from Taiwan and about 85 per cent of the finished products exported to their existing overseas markets (Qin 1992, p.37). Some midstream factories even invested with upstream and/or downstream factories and formed a self–sufficient and self–sustained operational system, almost wholly independent of the local economy (Kong 1991, p.34).

Obviously, as most WFEs tend to be vertically integrated into their parent corporations abroad, their concern is to maintain their own international production network rather than to set up links with the local economy. Thus, it may be unrealistic to expect the WFEs in Xiamen to develop economic and technological links with the local Chinese companies.

The third problem has been the preponderance of small–sized projects in FDI. In spite of the enormous effort made by the Xiamen authorities to attract large–sized FDI projects, especially those from Western multi–nationals, small–sized projects still accounted for 97.7 per cent of the total FDI projects in operation in 1994 while medium–sized projects constituted 1.9 per cent. Only three firms could be classified as large–sized projects (EC 1995, p.330).[7] Without doubt, the small size of most of the FIEs has considerably restricted their impact on the local industrial restructuring. As can be seen from Table 9.7, from 1986 to 1994 the overall enterprise structure in Xiamen experienced only a small change, with the proportion of small–sized enterprises remaining uncomfortably large (about 96.3 per cent). This will inevitably hinder the enterprises from exploiting economies of scale in the wider export market, crucial to the success of export–led industrialisation.

Table 9.6 Composition of the FIEs in Xiamen by type of contract, 1981–94

Category	1981–85		1986		1987		1988		1989		1990		1991		1992		1993		1994	
	No.	%	No.	%	No.	%	No.	%	No.	%	No.	%	No.	%	No.	%	No.	%	No.	%
Wholly foreign-owned enterprises	12	5.7	5	14.7	13	26.0	79	43.9	136	67.7	195	78.6	125	58.7	254	57.4	345	52.7	413	59.7
Equity joint venture	134	63.5	26	76.5	31	62.0	87	48.3	55	27.4	36	14.5	54	25.3	126	28.4	219	33.4	215	31.1
Contractual manage-ment enterprises	65	30.8	3	8.8	6	12.0	14	7.8	10	5.0	17	6.9	34	16.0	63	14.2	91	13.9	64	9.2
Total	211	100.0	34	100.0	50	100.0	180	100.0	201	100.0	248	100.0	213	100.0	443	100.0	655	100.0	592	100.0

Sources: EC (19 90, p.328; 1991, p.290; 1992, p.314; 1993, p.303; 1994, p.321; 1995, p.376).

Table 9.7   Composition of industrial enterprises in Xiamen by size, 1986 and 1994

Category	1986			1994		
	No.	% of total no.	% of GVIO	No.	% of total no.	% of GVIO
Large	4	0.2	3.8	9	0.6	15.7
Medium	12	0.7	22.4	47	3.1	21.0
Small	1,677	99.1	73.8	1,472	96.3	63.3
Total	1,693	100.0	100.0	1,528	100.0	100.0

Sourcse: Xiamen Statistical Bureau (1986, pp.37–8), EC (1995, pp.320–1).

The final main problem has been limited technology transfer from the FIEs to the local enterprises. The high labour–intensity of the FIEs was also a key reason for this problem. Most of the FIEs in Xiamen were engaged in the production of light industrial/consumer goods destined for their existing overseas markets, and hence tended to apply simple and standardised technology and equipment, which require little skill to operate. A survey shows that about 75 per cent of the FIEs used simple and, in some cases, second–hand machines imported from abroad, manufacturing such goods as footwear, clothing, toys, umbrellas, handicrafts, luggage and sporting equipment. Indeed, some Taiwanese firms even used less capital per unit of labour than the local Chinese SOEs (*Xiamen Statistical Bureau*, 1990, p.25). Needless to say, it is quite difficult, if not impossible, to use these FIEs to promote the technological transformation of the local enterprises.

As a result of the above four problems in utilising FDI, the FIEs have played only a limited role in facilitating the industrial restructuring in Xiamen. Not surprisingly, the performance of the SOE sector in Xiamen, as with most places in China, continued to deteriorate. In 1994, for example, the sector made a net loss of 149 million yuan, or 27.2 per cent of the SEZ's total industrial loss (EC 1995, p.337).

Furthermore, many old structural problems remained largely unsolved. In addition to the disappointingly large share of small–sized enterprises in the local industry, as shown in Table 9.7, infrastructure 'bottlenecks' continued to frustrate economic growth. Between 1980 and 1994, the manufacturing sector on the whole expanded at a rate of 20.3 per cent per annum whereas the infrastructure sector, composed of water and power supplies, passenger and freight transports, and harbour facilities, was lagging behind, with a growth rate of only 11 per cent (EC, 1995, pp.297, 300).

CONCLUSION

This chapter has sought to assess the performance of the Xiamen authorities' strategy of utilising FDI over the period 1980–95. It shows that Xiamen was still far away from fulfilling its goal of using FDI to facilitate the restructuring of local, long–established enterprises, despite the fact that the infusion of foreign capital has, to some extent, improved its overall industrial structure. There were three reasons for this. First, although the newly established electronics sector has emerged as the largest industry in the local economy, it was by and large a foreign–transplanted, labour–intensive industry and had limited forward and/or backward linkage with other industries. Naturally, it could not function as a 'leading industry' to stimulate the technological transformation of other industries through linkage effects, as expected by the authorities.

Second, although the FIE sector had become a dominant manufacturing and exporting force in the local economy, a considerable part of it was still not integrated into the local economy and thus, to a large degree, did not interact with the local enterprises. As many FIEs were engaged in enclave–type export–processing operations, it was hard for them to transfer technology and/or management expertise to the local enterprises.

Finally, the small size and relatively high labour intensity of most of the FIEs have further restricted their impact on local industrial restructuring.

Thus, the Xiamen experiment highlights the importance of a basic issue, that is, having a more realistic expectation of the role of FDI projects in developing countries. FDI may be used to create jobs, increase foreign exchange earnings, and indeed promote the prosperity of the local economy, but there are difficulties in using it to facilitate the restructuring of local, long–established industry because it will inevitably conflict with the objectives of FDI in developing countries. In other words, the Xiamen experience has proved that the strategy of using FDI to facilitate the restructuring of such enterprises is, at least for the time being, an unduly high expectation on the role of FDI.

In fact, with the opening of the direct shipping link with Taiwan, it is perhaps high time for Xiamen to reassess its comparative advantages *vis-à-vis* other Chinese SEZs and coastal cities. This may well lead to the readjustment of its industrial restructuring policy. As a city possessing a superior seaport and airport in southeastern China, Xiamen has great potential to become the transit centre to handle both cargo and passengers travelling between Taiwan and the mainland, a large part of which is currently handled by Hong Kong. This means that modernising the transport and tourist sectors, especially the seaport, should become the new priority of its industrial restructuring in order to cope with the imminent boom of *entrepôt* trade and tourism. In doing so, Xiamen will embark on the road of historic transformation from a manufacturing–dominated economy to a services–dominated one.

NOTES

1. However, the formal construction of the SEZ did not start until October 1981.
2. For the national figures, *Jingrong Shibao* (Financial News) (Beijing), 29/02/96, p.1; *Lianhe Zaobao* (United Morning Newspaper) (Singapore), 4/3/96, p.14; and SSB 1995 *Zhongguo nianjian 1995* (People's Republic of China Yearbook 1995), pp.150, 152; and for Xiamen's pre–SEZ figures, EC, *Xiamen Jingji Tequ Nianjian 1986*, pp.110–23.
3. See Table 9.1 and *Shenzhen jingji tequ nianjian 1996* (Almanac of the Shenzhen SEZ 1996), China Statistical Publishing House, Beijing, p.66.
4. For the Tentative Provisions on Encouraging Foreign Investors to Participate in the Transformation of Existing Industrial Enterprises issued by the Xiamen People's Government on 30 September 1994, see *Xiamen jingji tequ nianjian 1995*, pp.464–5.
5. *China Economic News* (Beijing), 17/6/96, No. 22, pp.22–3. For more information and analyses of FDI development in Fujian Province, see Luo and Ash (1996, pp.123–52).
6. For more information and analyses about Taiwanese investment in Xiamen, see Luo and Howe (1993, pp.746–69).
7. In China, the size of industrial enterprises is normally classified on the basis of their production capacities. In this case, however, the FDI projects are divided according to the number of employees, with those having 100 employees or below classified as small–sized firms, those between 101 and 500 as medium sized, and those with 501 and above as large sized.

REFERENCES

Basile, A. and Germidis, D., 1984. *Investing in free export processing zones*. OECD, Paris.
Chen, Qilin, 1995. 'The industrial structure in China's SEZs', *Fujian xuekan* (The Fujian Academic Journal), January.
EC (Editorial Committee), various issues. *Xiamen jingji tequ nianjian* (Almanac of the Xiamen SEZ), Statistical Publishing House of China, Beijing.
EG (Editorial Group), 1989. *Xiamen jingji shehui fazhang zhanlue 1985–2000* (The strategy of socio–economic development in Xiamen 1985–2000). Lujiang Publishing House, Xiamen.
Fujian Statistical Bureau, 1985. *Fujian jingji nianjian 1985* (Almanac of the Fujian economy 1985), Fujian People's Publishing House, Fuzhou.
Jingrong Shibao (Financial News), Beijing, 29/02/96.
Kong, Zhang, 1991. 'Assessment of Taiwanese investment in Xiamen', *Gang'ao jingji* (Hong Kong and Macau Economies), Guangzhou, June.
Lianhe Zaobao (United Morning Newspaper), Singapore, 4/3/96.
Lu, Yonghui, 1996. 'On Xiamen's role in the southwestern Fujian economy', *Tequ jingji* (The SEZ Economy), Shenzhen, June.

Luo, Qi and Ash, R., 1996. 'The economic challenge' in B. Hook (ed.), *Fujian: gateway to Taiwan*, Oxford University Press, Hong Kong.

Luo, Qi and Howe, C., 1993. 'Direct investment and economic integration in the Asia Pacific: the case of Taiwanese investment in Xiamen', *China Quarterly*, December.

Qin, Xuezhen, 1992. 'An analysis of wholly foreign–owned enterprises in the Xiamen SEZ', *Xiamen tequ yanjiu* (Studies of the Xiamen SEZ), Xiamen, No. 4.

State Statistical Bureau (SSB), 1981. *Zhongguo nianjian 1981* (People's Republic of China yearbook 1981), Yearbook Publishing House of China, Beijing.

State Statistical Bureau (SSB), 1995. *Zhongguo nianjian 1995* (People's Republic of China yearbook 1995), Yearbook Publishing House of China, Beijing.

Xiamen Statistical Bureau, various issues. *Xiamen tongji nianjian*, Statistical Publishing House of China, Beijing.

10. FDI and Economic Development in Guangdong

Yisheng Lan

INTRODUCTION

Guangdong has been a leader in China for the last 18 years in introducing foreign capital, especially foreign direct investment (FDI), and maintaining impressive economic growth. Getting into the 1990s, the share of FDI in total foreign capital has risen further and FDI has been playing a more important role in the provincial economic development. In 1995, the actual foreign direct investment in Guangdong was US$10.18 billion, which took up 27 per cent of the country's yearly intake. By the end of 1995, the number of registered foreign–invested enterprises (FIEs), *sanzi qiye*, in Guangdong reached 59,600, which was 25.5 per cent of the national figure (Guangdong Statistical Bureau 1996). The cumulative sum of actual FDI in Guangdong from 1979 to 1995 was US$38.8 billion, which was 29.1 per cent of the national figure of US$133.2 billion.

Since 1994, however, Guangdong has been facing more difficulties in utilising FDI to develop the local economy, and whether Guangdong can keep its top position in China in hosting FDI is questionable. Factors such as the loss of preferential economic policies, rising labour and land costs and poor public security in some cities have put Guangdong into an unprecedentedly difficult situation in attracting foreign capital. To keep the top position in China with FDI and economic development, the Guangdong provincial government has put into effect some new measures to encourage foreign investors.

FDI AND ECONOMIC DEVELOPMENT IN GUANGDONG

The economic reform and openness of China since 1979 has led to the most rapid economic growth in its history. Guangdong has benefited from and contributed much to this process and has become the leading economic giant of the country. From 1979 to 1995, the real average annual GDP growth of Guangdong was 14.2 per cent (China as whole had 8 per cent), even faster than Hong Kong, Taiwan, Singapore and Korea at their 'take–off' period; the urban resident income per capita increased from RMB402 to RMB6,850 yuan; and the rural resident income per capita increased from RMB193 to RMB2,699 yuan (Zhou et al. 1996). In 1994, the population of Guangdong was 66.91 million, 5.6 per cent of the nation, and its land was only 1.9 per cent of the whole country, but its yearly GDP was 9.7 per cent, fixed asset investment 13.4 per cent, residents' saving 11.8 per cent, import value 29.6 per cent, export value 38.8 per cent, actual foreign investment 25 per cent, tourist foreign exchange revenue 15.6 per cent and consumption goods retail sales 11.5 per cent of the nation (Guangdong Statistical Bureau 1995, pp.114–5).

The incredible economic achievements of Guangdong over the past 18 years have obviously been, to a great extent, the result of successful use of foreign capital. Guangdong has had both the most foreign capital and the fastest economic growth among all the provinces in China since 1979. The annual GDP and actual FDI growth rate between 1980 and 1995 was 14 per cent and 34 per cent, respectively. Foreign capital, FDI in particular, has helped to create the economic miracle of Guangdong (see Figure 10.1).

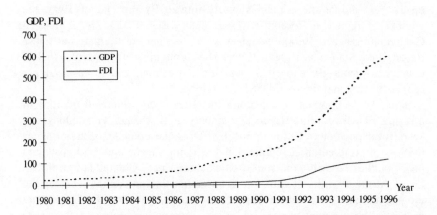

Sources: Guangdong Statistical Bureau (various years), GSB (1996).

Figure 10.1   Actual FDI and GDP in Guangdong (FDI in US$100 million, GDP in billion RMB)

FDI has made a tremendous contribution to output, employment and export growth and has been playing a more and more important role in Guangdong. Compared to the seventh 'Five–year–plan' period (1986–90), the share of actual FDI in total realised foreign capital inflow in Guangdong in the eighth 'Five–year–plan' period (1991–95) rose from 50.2 per cent to 79.8 per cent, while the share of realised foreign loans and other forms foreign capital in the total realised foreign capital inflow decreased to 20.2 per cent (see Figure 10.2). In 1995, the industrial FIEs completed production value of RMB282 billion yuan in Guangdong, which took up 36.5 per cent of the total provincial industrial production value, and the percentage was over 50 per cent in Shenzhen, Zhuhai, Shantou and Huizhou (Chen 1996). The export value of FIEs in 1996 was US$30.7 billion, which took up 51.7 per cent of the yearly provincial exports, US$59.4 billion. Now about one–third of the fixed asset investment in Guangdong comes from foreign resources.

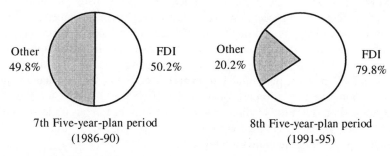

Other 49.8%	FDI 50.2%	
7th Five-year-plan period (1986-90)		

Other 20.2%	FDI 79.8%
8th Five-year-plan period (1991-95)	

Sources:　Guangdong Statistical Bureau (various years).

Figure 10.2　Share of actual FDI in total realised foreign capital inflow in Guangdong

The realised foreign capital from 1986 to 1995 took one–quarter to one–third of fixed assets investment in Guangdong (Guangdong Statistical Bureau 1987–96). In the three special economic zones, the share was even higher. The cumulative sum of realised foreign capital from 1980 to 1995 in Guangdong reached US$53 billion. Of the realised foreign capital, more than two–thirds was FDI. This is essential for the local economic development, particularly at its early stage when capital shortage would very likely result in a bottleneck.

Given the ambitious development goals set by the provincial government for the year 2000 and the year 2010, the domestic capital supply could hardly meet the huge investment demand. By 2000, GDP per capita should reach RMB7000 yuan, which requires a 13.4 per cent annual growth rate over the 1990s. By 2010, GDP per capita should reach RMB20,000 yuan, which requires 12.4 per cent per annum growth on average between 2001 and 2010 (Fu 1993). To maintain the high per annum growth, investment in these periods will certainly need to be increased on a larger scale and beyond the domestic capital supply capability.[1] Therefore foreign capital will be needed continue to play an important, or even decisive, role in the future development.

By the end of 1995, more than 6,000 established manufacturing enterprises, about two–thirds of all the existing manufacturing firms in Guangdong, improved their production operation by introducing new technology, equipment, management skills and expertise that were brought by foreign investors or partners. In recent years, some state–owned, deficit–making enterprises have been sold or rented to foreign investors. Most of them have made ends meet by improving management, introducing new products and raising production efficiency.

Most FIEs are export–market oriented (especially firms involved in manufacturing easy–processing and labour–intensive products), both because the Chinese government requires that FIEs balance their foreign exchange accounts and the obvious advantage of China in labour–intensive production. FIEs helped to establish Guangdong's leading position in China's foreign trade, particularly in exports (see Figure 10.3). Guangdong had a cumulative export/import trade volume of US$382.3 billion from 1979 to 1995 and has been the leading province in China in foreign trade volume since 1986.[2] In 1996, Guangdong's exports were US$59.35 billion, which was 39.3 per cent of the national total.

CURRENT SITUATION OF FDI IN GUANGDONG

Hong Kong has been the leading FDI investor in Guangdong. In 1995, it had actual FDI of US$8 billion in Guangdong, which accounted for 78.1 per cent of the provincial yearly intake. Other major investors for the year included Japan 4.1 per cent; Taiwan 3.5 per cent; the United States 3.3 per cent; Macau 2.5 per cent; and Singapore 2.2 per cent. Looking through the 1990–96 period, we find that some changes happened to the FDI in Guangdong.

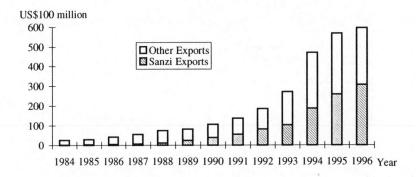

Sources: Guangdong Statistical Bureau (various years), GSB (1996).

Figure 10.3 Export composition in Guangdong, 1984–96

New Features of Slow Growth

Both the contracted FDI and the actual FDI experienced rapid growth in the 1991–93 period, then slowed down and even decreased in the 1994–96 period (see Figure 10.4). The obvious reasons for such a great fluctuation were Deng Xiaoping's South speech in Shenzhen, Zhuhai and so on, in 1992, which stimulated a new wave of foreign investment, and the Central government's macroeconomic adjustment and control policies, which firmly cut the total domestic investment scale to ease the serious inflationary pressure. Other reasons include the weakening of the advantageous position of Guangdong since 1993 when the Central government gradually unified its policies towards foreign investment all over the country, so that Guangdong, particularly its special economic zones (SEZs), that is, Shenzhen, Zhuhai and Shantou, no longer hold the policy advantages in attracting FDI projects.

Investment Diversified Activities

In the 1980s, FDI in Guangdong was focused mainly on the manufacturing industries such as textiles, clothes, shoes, toys, and electronics components. Since 1990, more and more capital has been invested in real estate, transportation, telecommunication and other service sectors (see Figure 10.5).

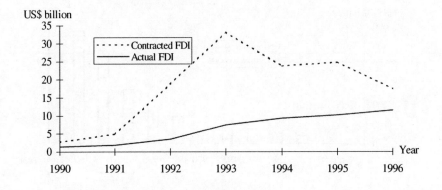

Sources: Guangdong Statistical Bureau (various years); GSB (1996).

Figure 10.4   Yearly contracted and actual FDI in Guangdong, 1990–96

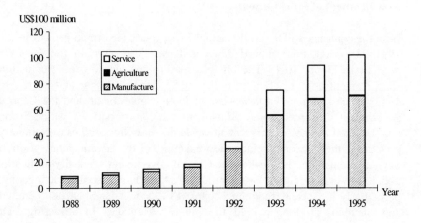

Sources: Guangdong Statistical Bureau (various years).

Figure 10.5   Sectoral shares of actual FDI in Guangdong, 1988–95

Large–scale Investment

In the 1991–95 period, the average volume of foreign–invested projects was US$2.12 million and the average scale of the projects approved in 1995 was US$3.03 million. This is double or even triple the figures for the 1986–90 period of US$0.93 million. In 1996, the average volume reached US$3.37

million. This change partly reflected the trend that multinational corp–orations have become more interested in investing in China, and Guangdong is one of major target areas. Quite a few big international business players, such as AT&T, GE, GMC, Pepsi, Canon, Mitsubishi, Panasonic, BHP and Philips, have now invested in projects in Guangdong.

Changing Distribution

In the 1980s, FDI in Guangdong concentrated on the three SEZs and the Pearl River Delta region. Getting into the 1990s, FDI has been spreading further into the East, West and North mountain area, and their share of the provincial FDI rose from 25 per cent in 1990 to 31.2 per cent in 1995.

Structure Change

While all three kinds of foreign–invested ventures maintained upward trends into the 1990s, the share of wholly foreign–owned ventures increased even faster than equity joint ventures and cooperative ventures. The share of wholly foreign–owned venture investment within total realised FDI rose from 14.7 per cent in 1989 to 25 per cent in 1995 (see Figure 10.6). This shows that the share of equity joint ventures decreased from 48.3 to 35.1 per cent while the share of cooperative ventures rose from 37.1 to 40 per cent, which implied that more and more joint–venture projects may now be involved with technique transfer and cooperation instead of financial input only.

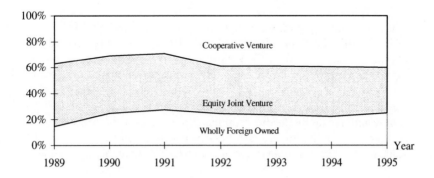

Source: Guangdong Statistical Bureau (1990).

Figure 10.6   Structure change of actual FDI in Guangdong, 1989–95

The Difficulties and Problems

The loss of preferential policies and higher labour and land costs makes Guangdong less attractive to some foreign investors   Unified policies and fair competition for all the provinces/municipalities/autonomous regions are now the basic principles of the Chinese government concerning FDI, which means that taxation, import duties, foreign–invested project approvals and other regulations related to FDI are basically the same throughout the country. Guangdong has been pulled down from its advantageous position created by the Central government's preferential policies, which contributed much to Guangdong's rapid foreign investment development and externally oriented economic growth. At the same time, after 18 years of rapid economic growth, land costs, office rents and wage levels in Guangdong are higher than in most other provinces, which is discouraging foreign investors. The cheaper land and labour competition comes not only from other provinces, but also from some low–income neighbouring countries like Vietnam.

'Soft' environment for foreign investment needs to be improved   In recent years, although infrastructure, such as transportation and utilities, has been greatly improved, the problems of crime and public security in some cities of Guangdong have become serious, which makes foreign investors worried about property safety and social stability. Safety and profitability are always two major concerns of foreign investors. In addition, corruption and wilful levy by some government officials on local enterprises are also major headaches for foreign investors.

The percentage of realised FDI from total contracted FDI is low   From 1979 to 1995, the cumulative contracted FDI was valued at US$123 billion, but the realised sum was US$39 billion, that is, 31.6 per cent. Even though the 1995 figure rose to 41 per cent, it is still well below reasonable expectations. The main reasons for this are the lack of reliable feasibility analysis on investment projects, being short of domestic–support capital supply and having ineffective contracts. Some investment projects have little economic feasibility but are rashly pushed by local officials because of their value for the cadres to show as their achievements to higher authorities.

Industrial relations in some FIEs become tense   Some investors, especially some of those from Hong Kong, Macau, Taiwan and Korea, are not particularly concerned about their employees' working conditions and often ignore the requirements of the state Labour Laws. The long working hours, wilful cuts of wages and poor working and living conditions stimulate workers' antagonism. Some workplace accidents, such as fires and bodily injury caused by poor and careless management, have raised workers' anger and made industrial relations in these FIEs very tense. If these problems cannot be solved or relieved soon, they could undermine the future development of FDI.[3]

PROSPECTS

Relatively developed economy, market mechanism and infrastructure The rapid economic growth since 1979 established Guangdong's leading economic position over the other provinces (see Table 10.1). More importantly, the market and market mechanism have been better developed in Guangdong than in other provinces. Further, partly with the help of FDI, transportation, telecommunication and other infrastructure in Guangdong have been greatly improved within this period. Guangdong now leads the nation in per capita telephone (including mobile phone) quantity, highway length, port capacity, airline passenger and cargo transportation and so on. The newly–completed Guangzhou–Meizhou–Shantou Railway, Guangzhou–Shenzhen Super–highway and Shenzhen–Shantou Super–highway, plus other railway, highway, seaport and airport development projects have made Guangdong more accessible to foreign investors and more integrated with other parts of the world economy, Hong Kong's economy in particular. And one of the three Internet outlets of China is in Guangzhou. All of this will certainly give some weight to Guangdong when foreign investors make their

Table 10.1   Some economic indicators of five major provinces of China

| | GDP (RMB bn) | | | | Export (US$ bn) | | Govt revenue (RMB bn) | |
| | 1985 | | 1995 | | 1994 | | 1994 | |
	Value	Place	Value	Place	Value	Place	Value	Place
Guangdong	55.30	4	538.2	1	49.99	1	29.87	1
Jiangsu	65.20	1	515.5	2	8.93	3	13.64	5
Shandong	63.10	2	500.2	3	7.08	5	13.33	7
Sichuan	58.50	3	353.4	4	2.25	8	13.55	6
Zhejiang	41.20	8	352.4	5	6.26	7	9.46	10

Note: Place is the position among all the 30 provincial units of mainland China.

Sources: State Statistical Bureau (various years).

location choices, especially at the time when we are moving towards the more efficient information era of the 21st century.

The potential both to develop high–tech industries and to find low–cost production sites for labour–intensive manufacturing within the province
The economic development of Guangdong has been quite unbalanced between different districts. As early birds, three SEZs and the Pearl River Delta have hosted most foreign investment and enjoyed faster economic growth due to preferential government policy, better infrastructure and easier access to foreign investors. The unbalanced economic development in Guangdong allows foreign investors potential both to introduce more advanced technology and equipment into some areas in order to raise profits and to find low–cost locations in other areas so as to keep easy–processing, labour–intensive products profitable.

With Guangzhou, Shenzhen, Zhuhai and their satellite cities, the Pearl River Delta has had the most rapid economic growth both in Guangdong and in China for the past 18 years and is the comparatively developed area in Guangdong. The Delta has a population of 21 million and an area of 41,596 square kilometres, which account for 31 per cent and 23.4 per cent, respectively, of the whole province. It created 70 per cent and over 80 per cent of the provincial GDP and exports in 1996. Because of the rapid economic development and income rise, thousands of talented, well–educated and mostly young people, have been attracted into this area from all over the country in past years. Therefore the Delta now has one of the most–educated and skilled labour forces in China.[4] This is a major advantage for Guangdong in attracting high–tech and knowledge–intensive FDI projects over most other provinces. In fact, the provincial government and some municipal governments such as Guangzhou, Shenzhen and Zhuhai have shifted their policy incentives towards such FDI projects from the traditional, labour–intensive FDI projects.

At the same time, since the gap in income level and labour cost between these relatively developed areas and other backward areas could be greater than the difference between Guangdong and other neighbouring provinces (see Figure 10.7), it is possible for foreign investors to find cheap labour and land within the province and keep their labour–intensive products profitable for a few years. In 1995, the average wage of all formal employees in Jieyang city and Heyuan city (both in Guangdong province), was RMB4,553 and RMB4,678 yuan, respectively, about one–third of that of Shenzhen, RMB12,276 yuan, and less than one–tenth of the average Hong Kong manufacturing worker's salary, of HK$62,000, and lower than that of the neighbouring provinces such as Fujian, Hunan and the national average.

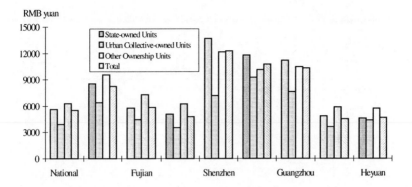

Sources: State Statistical Bureau (various years); Guangdong Statistical Bureau (1996).

Figure 10.7 Average wage of formal employees in 1995 (RMB yuan)

The close relation and economic integration with Hong Kong Hong Kong is the largest FDI investor in Guangdong, and there are over 2,300 Hong Kong invested enterprises and 80 thousand factories processing export goods for Hong Kong within the Pearl River Delta alone. It is estimated that the Hong Kong capital employs more than 3 million workers in the Delta (*Zhongguo Waizi* 1997). So Guangdong, and the Pearl River Delta in particular, has become a huge factory for Hong Kong's re–exports. The actual FDI from Hong Kong takes the lion's share of the total actual FDI in Guangdong (see Figure 10.8). Hong Kong is both the major export market and import origin of Guangdong. The externally oriented economy of Guangdong is in fact the Hong Kong–oriented economy.[5] In 1995, Guangdong's exports to and imports from Hong Kong were US$48.45 billion and US$30.35 billion, respectively, 87 per cent and 79.5 per cent of its total exports and imports. The financial and economic ties between Guangdong and Hong Kong have become quite strong over the past 18 years.

The close economic relations and geographic connection between Guangdong and Hong Kong give Guangdong not only opportunities to share the prosperity of Hong Kong but also a unique position among Chinese provinces, that is, it could have a greater influence on Hong Kong's economy. This will give Guangdong more weight in the Central government policy–making process, especially in this crucial period when Hong Kong's prosperity is important in keeping the local people's faith in its future, to set a successful example of national unity for Macau and Taiwan, and to show the world the ability of the Chinese government to maintain Hong Kong as one of the major financial, trade and shipping centres in the world, after its

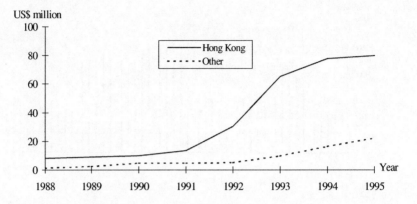

Sources: Guangdong Statistical Bureau (various years).

*Figure 10.8   Hong Kong's share of the total actual FDI in Guangdong,
                1988–95*

return to Chinese sovereignty. The Central government may find it ne–
cessary to keep Guangdong's economy dynamic and prosperous in order to
maintain Hong Kong's prosperity.

The established ties with foreign investors and clients As the major export
producer and FDI host of China, Guangdong has established broader and
stronger economic ties with foreign investors and clients, and has
accumulated more experience in dealing with foreign investors and
developing markets abroad than other provinces. And as one of the main
origins of overseas Chinese, Guangdong finds it easier to appeal to these
compatriot investors.[6]

Deficit–making state–owned enterprises As the coastal front, Guangdong
had received less state capital input from the Central government than most
inland provinces from the 1950s to the 1970s. This investment policy led to
a comparatively smaller state–owned sector and fewer large state–owned
enterprises (SOEs) in Guangdong. This used to be considered a weakness of
Guangdong and the major reason for its poor and backward industrial base
in that period. But now it has become one of the advantages of Guangdong
because it has fewer human–powered, poorly equipped, low–efficiency, and
deficit–making state–owned enterprises, which in many inland provinces
have become the main absorbers of government revenue and most
importantly, the cause of unemployment or underlying unemployment.

It is also interesting to note that, because most of the SOEs in Guangdong were set up later in the 1980s and 1990s, they have relatively advanced technology and equipment and a mainly market–oriented management mechanism, and have a better performance record than those in inland provinces. In fact, Guangdong has been leading the nation in holding cumulative state assets since 1993. In 1995, SOEs held 40.8 per cent of the total industrial input capital in Guangdong, while FIEs held 40.2 per cent and collective ownership enterprises held 14.4 per cent (Zhou et al. 1996). SOEs are a major resource and contributor to the provincial revenue.

Foreign investment through the stock market The common experience is that foreign capital involvement usually starts with loans then extends to joint ventures, and then to portfolio investment. Foreign investors have become more and more interested in the listed shareholding companies in China.[7] Since the shareholding companies have had to pass a complicated assessment process to list their shares on the market, they have better credit worthiness, and foreign investors are also more interested in considering them as partners for joint ventures than other enterprises.[8] As Guangdong hosts one of the two stock exchanges in China (Shenzhen and Shanghai) and has more listed companies than other provinces, it has benefited already, and will benefit more from this trend in the future.

NEW POLICIES TO ENCOURAGE FOREIGN DIRECT INVESTMENT

Since the Central government has turned its main attention to speeding up the middle and western areas' economic growth to narrow the gap of economic development and income levels between the East and the West, Guangdong can no longer enjoy the favourable position in the Central government policy–making process that it held from the early 1980s to the early 1990s. It has to be totally self–reliant to keep its leading position in introducing foreign capital and outward–oriented economic development. Being aware of the difficulties it is facing, the Guangdong provincial government has decided to adopt a more positive and encouraging attitude and policy towards foreign investment and promised an orderly and efficient part opening of the local market to foreign investors in order to attract foreign capital. The basic idea and approach is to swap part of the local market and state ownership for foreign capital and technology. Some new policies were put into effect in 1996.

Loosen Restriction on Domestic Sales Share of FIE Products

- For joint ventures and cooperative production projects that encourage the development of hi–tech industries, with foreign capital taking 50 per cent or more of the total invested capital, up to 50 per cent of their products could be sold on the domestic market if the total investment amount is below US$5 million; up to 60 per cent could be sold domestically if the total investment is between US$5 million and US$15 million; up to 100 per cent if the investment is over US$15 million (Fu 1996, p.76).
- For joint ventures in agriculture such as cultivation with high technology, high efficiency and high productivity, up to 100 per cent of their products could be sold on the domestic market regardless of the invested amount. If the invested projects are totally owned by foreign capital, up to 40 per cent of their products could be sold domestically (Fu 1996, p.76).
- If foreign investors purchase state–owned enterprises evaluated by the State Assets Administration Bureau and take 25 per cent or more of the ownership, up to 60 per cent of the enterprise products could be sold domestically.
- If foreign investors invest in the encouraging industries in mountain or island cities/counties with total investment being over US$1.5 million and foreign capital more than 50 per cent, up to 100 per cent of the products could be sold domestically.[9]

Gradually Grant Foreign–funded Enterprises 'Local Status'

FIEs used to have both concessional treatment such as income tax waivers and tariff exemptions on capital goods imports, and discriminatory treatment such as local market access restrictions and investment sector restrictions. Now the Chinese government is considering removing these 'treatments' on FIEs step by step. Some preferential policies towards FIEs, for example, two–year waivers and three–year half waivers on their income tax, have been rescinded. Meanwhile more industries and business areas such as banking, insurance, securities, foreign trade, retailing, tourism, transportation, real estate, infrastructure, accountancy and legal consultancy are either newly opened to FDI or opened wider to FDI, for example, allowing wholly foreign–owned enterprises to enter some sectors. Guangdong is quite active in this direction and is sure to take more steps towards this goal earlier than most other provinces.

Encourage More Multinational Corporations to Invest in Guangdong

Even though Guangdong is well ahead of other provinces in hosting more foreign capital, the average value of FDI projects in Guangdong had been below the national average for a long period until 1993. That reflected the fact that most FIEs in Guangdong were from relatively smaller investors in Hong Kong, which usually meant less–advanced technology and management skills in the invested projects. The situation has changed since 1994 when more big investors expressed an interest in Guangdong. More investment from multinational corporations with advanced technology and management would raise the quality of FIEs in favour of restructuring the local economy to high–technology and high–efficiency bases. Such FIEs, from the experience so far, also have less trouble with industrial relations than smaller FIEs.

In order to attract more multinational corporations to Guangdong, the provincial government has put into effect some policies in favour of big investors, particularly if they invest in infrastructure projects and high–tech industries. The fact that the average value of FDI projects increased quite substantially in 1995 and 1996 reflects some active results from this effort. It can also be viewed as a signal that FIEs in Guangdong are probably in the transition from traditionally more labour–intensive projects to more capital/technology–intensive investment projects.

The provincial government is also enforcing laws and regulations to improve the social environment for FDI: (i) punish criminals firmly according to the state criminal law and more effectively protect the lives and property of foreign investors and their employees; (ii) enforce the state Labour Laws within FIEs to protect the legal interests of employees and fair competition among FIEs; (iii) establish trade unions to carry on collective bargaining and encourage equal, cooperative, mutual–benefit industrial relations within FIEs; (iv) enforce the industrial property rights protection law to ease the worry and concern of foreign partners on technology transfer; (v) increase the transparency of FDI project approval and other FDI–related policies and management; (vi) punish corrupt officials and lift illegal levies or charges on FIEs.

CONCLUSION

Facing more difficulties than in the past, Guangdong may be unable to maintain FDI inflow and economic growth at the pace of the past 18 years, but it still holds an obviously advanced position over other provinces in hosting FDI and developing an outward–oriented economy. Being aware of

224 Foreign Direct Investment and Regional Economies

the challenge it faces, the Guangdong government has put some new policies into effect to overcome present difficulties. With its established advantageous position, that is, with better infrastructure, a higher–quality labour force and relatively developed market mechanism and economic ties with foreign resources, and the trend that more and more multinational corporations are entering the province, Guangdong has the potential to develop more high–tech, capital/technology–intensive FIEs. Meanwhile, with the cheap labour and land in some relatively backward areas of the province, it also has the potential for shifting labour–intensive FDI projects to these areas from the Pearl River Delta and maintaining some further development in this field. Therefore it is very unlikely that Guangdong will lose its leading economic position in China in the near future. Its integration with Hong Kong will also contribute to its future prosperity. If most of the new policies are carried out as expected, Guangdong could keep its top position in China for at least another decade.

NOTES

1. Estimated by the State Statistical Bureau of China, at the annual GDP growth of 8–9 per cent, the national cumulative sum of FDI in the 1996–2000 period will be US$230–270 billion. See *People's Daily* (Overseas edition), 24 March 1997.
2. Calculated from Statistical Yearbooks of Guangdong (1982–96).
3. In the International Conference on Labour Flow and Coastal Area Economic Development in China at Shantou University, Guangdong, in November 1995, some scholars from China, Australia, the UK and the US pointed out this problem in their papers. This collection of papers is to be published.
4. Since 1993, it has been very difficult, if not impossible, for people without Master/Doctor degrees or higher academic/technician qualifications to get permanent residency in Guangzhou, Shenzhen and Zhuhai.
5. In 1996, the export dependency rate (export to GDP ratio) of Guangdong was 82 per cent, the highest among all China's provinces.
6. Take the example of Chao–Shan area, which includes Chaozhou, Shantou, Jieyang and Shanwei, where there is a popular saying: 'One Chao–Shan in China and another Chao–Shan abroad', which means, in addition to the 20 million population in Chao–Shan area, there are over 10 million overseas Chinese who are of Chao–Shan origin.
7. By March 1997, 87 Chinese companies had issued 8.99 billion B–shares, a special category of shares for foreign investors, and totally raised capital of about US$3 billion. In addition, 29 Chinese companies sell their stocks on other stock exchanges outside mainland China (out of them, 22 are in Hong Kong, two in New York, four in both Hong Kong and New York and one in both Hong Kong and London), which raised capital of US$5.9 billion. See Lan Yisheng: 'Stock market in China: problems and prospects for domestic investment and foreign investment', CERC of Adelaide University working papers, 1997 (forthcoming).
8. See note 7.
9. There are a total of 50 counties in the East, West and North mountain areas and islands where FDIs have this incentive.

REFERENCES

Chen, Linhui and Jin, Dui, 1996. 'The important measures of Guangdong in utilising foreign capital', *Guangdong Da Jingmao*, November, p.32.

Fu, Xiaoping, 1993. 'Utilise foreign capital sufficiently to promote economic construction', *Enlightenment of reform and openness in Guangdong*, Guangdong, People's Publishing House, April, pp.167–76.

Fu, Xiaoping, 1996. 'The new preferential treatments to attract foreign investment', *Guangdong Da Jingmao*, August, p.76.

GSB (Guangdong Statistical Bureau), 1996. *Statistical bulletin on the economic and social development of Guangdong in 1996*, Statistical Publishing House of China, Beijing.

Guangdong Statistical Bureau, various years. *Statistical yearbook of Guangdong*, Statistical Publishing House of China, Beijing.

State Statistical Bureau, various years. *China statistical yearbook*, Statistical Publishing House of China, Beijing.

Zhongguo Waizi, 1997. 'Hong Kong's return and Hong Kong capital in the mainland', *Foreign capital in China*, January.

Zhou, Liao–gang, Zhang, J., Gao, Wei–wu and Feng, Yu–hua, 1996. 'Viewing the combination of market economy system with the basic socialist system from the practice of Guangdong', *Xueshu Yanjiu* (Academic Research), No. 12.

Index

econometric
  analysis 48
  studies 140
economic
  efficiency 185, 188
  growth centres 197
  sanctions 16
  and technological development zones
      14, 45
economies
  export–oriented 194
  newly industrialising 72, 157
  planned 25
    centrally 12
    state 186
  of scale 73, 182, 186, 203
efficiency 36–7, 136, 222
  allocative 149
  measurement 66
  operational 33
  production 212
  productive 28
  technical 60–2
  technological 74
employment and compensation systems
    187
enterprise
  contractual management 198
  export–oriented–type 174
  foreign–funded 71
  foreign–invested 5, 13, 209–10
  foreign–owned 161
  Hong Kong invested 219
  industrial 207
  small–scale 174
  small–sized 203, 205
  state–owned 33, 86, 149, 161, 174,
      198, 220
    systems 187
  technologically advanced 160
  wholly foreign–owned 198
entrepôt
  centre 182
  trade and tourism 207
entry barriers 4
error–components 48
euphoria 160

export composition 179
export–led
  growth 38
  industrialisation 72, 203
export–oriented FDI 72
export–promotion strategy 4
externalities 57
extrapolation 47

factor
  endowment 73, 85, 101
    approach 102
    relative 74
  intensities 102
  movements 102
  price equalisation 102
  proportion asymmetries 74
family–based management 174
FDI–led growth 140
fixed effect 48
foreign exchange
  control 114
  swap centres 160
foreign–invested
  firms 23, 25, 30
  ventures 176
Frankel, J. 86, 92, 97

generalised least square 48
geographical distribution 42
globalisation 140
government interference 186
Granger, C.W.J. 150
Granger causality 144
Granger no–causality 144–5, 149
  test 144, 147
gravity model 86, 91–2

heteroscedasticity 48, 88, 92
Hsiao, C. 48
human capital 3, 101
  minimum threshold stock of 4

import substitution 161
  strategy 4
increasing returns to scale 182, 184,
    187

marketplace 12
maximisation 136
measurement error 62
middle class 150
minimisation 136
monetary policy 25
most favoured nation 184
multicollinearity 50
multinational corporations 6

national
    austerity programme 161
    treatment 222
    unity 219
nationalisation 189
new growth
    framework 57
    theory 3, 140
        framework 5

Ohlin, B. 101–2
oligopolistic market structure 73
open-door policy 13, 42, 71, 75
ordinary least square 48, 88, 146
overseas–funded banks 174
ownership
    advantages 73, 97
    control 3
    foreign 15
    structure 115

partial adjustment model 42
patents 4
perfect
    capital mobility 102
    substitutes 102
performance measurement 57
Pomfret, R. 7, 142, 157, 160
portfolio diversification 2–3
preferential treatment 15
price formula 118
product differentiation 73
product–cycle model 73
production
    capacities 3
    cycle model 1
productivity 36–7, 100, 103, 143, 222

factor 37, 101
    industrial 53
profit repatriation 114
property
    development 18
    investment 18
    rights 19
        protection law 223
    safety 216
purchasing power parity 78

quality of foreign investment 39

rate of return 181
real estate 173
    market 18
realisation ratio 161, 166
regional protectionism 182
research and development 3, 57
    intensity 54
Romer, D. 86, 97
round–tripping funds 7

sectoral distribution 20
sensitivity analysis 45
simultaneity 45
    bias 140, 142, 146, 149
skilled labour 180, 182, 218
    supply 183
social
    environment 223
    stability 216
special economic zones 2, 5, 13, 45,
        114, 158, 188, 194, 213
specialisation 57
spillover
    effect 5, 149
    of new technologies 30
    skill 4
stability and rank conditions 146
statistical
    inference 147
    noise 62
stochastic frontier method 60
stock exchanges 221, 224

tariff